Soldier, Sailor

Gloria Virtutis Umbra

ENDPAPERS

Upper left: school bills of 1832 for the three sons of the 2nd Earl of Longford at Winchester (£218 1s 11d for half a year). Lower left: black-edged sheet, dated 1831, enclosing Kitty's hair after her death. Upper centre and right: packets of bills from the Grand Tour of the 2nd Earl, 1793–5, Centre: letter from Ellen Gwynn to the 2nd Earl in 1815 enquiring about her child, the natural daughter of his brother, General Sir Edward Pakenham, who had been killed earlier that year at the Battle of New Orleans. Centre: four account books of the 2nd Earl, including his 'manifesto and memorandum' of January 1808 of 'Fun, Folly & Frolic' ending on his marriage in 1817.

Soldier, Sailor

An Intimate Portrait of
an Irish Family

ELIZA PAKENHAM

Weidenfeld & Nicolson
LONDON

First published in Great Britain in 2007
by Weidenfeld & Nicolson
An Hachette Livre UK company

1 3 5 7 9 10 8 6 4 2

A CIP catalogue record for this book
is available from the British Library.

ISBN 978 0 297 84377 1

Typeset at The Spartan Press Ltd,
Lymington, Hants

Printed and bound at Mackays of Chatham plc,
Chatham, Kent

The Orion Publishing Group's policy is to use papers that
are natural, renewable and recyclable products and made
from wood grown in sustainable forests. The logging and
manufacturing processes are expected to conform to the
environmental regulations of the country of origin.

Weidenfeld & Nicolson

The Orion Publishing Group Ltd
Orion House
5 Upper St Martin's Lane
London WC2H 9EA

www.orionbooks.co.uk

In memory of my grandmother,
Elizabeth Longford

CONTENTS

ILLUSTRATIONS

Helen Hamilton and Bess Stewart, undated.

Kitty, Duchess of Wellington by Thomas Lawrence, 1814. (© The Trustees of the Stratfield Saye Preservation Trust.)

'The Storming of Badajoz', 6 April 1812 (coloured engraving), from 'The Victories of Wellington' engraved by T. Fielding, published 1819 (after Richard Westall) (private collection/Bridgeman Art Library).

The Hon. Sir Hercules Pakenham by William Egley after John Engleheart, 1855 (© Bonhams 1793 Ltd).

SECTION THREE

'The Battle of Salamanca', 22 July 1812 (coloured engraving), from 'The Victories of Wellington' engraved by T. Fielding, published 1819 (after Richard Westall) (private collection/Bridgeman Art Library).

The Duke of Wellington by Sir Thomas Lawrence, 1814 (private collection/Bridgeman Art Library).

General Sir Edward Pakenham by Martin Cregan/St Croix Commemorative Sword (© Peter Finer Ltd).

'The Battle of New Orleans', 8 January 1815 engraved by J. Yeager and published 1817 (private collection/Bridgeman Art Library).

Thomas, 2nd Earl of Longford by Sir Martin Archer Shee.

Georgiana, Countess of Longford by Martin Cregan, c.1817.

'A Sketch in the Park', lithograph published July 1834, artist unknown (© The Trustees of the Stratfield Saye Preservation Trust).

Catherine, 1st Duchess of Wellington seated at an easel, May 1825, by John Hayter. (© The Trustees of the Stratfield Saye Preservation Trust. Photograph: Photographic Survey, Courtauld Institute of Art.)

Edward Pakenham, William Pakenham, Thomas Pakenham, Charles Reginald Pakenham (on dog), c.1823.

Arthur Richard, Marquess of Douro, Lord Charles Wellesley and the Hon. Gerald Valerian Wellesley with Stratfield Saye House in the distance, by Richard Barrett Davis (© The Trustees of the Stratfield Saye Preservation Trust).

Georgiana Longford with Katherine Pakenham, Georgie Pakenham and Louisa Pakenham, 1833, by Miss E. Scott.

Tullynally (Pakenham Hall), June 2007 (photograph © Thomas Pakenham).

Endpapers: Tullynally archives © Thomas Pakenham

All unattributed images © Thomas Pakenham, with photographs by David Davison Associates.

Ireland

Locations of houses and sites associated with the Pakenham family

N
W   E
S

HMS *Saldanha* shipwrecked 1811

Lough Swilly

Rathmullan •

Letterkenny •

LONDONDERRY

ANTRIM

□ TYRCALLEN HOUSE

DONEGAL

U L S T E R

Lough Neagh

General Humbert lands August 1798

Killala Bay

□ BROWN HALL

TYRONE

LANGFORD LODGE □

• Belfast

FERMANAGH

ARMAGH

DOWN

SLIGO

LEITRIM

MONAGHAN

□ CARPENHAM

MAYO

General Humbert defeated at Ballinamuck 1798

• Cavan

LOUTH

C O N N A U G H T

ROSCOMMON

CAVAN

Longford •

• Granard

LONGFORD

EDGEWORTHSTOWN □

□ PAKENHAM HALL

• Castlepollard

MEATH

COOLURE □

• Mullingar

• Trim

WESTMEATH

SUMMERHILL □

DUBLIN

GALWAY

CARTON HOUSE □

CASTLETOWN HOUSE □

• Dublin

KING'S COUNTY

KILDARE

L E I N S T E R

CLARE

QUEEN'S COUNTY

WICKLOW

Atlantic Ocean

CARLOW

Irish Sea

LIMERICK

TIPPERARY

KILKENNY

WEXFORD

M U N S T E R

WATERFORD

KERRY

CORK

0   20   40   60   80 miles

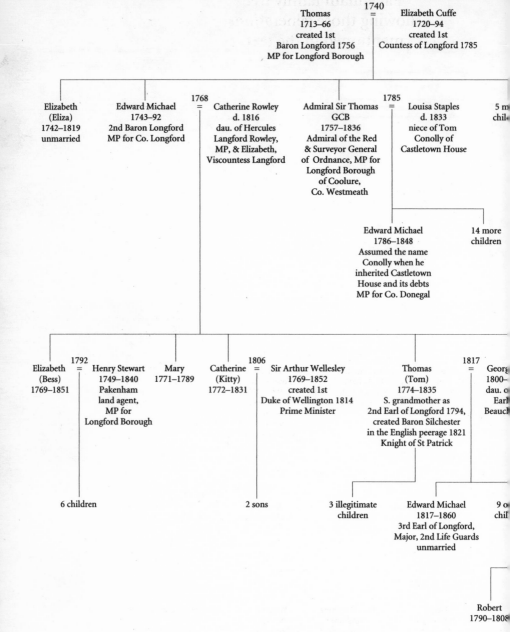

1740

Thomas
1713–66
created 1st
Baron Longford 1756
MP for Longford Borough
=
Elizabeth Cuffe
1720–94
created 1st
Countess of Longford 1785

Elizabeth
(Eliza)
1742–1819
unmarried

Edward Michael
1743–92
2nd Baron Longford
MP for Co. Longford
= 1768
Catherine Rowley
d. 1816
dau. of Hercules
Langford Rowley,
MP, & Elizabeth,
Viscountess Langford

Admiral Sir Thomas
GCB
1757–1836
Admiral of the Red
& Surveyor General
of Ordnance, MP for
Longford Borough
of Coolure,
Co. Westmeath
= 1785
Louisa Staples
d. 1833
niece of Tom
Conolly of
Castletown House

5 m[ore]
chil[dren]

Edward Michael
1786–1848
Assumed the name
Conolly when he
inherited Castletown
House and its debts
MP for Co. Donegal

14 more
children

Elizabeth
(Bess)
1769–1851
= 1792
Henry Stewart
1749–1840
Pakenham
land agent,
MP for
Longford Borough

Mary
1771–1789

Catherine
(Kitty)
1772–1831
= 1806
Sir Arthur Wellesley
1769–1852
created 1st
Duke of Wellington 1814
Prime Minister

Thomas
(Tom)
1774–1835
S. grandmother as
2nd Earl of Longford 1794,
created Baron Silchester
in the English peerage 1821
Knight of St Patrick
= 1817
Georg[iana]
1800–
dau. o[f]
Earl
Beauc[hamp]

6 children

2 sons

3 illegitimate
children

Edward Michael
1817–1860
3rd Earl of Longford,
Major, 2nd Life Guards
unmarried

9 o[ther]
chil[dren]

Robert
1790–1808

Pakenham family tree
showing those generations
mentioned in the text

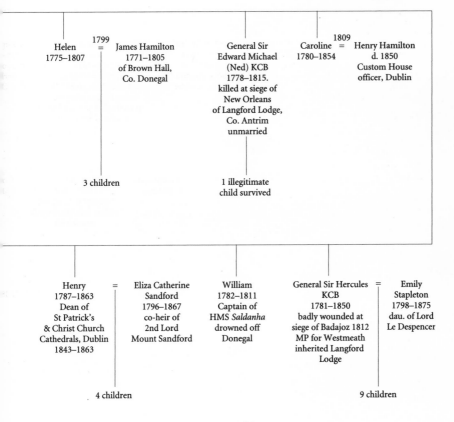

Helen
1775–1807

1799
=

James Hamilton
1771–1805
of Brown Hall,
Co. Donegal

General Sir
Edward Michael
(Ned) KCB
1778–1815.
killed at siege of
New Orleans
of Langford Lodge,
Co. Antrim
unmarried

Caroline
1780–1854

1809
=

Henry Hamilton
d. 1850
Custom House
officer, Dublin

3 children

1 illegitimate
child survived

Henry
1787–1863
Dean of
St Patrick's
& Christ Church
Cathedrals, Dublin
1843–1863

=

Eliza Catherine
Sandford
1796–1867
co-heir of
2nd Lord
Mount Sandford

William
1782–1811
Captain of
HMS *Saldanha*
drowned off
Donegal

General Sir Hercules
KCB
1781–1850
badly wounded at
siege of Badajoz 1812
MP for Westmeath
inherited Langford
Lodge

=

Emily
Stapleton
1798–1875
dau. of Lord
Le Despencer

4 children

9 children

ACKNOWLEDGEMENTS

My research into the Pakenham family has largely been conducted in Ireland at Tullynally. Without the help of the detailed calendar compiled there by A.P.W. Malcomson whilst Director of the Public Record Office of Northern Ireland, it would never have been begun. Similarly, the late Miss R.F. Butler's and the late Mrs Christina Colvin's calendars of the Edgeworth manuscripts at the National Library of Ireland and the Bodleian Library in Oxford were invaluable to my unearthing of so many references to the Pakenhams in the Edgeworth letters. I would like to express my gratitude to Professor Howard Colvin and Dr David Butler for giving their permission for me to quote from the Edgeworth papers.

Three private collections of manuscripts have been essential to my research. Lucinda Stewart's extraordinary kindness in allowing me to rifle through her archive collection in Howth, not to mention cooking me a delicious lunch every day for two weeks, will always be remembered. I have also been privileged to have been given access to the Wellington papers at Stratfield Saye, by kind permission of the Duke of Wellington and Lord Douro. Thirdly, Lord Mulgrave's willingness to share his family archive with the descendants of his illustrious ancestor's friend has been more than generous.

For their permission to draw on unpublished material, I would like to thank the following institutions: The Board of the National Library of Ireland; Armagh County Museum; Bodleian Library, Oxford; The British Library; Centre for Kentish Studies; Cheshire Record Office; Christies of London; Irish Art Research Centre, TCD; Hartley Library, Southampton University; Irish Architectural Archive; National Archives of Ireland; National Army Museum, London; National Library of Wales; Public Record Office of Northern Ireland; Public Record Office, London; Somerset Record Office; Suffolk Record Office; The Board of Trinity College Dublin; Westmeath

County Library. Letters quoted from the Wellington Papers in the University of Southampton are by permission of Her Majesty's Stationery Office.

Several people have kindly read versions of this book and given me invaluable advice on how to proceed. In particular I would like to thank my mother, Valerie Pakenham, who spent many hours reading it with a red pencil in her hand. My father, Thomas Pakenham; Anthony Malcomson; Linda Kelly, Annabelle Chisholm and Maria Winner were all both encouraging and wise in their remarks. And without the patient and practical help of my husband, Alex Chisholm, I would never have finished the book.

Many friends and professionals have been helpful to me in the various stages of writing, and I apologise to those whose names I have accidentally omitted. Amanda Foreman, Tif Loehnis, Flora Fraser and Mike Shaw (now retired) at Curtis Brown gave me excellent advice early on. Others helped me with reading lists, to uncover lost gems, to find illustrations and in innumerable essentials, in particular: Sean Barden, Caroline Bonham, Nicholas Brooksbank, Bruce Campbell, Edward Clive, David Davies, David Davison, Tom Desmond, Mel Fall, Peter Finer, Desmond Fitzgerald, David Fleming, Charles Forde, Antonia Fraser, Arthur French, Maurice French, Sir Peter Froggatt, Christopher Gray, David Griffin, Clive Hamilton, Colin Harris, David Hunter, Marian Keaney, Laurence Kelly, Dr Noel Kissane, Gerard Lyne, Nigel and Anna McNair Scott, Eddie McParland, Alan Masterson, Kate Mayne, Kevin B. Nowlan, Robert O'Byrne, Freddie O'Dwyer, John O'Raw, Clare Pakenham, Michael R. Pakenham, Dermot Pakenham, Fred Pakenham, Ned Pakenham, Betty Rizzo, Peter Rowley-Conwy, Daphne Shackleton, the Sheehys, Ian Wilson, Jeremy Williams, Borgislav Winner, Dr Christopher Woods, Dr Chris Woolgar.

Lastly I would like to thank my publisher Michael Dover at Weidenfeld & Nicolson, my agent Camilla Goslett at Curtis Brown, and my editor Linden Lawson for all their help.

Because the stories that follow are all interlinked, the reader will find an overlap in the narrative chronology, which runs more in a series of serpentine bends than a linear progression.

Spelling, grammar and punctuation have been left as in the originals throughout.

Introduction

I am standing in the dining room of my father's house* in Ireland,
gazing up at ten Pakenham family portraits. They have always
been friendly acquaintances. Once, years ago, I saw some of them
taken down to be cleaned, and then hung up again on the walls, a
safe distance from marauding children. But today it seems that this
is the first time I am really looking at them. Thomas, Elizabeth,
Edward, Catherine, Thomas, Georgiana, Hercules, Edward, William,
Thomas. What thoughts went on behind those passive, chalky faces?
How can I bring them out of the shadows?

I begin with a lady. Elizabeth Cuffe, born in 1720, married in 1740,
and painted soon after. She was the first figure in the circle of family
portraits that I remember noticing. Not because she is particularly
pretty: the long hair drawn back from her high forehead looks pale
and mousy, her chin is surely a little weak, and her lips are thin
and unsmiling. But there is a gentleness in her brown eyes, and a
homeliness in the plain expanse of chalk-white breast. Here is the
family matriarch, who looks so fragile, and young, but who was
highly literary and well-read – and who brought a fortune and a title
to the Pakenhams. You can find her fingerprints in the library which
she created, in the small leather volumes autographed with her three
successive names. Elizabeth Cuffe, Elizabeth Pakenham, Elizabeth
Longford.

Facing her across the room is Thomas, her new husband. His is a

* Now called Tullynally, but known as Pakenham Hall in the eighteenth and
nineteenth centuries.

I

softer, fuller face, with Cupid's bow lips, curling brown hair and a hint of a smile in his eyes. Compared to his wife, he looks rather dashing, his blue velvet coat gleams, the gold buttons on his waistcoat still catch the light. He is most certainly pleased with his position. A clever but profligate squire descended from 'Adventurer' soldiers who had come to Ireland a hundred years before, his future is now promising. Through his wife he is allied to some of the most prominent families in Ireland. In a few years' time, he will be made Baron Longford.

Further along the wall is Thomas's son, Edward Michael, the naval Captain. Fair-haired and young-looking in his smart blue uniform, he has his mother's gentle eyes, and her serious character. His contemporaries recalled him as plain-speaking and practical, the archetype of a 'well-born, well-bred' naval officer. He too made a marriage to a lady who brought the Pakenhams increased wealth and status. Her name was Catherine, and she was the daughter of one of the greatest landowners in County Meath, Hercules Langford Rowley, MP. In the twenty-four years of their marriage, Edward was often away fighting at sea. Between them, however, they produced eleven children. She was known as the 'mother of heroes'.

Edward and Catherine's eldest son was Tom, the 2nd Earl of Longford. He gets the title from his grandmother, his poor father having died too young to inherit it. In his portrait there is nothing of the military. He has a self-indulgent look about him, his thick brown hair and flowing white cravat hint at a pleasure-filled, sensuous life. It is hardly a surprise to discover that his sleepy eyes hide the knowledge of his three illegitimate children, by different women. On the other hand the portrait of his wife Georgiana has the pinched air of a girl made to grow up too soon: married at nineteen, she was widowed at thirty-five.

And then, blazing in his scarlet uniform, is the man I like best of all, Ned (Edward). Tom's younger brother is the darling of the family and hangs full-length in a gilt frame; his silver star of Bath gleams on his breast, and the epaulettes of a General gild his shoulder. Such a gentle, handsome face, with large expressive eyes and an almost girlish complexion, scarcely seems suitable for a man who has been a soldier for twenty years. In his hand is a parchment which reads simply '17 April, Toulouse, 1814', the date of the Armistice signed by the French during the Peninsular War. He looks every inch the hero. It is hard to believe that his life was to end in a catastrophic defeat.

There are later portraits too, of Admirals, Generals and Brigadiers; those who died in their prime and those who lived on into sedentary old age. But there is one missing ghost at this feast. Kitty, the naval Captain's daughter, has no proper portrait in the house. It is a strange omission perhaps, since her marriage brought a more valuable alliance than any other in the family. Her husband was Arthur Wellesley, 1st Duke of Wellington and conqueror of Napoleon. Yet, when he first proposed, Wellesley had been dismissed by the Longfords as not good enough for Kitty.

The Duke of Wellington features in hundreds of memoirs: his wife is generally overlooked. Wholly unsuitable for the great man, always foolish, never loved. Even my dear grandmother, whose biography of Wellington is a *tour de force*, had limited sympathy for her. When I insisted to her that there was more to Wellington's wife than had yet been explained, she replied: 'You will be the one to find it'. How could I then not help feeling responsible for Kitty, as though I personally had been given the task of rehabilitating her? I hope I have brought her a little further into the light.

Upstairs, the old nursery is now lined with carefully numbered cardboard boxes. Here are the records of three hundred years. Letters, journals, account books, bills reach to the ceiling. I search them for intimate details: lost children who feature on no family trees, whose existence remains only in codicils and private letters; desperate prayers composed at times of personal agony, slipped between the pages of a bible. I convince myself that a thousand hidden things still remain waiting for me to find them. I scratch in the rusty corners of old suitcases and grope in the spaces behind letter-books. I follow a paper trail to other places, to libraries public and private, even to a seaside attic in Dublin where I discover twenty-five tin trunks stuffed with Pakenham letters, almost entirely covered in soot. Under the black dust, the bundles are still tied with pink ribbons.

In the midst of all this material, one generation stands out.

Sometimes their words flow so thick and fast, I find it hard to keep my cast of characters together. These are the ticker-tape exchanges of the Napoleonic generation, who lived most of their prime when Bonaparte was the scourge of Europe. Four brothers and four sisters who survived into adulthood, all writing about each other, to each other, for each other. A hugely united, affectionate family. And most vitally of all, there was a letter-writer of genius in their circle. With the lightest flick of her pen she brings life to the canvas on which they appear. This was Maria Edgeworth, the Pakenhams' novelist neighbour. For thirty years her letters illuminate their lives.

I have something else that will help to set the scene. It is a careful pencil sketch made in the journal of George Edward Pakenham, the great-uncle of the Napoleonic generation of Pakenhams. He came to stay with his elder brother in Ireland in the autumn of 1737. It shows the place where they were all brought up as it was at the time of their grandfather, Thomas Pakenham. The foreground is all fields and hills, a pack of hounds and huntsmen chasing a fox, just visible leaping away in the corner. Beyond, on the opposite slope, is an elaborate formal garden of avenues, canals and basins, laid out like a miniature Versailles. Far away in the distance is the house, a plain square box, as small as a postage stamp, Pakenham Hall, Westmeath.

The scene looks bucolic. In his journal George Edward can't help a touch of envy creeping into his description. His brother's house was a bustling, prosperous place with 'a steward, a butler, gardener and several helpers . . . ten men in livery, 8 or 10 hunters, a fine pack of hounds and a set of horses' – in short, all that a fox-hunting squire could desire. But even a hard-up younger brother could see there were drawbacks to owning an Irish estate. He found his brother's fellow squires boorish and drunken; and the peasantry were miserably poor and (to his English Protestant eyes) kept in a state of ignorance and servitude by their local priests. And his brother's few surviving letters reveal a still dangerous and unsettled country, with bands of outlaws (probably dispossessed Catholics) hidden in the wild oak woods that edged the nearby lake of Derravaragh. Thomas Pakenham is only one generation removed from the civil wars of the late seventeeth century and the Battle of the Boyne.

The generation I have gone in search of saw their grandfather's house and its landscape transformed; the squire's square box begins to sprout towers and turrets and finally two huge battlemented wings as the family fortunes go from strength to strength. The formal avenues and canals have already given way to romantic parkland with Brownian clumps of trees. New walled gardens have been built and paths wind through the newly planted pleasure ground to a grotto and two ornamental lakes. When I walk out in a summer evening I look up through the canopied branches of the oaks, pines and beeches planted by my great-great-great-great-grandfather, Captain Lord Longford, and follow the garden paths laid out by his eldest son Thomas and his wife Georgiana.

The world beyond their gates was also in revolution. They were witnesses to the desperate duel played out for over twenty years between Revolutionary and Napoleonic France and her European rivals, which spilt into Ireland itself during the *annus horribilis* of 1798. And two of the brothers were front-row players in Wellington's army as he fought his way back and forth across Spain and Portugal in the Peninsular campaign. The family motto, *Gloria Virtutis Umbra*, can be translated as 'Glory is the Shadow of Virtue'. I had always assumed that this was an evangelical call to be dutiful above everything else, in a temporal world where glory could not last. But looking back on the conduct of this generation of my ancestors, I wonder if in fact they interpreted it another way. To be honourable, dutiful, and courageous was to be rewarded by the quality that followed these virtues like a shadow: glory.

Tullynally, 2007

Prologue

In December 1777, Captain Lord Longford took stock of his position:

> At this time I was as happily situated as it was possible for a man to be. My house of Pakenham Hall was repaired and made comfortable, the debts with which I found my estate encumbered were nearly discharged . . . my circumstances easy, though my income was not great . . . blest with the best of wives, with a promising and pleasing family of a son and four daughters, and happy in the company of my mother and sister; we passed our time in cheerfulness and content. This happy state of domestic tranquillity was interrupted by an event which I had long been apprehensive of, my being called upon . . . to take the command of a ship . . .[1]

It had been fourteen years since Edward had last stood on the quarterdeck. His naval life had begun at the age of sixteen, he had fought sea battles off North America and West Africa, and been held prisoner for more than a year by the Spanish. He had come back from the Seven Years' War against France and Spain with a captaincy and a reputation as a fair and humane commander. Since then he had inherited his father's title – and debts – and taken his seat in the Lords in the Dublin parliament. He had tried to keep his head down as far as politics were concerned; all his efforts had gone into improving his estate.

When the English journalist Arthur Young was writing his famous *Tour of Ireland*, he stopped for a few days at Pakenham Hall. There he discovered a landlord with agricultural practices after his own heart. The estate Longford had inherited in 1766 had been the scene of 'improvements' for a decade. Much of the boggy 'black bottom' land had been drained, the fields were planted with oats, barley and turnips, and tilled in rotation in just the way that the Royal Dublin Society would have approved. Even the tenants, though far poorer than their English equivalents, appeared well provided for, each with a cow or a pig and a small plot of land. And Captain Lord Longford believed in looking to the future: he was planting oak trees for the Navy that would take at least a century to realise their worth.

Britain had now been at war with its American colonies for two years. The protests against taxation that had begun with the 'Boston Tea Party' had led to armed clashes with the British Government forces at Lexington and Concord. The conflict had culminated in the disastrous Battle of Bunker Hill outside Boston on 17 June 1775. Although nominally victorious, the British had lost over a thousand men. On 4 July 1776, the United States Congress passed Jefferson's immortal Declaration of Independence. Hastily, the British Admiralty commissioned new ships, to the delight of young naval officers. Many expected that other European powers would soon be involved. (They were right: France declared war on Great Britain in February 1778, and Spain did likewise in June 1779.)

The Admiralty's call left Longford full of foreboding. He had long been ambivalent about the justness of the war. Like many Irishmen he felt a great deal of sympathy with the American colonists. The farmers and merchants of Massachusetts and beyond had had taxation imposed upon them by a Government to whom they sent no Members of Parliament. They had, he believed, been provoked beyond endurance by their colonial masters. Any protraction of the American conflict was an evil that could only ruin Ireland, and 'expose us as easy prey to the French'.[2] France, after all, had openly supported the Declaration of Independence by the American colonies. Moreover Longford had no faith in the Admiralty itself; he knew that the Navy had sunk to a dangerous low with poorly made ships and ill-trained men. Long gone were the glorious days of the

Seven Years' War. He wondered whether he himself would still be fit for such work after so many years on land. 'I suppose I shall be obliged to walk the Quarter-Deck with Franklin's *Marine Dictionary* under my Arm', he joked grimly to his old naval friend, Lord Mulgrave.*

As an officer in the Navy, such doubts had to be swallowed. And, if the conflict moved into Europe, it brought the prospect of prize money. 'Prize Money' had lured many a fine sailor into the Navy. The cargo of captured foreign ships was given as a reward to the captors, although it legally belonged to the Crown. When sold, the profits were divided amongst the officers and men according to their rank. Naval pay itself was notoriously poor. And Captain Lord Longford, after all his 'improvements', was pleased at the thought of such extra income – if indeed it was to be had. 'Very luckily', he concluded to Lord Mulgrave, 'I have finished my house & offices and it will not be amiss to make Monsieur or Don pay for them, tho' I can't say I think the chance of what we shall make that way is very great. I believe you and I will yet get more from Alum and Turf Bog than we shall by our Prize money.'[3]

By January 1778 Captain Lord Longford was in Deptford, fitting out the 64-gun *America* for his command. This new ship he quickly came to despise for its lack of seaworthiness, although Lord Mulgrave – now on the Admiralty board – had personally arranged it for him. In the meantime, as he appointed his officers and men, he was 'tormented' with endless demands for jobs. In particular 'young Irish Gentlemen . . . having grown too troublesome for their Friends at home' were sent over, 'generally without a farthing in their Pockets, which obliged me to receive them, or give them money to carry them back'. But his wife Catherine's strength of character helped to support him. Although pregnant with their sixth child, her 'degree of resolution and good sense' was admirable.

Longford had married Catherine Rowley in the summer of 1768.

---

* Captain Constantine Phipps had become Lord Mulgrave on his father's death in September 1775. The friends had first been at sea together during the Seven Years' War, 1756–63.

Her father, Hercules Langford Rowley, owned a vast mansion in nearby Meath called Summerhill. Of Presbyterian descent, he had sat in the House of Commons for fifty years by the time of his death and was considered 'of very great property'.[4] His income was £18,000* a year, partly because of Langford Lodge, the property owned by Catherine's mother, Viscountess Langford,† on the wild shores of Lough Neagh in County Antrim. And Summerhill, halfway between Dublin and Westmeath, was a convenient stopping place in the journey.

With the Captain's departure, the Pakenhams had left the country-side for the safety and convenience of Dublin. At least a regular garrison was stationed there. War had exposed Ireland's gentry to all the dangers of foreign invasion – a fear that had escalated now so many of the regular Army had been called abroad. By 1778 the usual quota of troops stationed in Ireland was down to a mere 4,000, who could hardly stretch to defend the whole country. Anxious to take action, even if the Government could not, the gentry in Ulster began to form regiments of 'Volunteers'. The idea soon spread across the country, each district quickly producing its own regiment in their gorgeously distinct uniforms, cut patriotically from Irish cloth.

The old house in Westmeath was closed up for the duration of the war, as a measure of economy, whilst the whole family squeezed into the family town house in Cavendish Row. Catherine made no objection; she had little interest in show. She kept only her maid and a footman, and left her carriage behind in Westmeath. With her came her spinster sister-in-law Eliza, her four daughters, and little Tom, the future Earl of Longford. They were welcomed by the Dowager Lady Longford, a widow of eleven years' standing, since the first Lord Longford had died of an apoplectic fit. Number 10 Cavendish Row had been built just under thirty years before and

---

* Equivalent to about £1.8 million today.
† Elizabeth Rowley, née Ormsby, had been made Viscountess Langford in her own right in 1766, a similarity in title to the Longford one which has often caused confusion.

faced the Rotunda ballroom and gardens across the road. In the nearby houses a number of relations were installed. And an hour's drive from Dublin were the great houses of two old friends of the Dowager's – the Leinsters of Carton, and the Conollys of Castletown.*

In Cavendish Row nobody complained of the squash. The two ladies Longford got on extremely well. They were highly maternal, affectionate women who found a great consolation in family life and a close circle of friends. Elizabeth, the Dowager Lady Longford, held a literary salon where, as one regular visitor put it, 'one was always sure to meet the cleverest people of this country'.[5] Her young cousin, Mr Edgeworth, remarked on her 'wit, humour, and a taste for literature . . . uncommon for women in her day'.[6] (It was Elizabeth whom he credited with making him the polymath and intellectual adventurer he was to become.) In spite of the war, social life in Dublin continued as frenetically as usual, with a great masquerade ball on St Patrick's Eve in March, where the Duke of Leinster appeared as a fruit-woman whose oranges miraculously changed to shamrocks as midnight struck. Two days later, on 19 March 1778, Catherine gave birth to a second son, and named him Edward.

By 13 June not only Lord Longford but his twenty-one-year-old naval brother, Thomas Pakenham, were under sail in the Channel. In North America, two years before, Thomas had distinguished himself by carrying the vital dispatches of General Clinton to General Howe[†] under the very noses of the American enemy. Now a bright-eyed Lieutenant of the *Courageux*, he sailed in the centre of Admiral Keppel's Channel squadron. Keppel's orders were to prevent the

---

* Emily Duchess of Leinster and Lady Louisa Conolly, née Lennox, were sisters and the daughters of the 2nd Duke of Richmond. The widowed Emily now lived in England and France, whilst Louisa lived with her husband, Tom Conolly. They were close correspondents. The Leinster family were distantly related to the Dowager Elizabeth Longford, whose husband had been in the same political set as the previous Duke of Leinster, Emily's husband. Both Carton and Castletown were grand Palladian houses.

† Brother of Admiral Howe, and brother-in-law of Tom Conolly, through his marriage to Frances Conolly.

two French fleets, based on Toulon and Brest, from combining. Meanwhile, in Dublin, the family anxiously waited for news. 'The poor Lady Longfords live in a constant dread', Lady Louisa Conolly reported to her sister Emily in France.

The war began with neither glory nor rewards. But the Captain's humane character soon revealed itself in the very first engagement. A French ship, the *Licorne*, which had already been captured, fired her 'whole broadside' into Longford's ship,[7] breaking all the rules of war by simultaneously 'hauling down her Colours and lowering all her sails'. Captain Lord Longford resisted the temptation to return fire. He later described the French ship's behaviour as the 'rash act of one wrong headed Man' for whose actions other people should not suffer. The news of the incident spread abroad: 'I never heard of anything so charming as Lord Longford's behaviour', gushed Lady Louisa Conolly to Emily, 'his humanity, command of temper, and prudence are equal to anything one ever heard of.'[8]

The Battle of Ushant* that followed on 27 July was inconclusive. Keppel's fleet sailed back to Plymouth with barely a sense of victory. And the weeks that followed Ushant were increasingly disheartening, as the *America* cruised the Mediterranean in search of the elusive French. Longford was battered by nothing but storms and the quarrelling of his officers. By the following summer, Longford was very thankful to be taking command of a new ship, the 74-gun *Alexander*, and sensibly he left 'several Irish young Gentlemen' behind him on the *America*. 'I believe my successor will not be much obliged to me', he joked.

In England fears of invasion grew. The defences of the coast appeared astonishingly poor. In 1779, the French Admiral D'Orvillier's fleet had joined France's new Spanish allies in the Bay of Biscay, and sixty-six ships of the line had even entered the English Channel. Fortunately a misunderstanding in their signalling system and the harsh westerly gales had made the 'great, unwieldy armada' quite powerless to attack. Meanwhile, in Ireland rumours of invasion were

---

* A hundred miles west of the French island of D'Ouessant, at the mouth of the Channel.

equally widespread. 'Indeed,' wrote the anxious Lady Louisa Conolly, 'I have no doubt but that we shall make a good defence against Spaniards and French; but if the Americans should come, it's impossible to guess at the consequences.'[9]

Young Thomas Pakenham, in the meantime, was doing well. Now promoted to Captain, he brought a goods convoy safely home from Jamaica, and pleased the merchants of Bristol so much with his care that they gave him a fifty-guinea sword. He was handed the command of the 28-gun *Crescent*, much to his delight.

Then there was an encounter which nearly scuppered his career. In May 1781, the *Crescent* and her fellow frigate the *Flora* came upon two large Dutch frigates. By this time, the Dutch had joined the French and Spanish. It seems the Captain of the *Flora* was intent on winning prizes, and once he had disarmed the first Dutch ship, remained at some distance from the battle between the *Crescent* and her larger Dutch assailant. The Dutch captain, 'a most humane, most gallant, most generous, and most honourable enemy' according to Longford, did everything he could to persuade Pakenham to surrender. But Thomas would not give in: for two and a half hours he let loose everything he had, but was finally entirely crippled by the loss of both his masts, which had fallen over the decks and disabled all his guns. 'In this situation without a Gun to fire or a Sail to set . . . 30 Men killed and 70 wounded, my Brother', wrote Longford, 'was under the necessity of Striking his Colours',* which he did. But the damaged Dutch ship did not claim its prize, and instead limped away from the *Crescent*. By the time the tardy *Flora* appeared, Pakenham was so indignant at her Captain's lack of support that he insisted on resigning the command of the *Crescent* to him. Having lost his ship, Thomas knew he would face trial in a public court martial.

The court martial was understanding. Unanimously they gave their opinion that 'the Hon Captain Pakenham throughout the action . . . behaved with the coolest & ablest judgement, and with

---

* To 'strike' one's colours meant to haul down the ship's flag and thus surrender.

the firmest and most determined resolution; and that he did not strike the Crescent's colours until he was totally unable to make the smallest defence'. The court could not 'dismiss Captain Pakenham without expressing their admiration of his conduct on this occasion'. Both officers and men were complimented on their iron discipline and bravery, with over half of their number killed or wounded.[*]

In the drawing room at Pakenham Hall, three oil paintings commemorate the scene. The first shows the brave *Crescent*, dwarfed by the Dutch frigates, firing with all its might, in true David and Goliath style. The second depicts the *Crescent* broken and immobilised, its flag tattered and sails ripped. In the third, a tiny figure wields an axe, in a desperate attempt to release the shattered mast. Out of sight of the artist, a grisly scene of multiple amputations was taking place below deck, with forty-nine limbs sawn off by the hard-pressed surgeon, and yet not one man dying of his injuries. This last detail may have been due to a peculiar cure put in place – 'each man had, by the desire of the surgeon, a bottle of Minorca Wine saturated with bark, hung over his hammock'.[10] The third painting is also the epilogue: there is the defeated Captain Pakenham being rowed away to the Admiral's flagship, to face the inevitable.

Captain Lord Longford himself continued the unexciting business of defending the Channel, taking what prizes he could. He had not changed his mind about the conduct of the war. 'Times are so altered, my dear friend,' he wrote to another old naval shipmate, William Cornwallis, 'since you and I first went to sea . . . and as I see no prospect of things mending this war, I wish most sincerely we were well out of it; so wishing you patience and potatoes, and greens and good health, I remain, &c.'[11]

By the end of 1782, the naval campaign was at an end. The American war had been largely over since General Charles Cornwallis – William's brother – had surrendered at Yorktown in October 1781. After five years of only the briefest of visits back to Ireland, Lord Longford, at least, was delighted to be dismissed from service. He

---

[*] The entire ship's complement was 198.

was tired out with naval life and naval politics. Crossing from Holyhead to Dublin by the packet ship, he paused only to hand over his prize money to his young land agent, Henry Stewart. He made a careful note in his account book that it added up to a healthy '£5,400', more than double his annual income. Then it was home, as fast as his mare could take him, to the turf fires and cosy hubbub of Pakenham Hall.

At home, all were waiting with open arms. The family had expanded; each shore leave of the Captain's had left another child 'on the stocks'. By now, little Tom, a fine boy of nearly nine, had three younger brothers (Edward, Hercules and William, born in 1778, 1781 and 1782 respectively), as well as being 'damnably encumbered', as the Captain put it, with five sisters.* Every daughter meant that an additional dowry would eventually have to be provided.

The Captain's neighbours clamoured to see the naval veteran. Twelve miles away at Edgeworthstown lived the Longfords' cousin, Richard Lovell Edgeworth. Married to his third wife – the first two had died – he had nine children, the third of whom, Maria, he was schooling to be his amanuensis. He was a progressive, liberal and enlightened landlord, and something of an amateur inventor. At this time he was experimenting away to add springs to carriages, perhaps inspired by the uncomfortable crossing of the 'vast Serbonian bog' that separated Edgeworthstown and Pakenham Hall. The two families were frequently visiting each other, in a tradition that had begun in Edgeworth's father's time. At Christmas there were plays of 'home-made manufacture' put on by the children; in January 1785, all flocked to Dublin's Ranelagh Gardens to see Mr Crosbie ascending in a hot-air balloon, dressed in his quilted satin breeches and leopard-skin hat, even if he never made it across the Irish Sea. In the same year, the Pakenhams were gratified by a step up in the Irish peerage. The Dowager Lady Longford was made a Countess, chiefly 'in consideration of the professional services of her two sons',[12] although no doubt their faithful voting with the Government had helped. It was a happy time at Pakenham Hall, as one friend reported when she

---

* Bess, Mary, Kitty, Helen and Caroline.

came to stay: 'nothing can be more united, more Friendly or more agreeable than the inhabitants of this House'.[13]

There had also been a welcome increase in the family fortunes. During Captain Lord Longford's absence at sea, he had inherited part of some large estates in Cork, Dublin and Hampshire.* This translated into an additional £1,200 a year in tenant rents. The windfall meant more substantial dowries for his five daughters, and more proper provision for Catherine in the event of his death. And most importantly of all, Edward Michael could now make a gift of £4,000 to his brother Thomas, and give him an independent estate. This was land along the shores of Lough Derravaragh, known as 'Coolure', two miles west of Pakenham Hall. With Thomas's own fortune of £2,000 and the prospect of Government employment, this made him a decidedly eligible prospect, for a younger son.

By 1785 Sophia Fitzgerald, the shyest of Emily Leinster's numerous daughters, was watching in trepidation as her friend, Louisa Staples,† was pursued by the young naval officer. Louisa, the motherless niece of Tom Conolly, had been brought up at Castletown with Sophia. Sophia hints in her journal[14] that Mr Pakenham 'vexed her' with his bumptious attentions, but the family liked him. On 24 June they were married, and Sophia Fitzgerald lost her best friend and ally to a Westmeath estate. 'Tom has an amiable unaffected pleasing girl for a wife', Longford reported to Mulgrave, unaware that this 'girl' would one day bring her husband the magnificent Conolly property of Castletown.

The marriage gave Thomas Pakenham a further notch up in his career. He now had a job at the Ordnance Office at Dublin Castle, to supplement his estate income. He and Louisa built a three-storey house looking south over Derravaragh. When Lady Louisa Conolly

---

* Charles Dunbar, descended from the wealthy seventeenth-century Primate Michael Boyle, had died childless in October 1778 leaving his property divided between the three heirs of the Primate who were descended through the latter's daughters: Lords Hillsborough, de Vesci and Longford.
† The daughter of Harriet Conolly and John Staples of County Tyrone. Her younger sister Henrietta was also brought up by Lady Louisa.

went to see it, she liked it very much: 'The Coolure House is in vast forwardness, and a sweet pretty thing it will be. Tom Pakenham and Louisa seem equally engaged about it, though in different lines. He minds the farm only, and leaves the house, plantation, and gardening entirely to her. But both agree in loving the place and wishing to spend their lives there.'

Even Lady Louisa Conolly's youngest sister Sarah Napier,* who was never so enthusiastic as Louisa, reckoned it 'the best family House possible', and 'very Cheap', due to the building skills of Lord Longford, who 'understands the useful part of the business'.[15] In the years that followed, Coolure became a second point of the compass for the extended Pakenham clan.

The Pakenham family kept on growing. By 1787 a fifth son, Henry, had arrived and Lord Longford was the father of ten. The older boys had already been sent away to Dr Carpendale's famous school in Armagh,[16] like young Robert Stewart, later Lord Castlereagh. (In fact Tom, according to one memoir, was behaving in a cruel fashion to a younger boy who was his 'fag'.)[17] Meanwhile, the elder Pakenham girls, Bess, Mary and Kitty, had been gathering every sort of accomplishment at home. They had been taught chiefly by a fierce French governess called Madame Blondel,[18] with separate masters for drawing, the pianoforte, and of course dancing. Mr Edgeworth often came over to see them, and admired Bess's beauty –

> Who can escape, what man alive?
> At least what man of twenty five?
> When e'en grey hairs & wrinkles court ye
> And men turn poets in your praise at forty.[19]

All the girls were unusually bookish. The library built up by the Dowager Lady Longford was their greatest resource; *Mémoires* in French and English stocked the shelves,[20] philosophies, histories and

---

* Previously Bunbury, the youngest of the four Lennox sisters. She lived in Ireland with her soldier husband Colonel George Napier.

novels, including the newest wonder, *Cecilia*[21] by Fanny Burney. Their mother Catherine believed in children doing as much as possible to entertain themselves. She taught them to take cuttings for their gardens, to read aloud and act in plays, to exercise by going for long walks and rides. No indulgence was given to high fashion; the young people were dressed as plainly as their parents. Catherine's greatest concern was that they should follow the Christian philosophy which had always sustained her. Practical Lord Longford took care of their physical health, arranging that all the children should be 'variolated'* against the scourge of smallpox. But there was little to be done against the other great killer, tuberculosis.

From the age of sixteen, a gentleman's daughters were on public display. In Ireland they were presented to the Lord Lieutenant at Dublin Castle, then chaperoned at a series of assemblies and balls. The Rotunda ballroom, just opposite the family house in Cavendish Row, was the most popular venue. As Dublin was proud to proclaim, it measured only twenty square feet less than the one at Bath, and held six formal assemblies a year. Since all the proceeds went to the hospital next door, it was considered as much a public duty as a pleasure to attend these 'conscription balls'. One particular type of entertainment was known as a 'promenade', where guests walked round and round the circular hall until the supper bell was rung. When a French visitor, the Chevalier de Latocnaye, came to see it in 1796, he could not help noting that it meant a rare chance for unchaperoned flirtation: 'The good mammas were not very numerous, and those who were present appeared to be absent minded. The young folk, on the other hand, were very numerous and making good use of their time – I think perhaps the Promenade attained its object along more lines than one.'[22]

By 1789, Bess, Mary and Kitty were already out in society. The Lord Lieutenant's aides-de-camp were charming dancing partners for

* An early form of inoculation that was introduced to society by Lady Mary Wortley Montagu in 1721; it involved deliberately injecting matter from smallpox pustules into the skin in the hope that a mild but preventative infection would result. Dr Jenner's much more successful inoculation was not developed until the 1790s.

them. Dashing Arthur Wesley for example,* whose family home at Dangan was only a mile from the Rowleys at Summerhill, danced with delicate little Kitty, the youngest of the trio. This 'charming young man. Handsome, fashioned, tall and elegant,'[23] was the younger brother of Lord Mornington, and an Army officer. Unfortunately the Mornington estate was badly in debt, Dangan Castle now mortgaged to the hilt, and the Mornington fortune fast disappearing. In fact, Arthur had been removed early from Eton since his mother could not afford the fees. No wonder perhaps that Lord Mornington later described his parents as 'Frivolous and careless personages like most of the Irish nobility of that time'.[24] Now that Arthur was serving at the levées and lodged in the Castle Yard, Kitty saw him frequently. So too did Thomas Pakenham, the girls' uncle, who had Arthur to stay at Coolure.

Then in July 1789 Mary, the second daughter, and the darling of her Rowley grandparents, caught a 'bilious fever' and died. Sadly Lord Longford ordered 'raven grey' cloth for his sons' mourning clothes. Her distraught grandparents commissioned Sir Thomas Banks to create a marble sculpture of the girl in prayer, with her pet dog beside her, for the mausoleum at Summerhill.†

By 1791, the threat of war once again hung over Ireland. The old enemy, France, now had a new revolutionary government and its citizen armies were already seen as threatening the European status quo.

Once again, faithful as ever to his country's call, Captain Lord Longford proposed himself for naval service. At forty-nine, he was now in constant ill-health: half-blind, and assailed with such congestion in his lungs that he was forced to sleep in a chair. But he had his quadrant packed and ready, and he hoped that the three-decker ship that Mulgrave was trying to arrange for him would mean he had

---

* Arthur began signing himself 'Wellesley' in 1798, following his brother Richard who had changed the family name to its earlier version.
† The inscription is said to have read: 'To the Hon. Miss Mary Pakenham, second daughter of Lord Longford who died 3rd July 1789 aged 17 years and is buried here.' But the mausoleum is a ruin.

not such a need of the telescope to observe the enemy. Every day he expected that the letter commissioning him would arrive.

The voyage was never made. By Easter 1792, the Captain was sinking. The fishing nets he liked to mend sat untouched in a basket beside his chair, his blind eyes unable to see the needle. With quiet resignation, he tried to impress upon Catherine the dictum he had followed all his life: 'As you wish for happiness, let moderation guide your desires, & candid integrity your actions; never allow yourself to seek for amusement or advancement from the Follys or Vices of Others; make our Children sensible that obtaining command of their desires is the only way to preserve independence or ensure Content.'

Finally, on 6 June 1792, the weeks of waiting came to an end. 'The late Lord Longford,' declared *Faulkner's Dublin Journal* the next day, 'who was truly great as well as noble, has transmitted to his heir an example of loyalty and virtue, which to imitate will exalt him more than his fortune or his titles.'

Less than a year later, the conflict that Captain Lord Longford had long anticipated broke out. In February 1793, a month after Louis XVI had been guillotined,* France declared war on Britain. This time at least Lady Longford did not have to suffer the grief of seeing her husband called away to sea. But one way or another, the new war with France was to overshadow the rest of her life.

* 2 January 1793. The priest who attended the monarch to the scaffold was Abbé Edgeworth, a cousin of Richard Lovell's.

1

An Untimely Proposal

For a long time, Catherine could not be comforted. She had never quite believed that her Edward could leave her. 'How much I might have learned for the good of our dear Children could I have borne to consider him as lost to us, even when I knew his danger.' The burden of such a large family seemed too much to bear. Who was to help her now? Her eldest son Tom was away at university in Glasgow, her father, old Mr Rowley, was in a declining state.

Comfort came from the family agent, Henry Stewart. A cheerful, practical man, he knew Longford's affairs better than anyone and shared many of his views. At forty-three, only six years younger than the Captain, he was like a favourite uncle to the children. To one of them, however, he appeared in a rather different light.

Bess, Catherine's eldest daughter, was now a vivacious girl of twenty-two. She had spent many of the previous years in Dublin or at grand, but lugubrious, Summerhill. There Bess had plenty of opportunity to meet Henry Stewart, under the doting eyes of her Rowley grandparents. When it emerged that she had become secretly engaged to him Catherine was surprised, but also delighted. 'It is the greatest comfort to me', she confessed to Henry's mother, 'to think my dear Bessie's happiness secure in such a companion as may often be wished for but seldom very seldom found.'[1] The Stewart family also approved of the match; the letters of congratulation poured in. 'I consider the connection the most eligible that Ireland could afford', wrote one of Henry's brothers.[2] Before the year was out, Bess and Henry were married.

Twenty-year-old Kitty was now the eldest daughter still at home.

Her sister's romantic love affair had opened her eyes. As she and Captain Arthur Wesley – handsome, musical, well-read, but badly paid – danced round and round the great hall of the Castle, how could Kitty fail to be smitten? Before too long the pair were openly courting; meeting at Summerhill or at Coolure under the cheerful gaze of Captain Pakenham and Louisa. When war broke out with France, the young officer made up his mind. In April 1793, Arthur proposed, and Kitty went straight to her mother.

But Catherine Longford, and her eldest son, were absolutely against the match. 'My mother', wrote Bess defensively forty years later, 'in denying the suit of Arthur Wellesley, acted from the best of motives.' It was not his lack of fortune that put her off, for according to Bess, 'when other & wealthier proposals were made [she] never pressed [Kitty's] acceptance or even shewed any influencing wish on the Subject'. One can only suspect that it was a case of bad timing; after all, Bess herself had recently married, and Catherine was still in shock after her husband's death. War had just been declared. In her depressed state, perhaps Catherine saw Wesley as too gay, too frivolous, all too likely to end up as the 'food for powder' his own mother had predicted. She determined that Kitty should wait.

Eighteen-year-old Lord Longford wrote to Wesley in no uncertain terms. The marriage was not to be allowed 'for prudential motives'. Longford, who would be an Earl once his grandmother had died, was not going to throw his pretty sister away on an Army captain whose elder brother was in such debt that he had had to sell the family home in Dublin, and whose grandmother had been retrieved from a sponging-house not long before. Both Arthur and Kitty were forbidden to see or write to each other again. With her acute sense of family duty, Kitty submitted. But what neither Longford nor his mother realised was that Wesley's dismissal had wounded Kitty's heart so deeply that it would remain unhealed. As for Arthur, his rejection by Lady Longford and her son rankled more than any could have predicted.

In the autumn of 1793 Tom, the new Lord Longford, was nineteen. He had just begun his 'Grand Tour' of the beauties of Europe. With his father's sober guidance removed, he was considered rather an over-exuberant youth; to prevent accidents, his mother arranged for him to be accompanied by a Mr Nott* – only a year or so older than himself, but a classical scholar of great erudition. Nott turned out to be 'as different as black to white' to Longford.

The two-year meander from Neufchâtel to Naples, visiting mountain panoramas and classical antiquities, was only a little inconvenienced by the Continental war. The territory of enemy France, of course, was out of bounds, with the National Convention in power and the guillotine in full swing. With that exception, Nott and Longford traipsed the conventional path: Switzerland, Austria and Italy. The roads were exceptionally bad at Mannheim, 'dreadfully cut up by artillery and camp wagons'; in some places the provisions were rustic to say the least, and horses hard to come by. Yet the proximity of gunfire only added to the excitement for Longford.

As the weeks passed, Mr Nott worried that the French appeared to be winning. Longford wouldn't let it trouble him; he relished all the war news they could glean, passing it on to his sister Bess in lively letters home.[3] He found his taste in landscape was for the pastoral rather than the dramatic, perhaps because it reminded him of the Westmeath countryside. In Switzerland, he confessed that he preferred the 'rich and fertile valley to ugly, black mountains and precipices. These afford a striking *coup d'oeil* for a moment, but once that is over (to me) it is very wearisome and uninteresting.' He went for long rides, learnt German fluently, and the fiddle too – in fact, he showed more interest in music and the local society than sculpture and antiquities. In Milan he admired the opera, and noticed the propensity of the people to stab each other over small matters. At Bologna he was delighted. 'Everyone here is a musician and most people have very fine voices.' At Vienna he was so impressed by the

---

* George Frederick Nott, Fellow of All Souls, who later became Prebendary of Winchester. When supervising the repairs to Winchester Cathedral, he fell on his head and never fully recovered. His love for Rome and Italy, however, remained with him all his life. When Henry Edward Fox met him there in 1828, his verdict was: 'He is like a character in a novel . . . too absurd for real life.'

music of an unknown composer, Ludwig van Beethoven, that he subscribed to two copies of the latter's first opus, the piano trios.[4] At Naples Longford was so pleased with the southern beauties that he and the young Lord Carmarthen gave a ball. He was also able to give Nott the slip – 'he seldom caught me there',[5] he admitted to his brother forty years later.

Rome, which followed, was a sad disappointment: 'I lived at Naples,' he concluded to Bess, 'and die at Rome.' By the time they reached the eternal city, Longford wanted nothing to do with the great works of art he was expected to admire. 'I am obliged to go poking in search of antiquities, to stand an hour hungry & cold under an ugly old pillar of marble while a prosing antiquarian harangues on the merits thereof & tries to persuade that it is vastly interesting – & all this because "it is the *custom*".' Nott, on the other hand, leapt about with excitement at the sight of a mere old stone or two. 'Nott is almost mad, at every old wall he stops and examines every stone to see if he can find any pretensions to antiquity . . . if any old arch or a pillar is to be heard of he runs off immediately and stays poking them till I send him word that I can wait no longer.'

On one subject Longford refused to allow any intimacy, and that was the state of his heart. 'I put a stop to all sentimental subjects (of which he proposes one or two every day) by refusing the one & when the other comes I *regularly* go to sleep –' he confessed to Bess. Nevertheless, gossip was rife, Longford's name and others of the Anglo-Irish circle were quickly linked by the expatriates in Italy. Later in the year, a few hints suggest he was pursuing his own sentimental journey. He had a habit of creeping out at night, when his moral guardian assumed he was asleep. The consequences may well have been long-lasting.* Yet in spite of their differences Longford enjoyed his innocent tutor's company: 'He is the best man in the world but knows nothing of it', Longford concluded to Bess as he began the slow stages back to '*the dear country* as we express it with more sincerity than gentility'. His own worldliness now confirmed, he arrived home just after his twenty-first birthday.

* See Chapter Seven.

Whilst his nephew was touring the Continent, Captain Thomas Pakenham had been fighting at sea. In early 1793 he had been issued with the command of the 74-gun *Invincible*. He left Ireland for Portsmouth, with all the energy and enthusiasm he brought to every job that came his way. His wife Louisa was left at Coolure with his cheerful advice ringing in her ears: ''Tis folly to fret'.

But fret she did. Eight years after her marriage, Louisa had changed from being the carefree playmate of Sophia Fitzgerald to the anxious mother of half a dozen children. She had had to become used to disruption. With Thomas now Surveyor General of the Ordnance in Dublin, as well as an MP, their establishment had been constantly moving between the Castle and Coolure, with stays in between at Castletown to see her adored aunt Lady Louisa Conolly. But she depended on her Captain, and missed him dreadfully. Now, with another baby expected, she could not even bring herself to go to Castletown, she could only wait at home for news. 'She has shown a most wonderful degree of sensibility far beyond what I suspected her capable of, and such *strong sense, prudence* and *Character* she amazes me', wrote Sarah Napier, adding sadly: 'I have no hope to give her, for I fear dear Thomas will not be allowed to come home or even stay in port long enough for her to go to him'.[6]

Louisa determined not to remain in Ireland. In March 1794 she sailed for Portsmouth with her tribe of children and the new baby, in order to be near Thomas should he get shore leave. Thankfully, the party arrived safely. The anxiety, however, did not go away, and Sarah Napier hoped that Mrs Pakenham would 'physic away her milk'[7] or she would fall ill. The Duchess of Leinster joined in the concerned chatter and promised Sarah to befriend Mrs Pakenham should she come to London: 'as an old acquaintance, a Dear Creature in herself, Louisa's child and Dear Sophy's friend, I think her entitled to every thing from us'.[8] But nobody could do very much. The Pakenhams had the briefest of reunions in Portsmouth, and then he was at sea again.

At the time the French fleet at Brest were desperate to reach the open Atlantic, in order to receive the badly needed supplies from their merchant convoy due from the United States. To prevent this, the Allied coalition was blockading the Channel. Admiral Howe had twenty-six ships of the line, whilst Admiral Villaret-Joyeuse of the French navy had thirty-one. With such relatively even numbers, Howe's plan was to bring about a series of single ship duels. On 29 May 1794 Captain Pakenham of the *Invincible*, in the van of Admiral Howe's fleet, received orders to engage with his opposite number in the French Admiral's armada, *Le Juste*. For two days the sea fog over the Atlantic made it impossible to detect the enemy. Then, on 1 June, the sun rose and the chase began; and the firing never stopped until noon. Even with his own masts torn to pieces by the cannonade, Pakenham refused to give up. He 'fir'd a musqet over [*Le Juste*] & desir'd her to strike, upon his doing which we sent a Boat on board'.[9] *Le Juste* was duly handed over to Admiral Howe, its 870 seamen made prisoners; amazingly, only fourteen of Pakenham's men had been killed. In the meantime, the famously evangelical Captain of the gallant *Defence*, 'Preaching Jimmy' Gambier, had signalled for help, all his masts and rigging shot to pieces. Pakenham came by in a boat and hailed his friend with his usual humour: 'Jemmy, whom the Lord loveth He chasteneth! Luff, Jemmy, luff!',* which cannot have gone down well with his friend. Captain Gambier replied by asking how many men Pakenham had lost. 'Damn me if I know', came the answer, 'they won't tell me, for fear I should stop their grog.'[10]

By noon on 1 June, Howe's fleet had their victory – at least they had not lost a single ship. For his part in the 'Glorious First', as it became known, Captain Pakenham was given a gold medal by the King. Returning to Portsmouth, the cheerful Captain fell into the arms of Louisa, and before long she had conceived an eighth child.

Back in Dublin, Bess Stewart gave birth to her first, her mother at her side. But the happy news was dampened by the continuing agitation in the countryside, with 'Defenders' – armed Catholics who had originated in the sectarian feuds in Ulster – now a threatening force

* 'Luff' is a naval order meaning to put the tiller towards the lee side so that the ship sails closer to the wind.

in the midlands. In nearby County Longford, cattle were mutilated, landowners were assaulted and even murdered by black-faced assassins. Maria Edgeworth wrote to her aunt that she checked carefully for traces of charcoal on the faces of those who came to the house, but it was a nervous joke. Mr Edgeworth, in the meantime, had come up with an amazing invention to help with the defence of Ireland against France. The 'tellograph', as he christened it, consisted of a semaphore system of hilltop signals to pass messages from one Government corps to another. The idea was that Dublin would be able to communicate swiftly with all coastal points of Ireland, an essential service in the event of an invasion. Lady Longford was more than happy to let him use a hill at Pakenham Hall as a point for the experiment. The system worked; in five minutes a signal was transmitted, received and replied to from Dr Daniel Beaufort's home at Collon in County Louth. Edgeworth, delighted, began working on submitting his plan to the Government.

Meanwhile, the younger Pakenham boys were growing up, and needed professions. The military was the obvious route – the present war made it the patriotic choice. The second son, Ned, following in the footsteps of his seventeenth-century ancestors, went into the Army. At sixteen, he was bought a commission in the 92nd Foot, as a Lieutenant of the regiment. His mother decided that he was too young to serve immediately, and arranged for him to spend the first year with a tutor in Wales, well away from the temptations of Dublin. Longford, almost as soon as he returned from Europe, took on the captaincy of the local yeomanry. At first there was not much for them to do except make an occasional tour of the neighbouring hotspots, keeping an eye on any disaffected elements that might use the opportunity of a foreign war. But this was a situation to which everyone was accustomed. 'I suppose you won't forgive me saying nothing of our Irish politics, as they sound so terrible', Sarah Napier explained to her cousin in England: 'That good-natured Mrs Crewe* wrote to beg of us to *take shelter* at Crewe Hall & we got her letter of *terrors* just as we were preparing for a ball at Castletown, where we

---

* A famous Whig hostess known as 'buff & blue Mrs Crewe'.

have passed a *very* merry Christmas, tho' *canons* are sent down to the county of Louth, within 20 miles of us!' she joked.[11] It was equally difficult for any of the young Pakenhams to believe that their peace would really be threatened. But, reading the Government spies' reports in the Ordnance Office in Dublin Castle, their uncle Thomas thought differently.

Hercules, meanwhile, was finishing school in Dublin, where Bess and Henry Stewart acted *in loco parentis*. The fourth brother, William, had been made a naval cadet at thirteen and sent out to the Indies with the help of the Captain's old friend, Admiral Duckworth. The rest of the family remained in the country. Kitty, Helen and Caroline, particularly now Bess had left home, attached themselves dutifully to their mother, who was soon mourning the death of her father.* Kitty, in particular, still much in demand in Dublin society, seemed to prefer not to leave the safe shadow of her extended family. With a great maternal instinct, she helped look after the various waifs and strays left at home: above all, poor little Robert – her parents' youngest child – crippled from a deformity of the spine brought on by measles. Perhaps using Robert's needs as an excuse, she gradually became more of a retiring figure. In private she was still mourning her handsome Arthur Wesley.

---

* Old Hercules Langford Rowley died at Langford House in Dublin in 1794. *Walker's Hibernian Magazine* reported the death of the oldest member of the House of Commons: 'He was seemingly in good health on Monday, but on the next day he put his hand to his forehead, and said to his servant: "Lord bless me, I believe I am going to die", and then expired without a groan or a struggle.' His heir, Hercules, died in March 1796.

2

Rebellion

❧

The summer of 1797 was election time in Ireland. In Westmeath, Captain Thomas Pakenham, MP for the neighbouring rotten borough of Longford, took a keen interest in which way the electors might vote. He drew up a table of four columns, and headed them *'Friends, Enemies, Doubtful* and *Unknown'*.

In principle the family had no control over the two county seats of Westmeath, although the Pakenhams were major landowners. How many would adhere to young Lord Longford's wishes, and vote for the candidates the family supported? How far had the spirit of discontent spread to the local freeholders?* There had already been a serious insurrection in the north, now crushed by the commander of the forces there, General Lake, who had proclaimed martial law. But what was the feeling in the midlands?

Since 1793 the political temperature in Ireland had been rising. To the radical dissenting elements in the north, the French 'Citizen' republic was an inspiration. There were even radicals among the ruling Anglo-Irish families. The most ardent of all was Lord Edward Fitzgerald, the Conollys' nephew and the brother of the Duke of Leinster. He had joined the 'United Irishmen', founded by Theobald Wolfe Tone and others in 1791, and was now one of its leaders. Their aim was a complete severance with Britain and the unification of all

---

* The 'forty-shilling' freeholders were the electorate for the county seats with that property qualification – i.e. their properly was worth a minimum of forty shillings per year. Lord Longford's influence was over the two *borough* seats of Longford town, which were less important than county seats as they had a smaller electorate, usually about fifteen freemen of the city.

'hearts' in Ireland under the banner of a French-style republic. Three years after its foundation, the movement had been declared illegal by the Government and gone underground.

As Surveyor General of the Ordnance in Dublin, Captain Pakenham was now in charge of moving Government munitions and armaments to strategic points. The Lord Lieutenant, Lord Camden, was leaving nothing to chance. He had suspended *habeas corpus* in 1796, and an uneasy atmosphere existed in the country. Pakenham's knowledge was especially valuable because of his naval experience: the main Irish waterways were considered soft targets for a foreign invasion. There had already been a horrible scare in late December 1796, when the French General Hoche's attempt to land his invasion force at Bantry Bay* in Cork had only failed because of the storms. 'Captain Pakenham is come and in great spirits – he thinks hardly a ship will get back', George Knox had reported from the Castle to Lord de Vesci.[1] But bad weather was not a reliable ally. And revelations by the captured French officers that they had expected to find their Irish allies waiting, made terrifying news.

In early 1797 Camden instructed the First Lord of the Admiralty, Earl Spencer, to keep Pakenham in Ireland. Spencer was pleased to concur, having already planned to ask Thomas to look into the arming of gunboats on the Shannon and Waterford rivers.[2] Louisa might have her husband back from the Navy, but his military duties were far from over. In the meantime, his election for the Longford borough seat was successful. But the election was succeeded by the imposition of martial law a year later. In Dublin, the atmosphere was growing more uneasy by the day. Government spies were everywhere, on the lookout for any conspiracy. The United Irishmen were known to be planning an insurrection, and on 12 March 1798 all but three of the Dublin Executive were arrested. By the 30th, Camden had ordered a curfew on the whole city. Lord Edward Fitzgerald had escaped and gone into hiding; there was now a price on his head.

Louisa Pakenham began to feel the awkwardness of her family

* The French had been persuaded to send a fleet by Wolfe Tone, who was on board the flagship.

situation. Edward Fitzgerald was her aunt Conolly's favourite nephew, the Duchess of Leinster's 'dearest Angel Eddy'; she had been brought up knowing him like a brother. His wife, Lady Pamela, had always 'quite delighted' her. On the other hand, Captain Pakenham, with his trusted position in the Castle, was naturally on the other side. She wrote nervously to her old childhood friend Sophia, now living in England, and Edward Fitzgerald's favourite sister. She tried to explain the clash of loyalties.

> I feel very much at a loss how to write to you, & yet when events have happened that give you so much concern, I cannot be silent. The arrest of a Number of Persons in Dublin last week, and the sudden departure of Ld Edward, has been too Publick a thing for you not to have heard of it . . . I know not, my Dearest Sophia, what may be your way of thinking about Politics, unfortunately for these countries few people at this moment feel impartial on that Subject. Mr Pakenham's situation & opinions attaches him strongly & of course me to the existing Government here but we do not & I hope we never shall let any opinions alter our private friendships . . . the Government have found this Act of Power necessary, & altho' we are not among them who blame them for it . . . we lament it so much in general as any people can do, & in particular most sincerely deplore the distress it has occasioned to our Friends . . . Lady Edward I believe does us the justice to believe this fully as she has conversed with me since with a degree of kindness that shows her good sense can distinguish between public necessity and private regard.[3]

Sarah Napier, however, did not believe for a moment that Thomas was sincere in his private sympathy. She wrote bitterly in her journal that 'Mr P. spoke as usual, of Edward, *fine flummery*, and said he only hoped in God he should not meet him, as it would be a sad struggle between his *duty* and his *friendship*'.*[4] Louisa Pakenham

---

* The quote continues: 'Louisa took all this, as it was intended she should; but when she was out of the room, Emily heard Sir G.S. express his *hopes that Lord Edward would be caught*, and she did not *hear* or *see* any-thing like a contradiction to this wish from any of the company.'

– like Louisa Conolly – could only pray that Edward had already got safely abroad.

The Conollys themselves were in far more difficult circumstances. Lord Camden's acting Chief Secretary, Lord Castlereagh, was married to Tom Conolly's niece, Amelia Hobart.[5] It meant that good Lady Louisa was hard put to say a word against the Castle people. In despair Tom Conolly rode about the neighbourhood of Celbridge and Leixlip, appealing to his tenants to give up their pikes.

Some weeks later, on 19 May, Thomas Pakenham was enjoying *Robin Hood* in Lady Castlereagh's box at the Theatre Royal with his wife and Emily Napier, Sarah's daughter. Next to them sat Lord Camden, anxious to prove that everything was now quiet in Dublin. Suddenly a whispered name caught the attention of the party: Lord Edward Fitzgerald had been captured! Not only that, but wounded in the act of shooting an officer! Camden hurried away, and the ladies begged to leave too, but Thomas pressed Louisa to keep Emily in the box, fearing that panic would follow if they were seen to go. Pakenham's position was now more awkward than ever. He could not help cursing that the young lunatic had not escaped abroad when he could, rather than let his dangerous zeal for democracy cause such pain to himself and others.

As for Louisa Pakenham, she was in despair. What could she say to Sophia? She wrote first one letter then another, fearing that her first letter had seemed 'very cold, but I know not what to say except that nothing can alter my affection for you, God Almighty comfort and support you all'.[6] None of Edward's family was even permitted to visit the wounded prisoner in Newgate. In England, his desperate mother had set off to reach her sick child: 'the child of her heart, & the idol of his family'.[7]

Four days after Edward Fitzgerald's capture, on 23 May, Lord Longford was returning to Westmeath in the Dublin coach. Dozing in the early morning light, he woke suddenly to find the coach jerking to a halt, the reins of the horses seized and the passengers ordered out by a gang of rebels. In the noise and confusion he jumped out just in time. 'Lord Longford was taken but has made his escape tho' he has not yet been found', reported a neighbour to his friend in Dublin, and continued more alarmingly: 'a gentleman just arrived from Trim says there are 5000 Rebels in battle array near Dunshaughlin but all in appearance *Black Guards*, ill-disciplined and armed with bad Pikes. But determined to Conquer or Dye every Military & Yeoman for many miles around. Gone to assist.'[8]

The rising had begun. The signal was the capture of the mail coaches on the radiating roads out of Dublin: insurrection had broken out at a number of points in the counties of Dublin, Kildare and Meath. At Naas in Kildare, Lord Gosford's militia fought off an attack of insurgents. Houses were being burnt by the militia in the search for rebel arms; on 26 May a band of 200 United Irishmen broke through Mr Conolly's gates and marched across the front lawn of Castletown under Lady Louisa's nose. The situation was considered so dangerous that Captain Pakenham's boys at school had to be brought to Dublin under military escort. All was panic and agitation; Ireland was now in a state of civil war. In the months that followed, 30,000 were to meet their deaths.[9]

Louisa Pakenham, deeply anxious 'in the present Crises of affairs', felt it her duty to stay with 'Mr P. who is harassed to death with Publick business'.[10] In Dublin she did what she could to glean information on the precarious state of Edward's health, whose wound had begun to fester, seeing his surgeon every day, and sending bulletins back to Castletown. She didn't dare go to Coolure, since though 'Dublin is perfectly quiet and safe . . . the country all round is in open Rebellion'.[11] Then, on 3 June, Louisa sent an express to Castletown. The family must come with all haste, Lord Edward was dying.

The account of Lord Edward Fitzgerald's last delirious hours, and Lady Louisa Conolly's desperate attempts to see him, has been told many times before. Lord Camden refused to allow Lady Louisa into Newgate. It was only when she begged Lord Clare, the Chancellor, to help her that she was admitted into the prison. In fact Clare was so touched by her distress that he showed Lady Louisa the 'tenderness of a Brother rather than a Friend', as Emily Napier much later described it, '& . . . cried like a woman when he saw [Edward] dying'.[12]

When the end came on 4 June, Louisa Pakenham, exhausted by sick children and her own family sorrows,* took up her pen to write to Sophia 'twenty times', but did not know what to say. Weeks later, she described to Sophia how she had spent the dreadful days in Dublin, 'in constant alarm, Mr Pakenham's business at the Ordnance obliging him to stay day and night at his Office, so that for all that time, I passed the night either watching at the Window for his return or when he would permit me walking about the Castleyard with him'.[13]

At Castletown, Lady Louisa could only 'go on like a machine'. She dreaded that a battle would break out nearby: 'Our house is a perfect garrison. Eighteen soldiers sleep in our saloon, and we are all blocked up and shut up except by the hall door and one door to the kitchen-yard, and are frequently ordered all into the house upon the alarm being given of the rebels being near Celbridge.'[14] Her pity was for the people, who she had no doubt were 'forced into rebellion' by a faction of agitators. She could not believe they would hurt their landlord.

Others were not so sanguine; everywhere houses were raided for arms. At Carton, the Duke of Leinster's butler bricked up the valuable plate in a wall. But the raids in Kildare were only short-lived outbreaks. In the south of the country a mass rising had taken place. On 30 May in Wexford, a local army of 20,000 had marched on Wexford town and proclaimed a republic. They were only finally defeated nearly a month later, on 21 June, in the brutal Battle of Vinegar Hill.

By the end of July Louisa Pakenham had retreated to England with her children. She went under orders from her husband, and took a house at Parkgate near Chester for a month, a small sea port where the Irish packets docked. By now, all the men of the Pakenham family who were old enough were involved in the fighting. Harry Stewart was with his corps in Donegal, Lord Longford with his yeomanry in

---

* Her brother, William Conolly Staples, died in March 1798 from consumption. His widow, Anne, was only seventeen, and was left with a newborn baby. She married Richard Napier, Lady Sarah Napier's fourth son, nineteen years later.

Westmeath, young Ned now a Major in the 23rd Light Dragoons under General Lake, and even seventeen-year-old Hercules riding with the Lawyers' Corps.

When Louisa returned to Ireland at the end of August, a Bill of Attainder against Edward Fitzgerald was being pushed through Parliament, dispossessing his wife and children of his estates. Sarah Napier was violent in her antipathy to all on the Government side. She only slightly held back her vitriol when it came to the Pakenhams:

> . . . on Sunday, Lord and Lady Castlereagh, Mr and Mrs P., Mr and Mrs F., have made a party to come and dine, and stay here [Castletown], because Lord Hobart comes; so that all Dublin will hear that the very people who passed the week in plunging daggers in Louisa's heart hallow the seventh day by a junket in her house! Mrs P. is indeed just landed from England, and Mr P., we have reason to believe, has avoided the house of Commons as much as he could . . .[15]

At the Castle, a few weeks before, Captain Thomas Pakenham welcomed the arrival of the new Lord Lieutenant, Marquess Charles Cornwallis. He was known to be a civilised character, and would approach the situation with honesty and lack of prejudice – or so Lady Louisa Conolly considered.[16] And Charles Cornwallis had known Tom Pakenham for ever – after all, Pakenham had fought under him in the American war, and Cornwallis's own naval brother William was a family friend of the Longfords. Like Lord Camden, Marquess Cornwallis thought Pakenham a safe bet for the defence of Ireland, if rather 'light-headed' and without much 'method',[17] and kept him at his post in the Ordnance. (Although another peer had referred to him as 'a very cunning quizzing Knave of a seaman'.) Cornwallis knew that Pakenham's naval expertise might well be vital if the French support expected for the rebels was to materialise.

Cornwallis had not long to wait. On 22 August 1,000 French troops under General Humbert disembarked at Killala in County

Mayo. Five days later they had gained a humiliating victory over General Lake at Castlebar,[18] where another 3,500 rebels had joined them. The Pakenhams' neighbour and Lake's subordinate, Lord Granard, had vainly tried to keep his militia from fleeing, but 'they ran away at the very first discharge of the French artillery and never looked behind till they got twenty miles off'[19] reported Lady Longford's niece Harriet.

In County Westmeath, United Irishmen began to assemble to meet their French allies; Lord Sunderlin, a Protestant grandee, found his house surrounded by rebels, and feared it would be burnt to the ground.[20] Only his reputation as a considerate landlord put off the attack. By early September Lord Longford was alone at Pakenham Hall, 'keeping garrison & . . . constantly watching the country about P. Hall with his very efficient Corps'.[21] Lady Longford had been in Dublin with the family when the rising broke out and had been urged not to return.[22] In Rutland Square* they waited anxiously for news. It came with a drum-roll. For by 5 September trouble was right on their doorstep, with several thousand rebels camped on the high ground outside a charitable institution known as Wilson's Hospital, just a few miles from Pakenham Hall.

At first light on 6 September Captain Lord Longford led his small troop of yeomanry† as fast as possible across the bog. He had sent an urgent message to Major Porter, commander of the garrison at Cavan, appealing for support. Just before Wilson's Hospital he halted, and waited with impatience for Major Porter and his Argyll Fencibles to join him. Only the day before Porter had routed an attack by an army of 1,000 rebels[23] on the nearby garrison at Granard in County Longford. Amongst the small, entrenched force camped on the town's famous Norman motte was Major Edward Pakenham with his Light Dragoons. As a cavalry regiment, the Light Dragoons had had little prospect of success against a line of pikes. Luckily for

---

* Cavendish Row had been renamed after the Lord Lieutenant, the Duke of Rutland, in 1795.
† From Castlepollard, the local market town, and the surrounding areas. They would have been his tenants.

Ned, Porter's men tipped the balance, and though the rebels tried to gain the advantage by stampeding the local cattle, by 3 o'clock in the afternoon they had been defeated. Several hundred were caught and some hanged.

Porter did not stop, but marched on to Westmeath, where he joined Lord Longford on the evening of the 6th. In all, their combined forces were only something like 350 men, against a rebel army of about 4,000, still camped in the grounds of the Hospital. But the rebels had lost heart when there was no sign of their French supporters. By dawn of 7 September they had been scattered by Longford and Porter's men, and Wilson's Hospital was deserted. All day the yeomanry rounded up the rebels; many drowned in a desperate attempt to flee across nearby Lough Owel. Only darkness halted the pursuit.

At Edgeworthstown, a very different scene was played out. Richard Lovell Edgeworth had recently returned to Ireland with his new wife, Frances Beaufort.* As the news of Westmeath's uprisings came through, Edgeworth decided to move his family from their relatively isolated home to Longford town nine miles away, where there was a regular garrison. Moments after the carriage and horses had left with an accompanying corps of Edgeworth's unarmed tenantry, a marching band of rebels had descended on his house. It was saved from burning only through the greatest coincidence: one of the leaders had once been lent money by Edgeworth's housekeeper and would not allow the others to enter the gates.[24] Meanwhile, Edgeworth arrived at Longford just as the news came through of victory for the Government forces at Granard.

To his indignation, Edgeworth now found himself under suspicion from the Protestant garrison. Why was Edgeworth's corps largely made up of Catholics? Why had the rebels not burnt his house? The yeomanry almost lynched Edgeworth's son Lovell when they found

---

* Oddly enough, when he reported to his children that he was going to be married for a fourth time, one of them suggested that 'Lady Longford' was to be the lucky bride. Frances was the daughter of Dr Daniel Augustus Beaufort of nearby County Louth, a clergyman famous for his map-making skills.

he had taken a telescope up onto the courthouse roof, as they assumed he was signalling to the rebels. The situation was saved by the arrival of their commanding officers, but only just. Edgeworth had been pelted with stones and insults.

By 7 September Humbert had crossed the Shannon with his army. Cornwallis aimed to cut them off before they reached Dublin, and sent General Lake north while he himself took a southerly route. Accordingly, on 8 September General John Cradock* and Captain Thomas Pakenham, in the van of Lake's pursuing army, came upon the rear of Humbert's forces at the small hamlet of Ballinamuck, in north County Longford. One Martin McLoughlin left a vivid recollection of the next scene:

> . . . when the small body of the advanced guard came near, some of the French began to throw down their arms; upon which Captain Pakenham and General Craddock, with about twenty dragoons, rode up and ordered the French to surrender, which they did . . . When they came up to the Irish recruits, Captain Pakenham called out to us to throw down our arms, and take to our heels as the only chance we had of saving our lives; but General Blake who commanded us swore he would do no such thing. He ordered Captain Pakenham and General Craddock to surrender themselves prisoners immediately. 'Damn me, Jack,' says the Captain to General Craddock, 'we are all in the wrong box – about ship my boy.' He then called out to General Blake, 'Why, blast your eyes! You are not going to fire at us, you scoundrel, are you? Do you see ten thousand men coming down the hill? If you fire a shot at us, they'll cut you to atoms.' – 'Surrender yourselves immediately,' cried Blake, 'or I'll pepper you by G-d.' – 'You may be damned for a rascal,' cried the Captain of the *Invincible*, spitting out a large quid of tobacco, 'Tom Pakenham was never born to be shot.' Then clapping spurs to their horses, General Craddock and he rode off as hard as they could gallop; and immediately a volley was sent after them by our party . . . [25]

---

* Created Baron Howden in 1819.

In a moment, Lieutenant-Colonel Innes and the Armagh Militia descended on the rebels with all the ferocity Pakenham had predicted. Humbert, caught between Lake and Cornwallis, had no choice but to turn and fight. It was a dismal affair, lasting all of half an hour before the French surrendered. Whilst they were marched away as prisoners, their Irish allies met a far worse fate. Many men were hung on the spot, whilst others were dragged away to the gibbets at Granard.[26]

The battle's aftermath showed a horrible scene. The hillside above Ballinamuck was covered with corpses, from a distance like 'flocks of sheep', the stripped bodies white and bloated. Yet when Maria Edgeworth visited the camp, she made no mention of them. The new Mrs Edgeworth even drew a sketch of the camp. The Edgeworth party must have been on the other side of the hill from where the slaughter had taken place. With surprising enthusiasm Maria described the site to one of her cousins. 'Perhaps you recollect', she wrote,

> a pretty turn in the road, where there is a little stream with a three-arched bridge: in the fields which rise in a gentle slope, on the right hand side of this stream, about sixty bell tents were pitched, the arms all ranged on the grass; before the tents, poles with little streamers fling here and there; groups of men leading their horses to water, others filling kettles and black pots, some cooking under the hedges; the various uniforms looked pretty; Highlanders gathering black-berries . . . Don't imagine that I am camp mad – I was only glad to see anything like order and civility after the horrors of Longford.[27]

The encounter with the Protestant yeomanry at Longford had been an unprecedented shock to the family. Richard Lovell Edgeworth himself was so disgusted by the sectarian violence shown up by the whole affair that he decided to leave Ireland for good, since he could not live amongst such 'warring savages'.[28] Only the calm advice of his father-in-law, Dr Beaufort, persuaded him to stay.

The evening after the battle, Thomas and Ned Pakenham, uncle and nephew, rode alongside Generals Cornwallis and Lake in search of a bed for the night. From another direction, General John Moore was making his way to the same rendezvous. Quite naturally, with Lord Longford's house so close to the scene of destruction, they made their billet at Pakenham Hall.

3

A Call for Union

For nearly a hundred years, since the Scottish parliament had been united with the English in 1707, the issue of an actual Parliamentary Union between Dublin and Westminster had been mooted. There had been a separate Irish parliament since the fifteenth century, an assembly that had had its legislative powers restricted and then nominally restored in 1720 and 1782 respectively, with the so-called 'Grattan's Parliament'.* Now the civil war had pushed the matter to the forefront of the political agenda. With the war against Revolutionary France continuing, a disaffected Ireland was an urgent problem to the Government. Both Cornwallis and Castlereagh, by now his permanent Chief Secretary, urged that the Union should be accomplished in the interests of Irish and English stability. Castlereagh, in particular, had come to see it as the only means by which the Emancipation of Irish Catholics could be achieved; such was the lobby against them in the Irish parliament.

Emancipation, in this context, meant chiefly the ability of a Catholic to have a parliamentary seat, although it also included the holding of high office in Government, the Army and the Law. It was the natural successor to the Act of 1793, whereby 30,000 Irish Catholics had been enfranchised. But George III, who remained stubbornly against any form of concession to the Catholics, wanted the rebellion to be used as a stick to suppress Catholic demands. In June 1798 he had

---

* The two Acts which had kept the Irish parliament under English control were repealed and amended in 1782, following the campaign of the Irish Volunteers and MPs, including Henry Grattan.

made this clear to his Prime Minister, William Pitt: '[General Corn-wallis] must not lose the present moment of terror for frightening the Supporters of the Castle into an Union with this Country, & no further indulgences must be granted to the Roman Catholics.'[1]

In fact, the issue of Catholic Emancipation brought two opposing groups in the Irish parliament together when it came to the question of a Union. While some saw the end of Protestant-controlled parliament as a precursor to a much needed remedy for the Catholics, others saw it as a guarantee such a revolution would never happen. To further complicate things, some of the Castle's traditional supporters were either against the measure, or at least unsure of their feelings. In November 1798 Castlereagh put the young Lord Longford at the top of the 'doubtful' list. The leaders of the Irish Whigs,* on the other hand, were in no doubt: the Ponsonbys, Lord Charlemont and the Duke of Leinster stood doggedly anti-Union. Tom Conolly was for it, yet was at pains to reassure his nephew-in-law, the Duke of Leinster, that he was still his most affectionate friend.

Once the news of a possible Union had become widely known, a flurry of pamphlets appeared denouncing the measure. 'Bushe, Barrington and Mr Jebb come forth in print tomorrow. Surely all Bedlam, not Parnassus is let out', Alexander Knox, the Under Secretary, complained to Castlereagh at this hailstorm of press activity. Although Knox was confident that eventually 'liberal terms and discreet management will bring forward a muster of men of no personal feelings . . . who will much outvote the political Stentors who are bellowing to the high heavens',[2] it was a provoking time. Passions were decidedly raised in the two Houses, with each side trying to win or cajole their supporters.

When the first vote[3] came to be taken on 23 January 1799, according to the partisan memoirs of the barrister Jonah Barrington,†

---

* Traditionally the 'Whigs' were the party of the country, and the 'Tories' the party of the monarch and court. In Ireland, a Whig club had been established by the Duke of Leinster in 1789.

† Jonah Barrington accepted the Escheatorship of Munster 14 January 1800, and therefore resigned his seat in parliament before the decisive vote of 6 February 1800.

secret messengers were dispatched in every direction, to bring in loitering or reluctant members – every emissary that Government could rely upon was busily employed the entire morning . . . Admiral Pakenham, a naturally friendly and good-hearted gentleman, that night acted like the captain of a press-gang, and actually *hauled* in some members who were desirous of retiring. He had declared he would act in *any* capacity, according to the exigencies of his party; and he did not shrink from his task.[4]

But at this point, at least, Pakenham's zeal was to no avail, and the Government won by only a single vote. As the session broke up the Marquess of Buckingham, the ex-Lord Lieutenant, reported that 'the mob drew the Speaker home, and then proceeded to hustle Lord Ormonde and Captain Pakenham; the latter drew a pistol, collared the first man who struck at him, and has secured him. They were dispersed by the first appearance of troops . . . Dublin is in a very unpleasant state.'[5]

In the face of such minimal support, Castlereagh was forced to withdraw the measure. The freeholders of numerous counties including County Longford had been split in two over the issue. One group sent in anti-Union petitions to the Castle, whilst their neighbours sent protests against such petitions. But Lord Longford, for one, wrote to Castlereagh that he would not sign a protest that only added to the trouble. A protest 'would have strongly the appearance of intending to push a measure against which the public mind has for the present shown itself so violently prejudiced'. Even with this caveat, Longford announced his loyalty to Government to be unquestioned. 'I have no difficulty in declaring that my opinion coincides with the sentiments expressed in the Protest; but, at present,' he continued to Lord Castlereagh, 'I think the first object is to tranquillize, by allowing the ferment to subside.'[6]

Seeing no alternative, Castlereagh raised the stakes. Whatever the cost, he was determined that 'nothing but the utmost effort to meet private interest can enable us to buy up the fee-simple of Irish corruption'.[7] Cornwallis, although he confessed to hating himself for being involved in such 'dirty business', and 'wishing to kick those whom my public duty obliges me to court',[8] supported Castlereagh. Accordingly, the promise of financial compensation was made to those who would lose their borough seats in the rearrangement of the constituencies. It was universally understood, after all, that a borough was a marketable piece of property. As for patronage, Castlereagh recognised that the price of victory would be a very heavy one.

For ten more months the debate continued. Even with his oiling of the wheels with the help of a Secret Service slush fund,[9] Castlereagh feared that the great baggage of the Union would fail to pass over the threshold. In order to be nearer the centre of operations, he leased Mornington House, the Earl of Mornington's old home in Upper Merrion Street. Here Lady Castlereagh gave dinner parties for the staunchest Government supporters. Across the Liffey, the octogenarian patriot and friend of Longford's father, Lord Pery, hosted a great meeting of the Antis in his house in Sackville Street.

By the summer of 1799, Longford was openly declaring himself a supporter. If he behaved without the zeal of his uncle Thomas, he was convinced that Union was the right step. Reports of foreign invasion continued; in parts of the country there were still bands of guerrillas attacking property and mutilating cattle, not to mention the widespread economic distress caused by a failed harvest. The embers of revolutionary fervour seemed all too likely to reignite. No, peace, security and prosperity were inherently tied up with Great Britain. His control over the Longford borough seats meant he was able to depose Henry Stewart, who had voted against the Union in January, from his seat – and put in his brother Ned. Longford's cousin, Lord Bective, in Kells, did much the same, chucking out one brother, Robert Taylor, in favour of a pro-Union cousin for the same reason. Bective's other brother, Clotworthy Taylor, was persuaded to change sides to the Union cause, a double crime in the eyes of Jonah Barrington. Many other families were split: Lord Clements voted against whilst his father the Earl of Leitrim gave his support; the Duke of Leinster – the leading figure amongst the anti-Union peers – had two brothers (Charles and Robert) who were pro-Union.

Lord Charles was subsequently made Baron Lecale; Clotworthy Taylor – who had married his first cousin, Fanny Rowley – was created Baron Langford in July 1800. Tom Conolly – and his wife Lady Louisa – were pro-Union in spite of their close relationship with Leinster; in fact Louisa declared it her 'favourite object' and went on to describe how her 'friends the Catholics are well inclined to it'.[10] Longford himself was not on the list of those who had been promised titular rewards. His loyalty, however, was not forgotten when the time came to choose the twenty-eight representative Irish peers for the Lords at Westminister.

By January 1800 Pitt and Castlereagh were surer of their majority, but a majority was a fragile thing. It was rumoured that the opposition had begun to play the Castle at their own game, raising large funds to 'buy' pro-Union seats. The pale figure of the great patriot himself, Henry Grattan, 'father' of the Irish parliament, was carried to the House to make a final appeal for rejection. Too ill to stand to make his speech, for two hours Grattan lectured the Commons on the freedom they would be forfeiting should they vote for the Union. ' "The thing which he proposes to buy is what cannot be sold – liberty," ' denounced Grattan, 'pointing an accusing finger at Castlereagh'.* It was said however, that Grattan only won some Catholic supporters over to the anti-Union cause. In the meantime, Richard Lovell Edgeworth fulminated against the 'fraud and farce' used to 'subjugate my country'. To punish the Government he declared he would vote with the Antis, although his own 'Opinion' was 'in Favour of the Union'. He then had his speeches published as a pamphlet.†

The Bill for an Act of Union passed in the Irish House of Commons on 7 June 1800. With characteristic melodrama, Jonah Barrington later recorded the moment although he had not been there:

---

* *The Rise of Castlereagh* by H. Montgomery Hyde, p. 344. In fact Henry Grattan lived another twenty years, sitting in Westminster once the Irish parliament had been dissolved.
† *The Substance of Three Speeches Delivered in the House of Commons, Ireland: February 6, March 4, and March 21 1800.*

At length, with an eye averted from the object which he hated, [Speaker Foster] proclaimed, with a subdued voice, 'the AYES have it.' The fatal sentence was now pronounced, for an instant he stood statue-like; then indignantly, and with disgust, flung the Bill upon the table, and sunk into his chair with an exhausted spirit. An independent country was thus degraded into a province – Ireland, as a nation was EXTINGUISHED.[11]

When the Bill went forward for its third reading in the Irish Lords on 13 June, it was a mere formality. Seventy-five peers voted for the 'ayes', Tom Longford amongst them; a stalwart twenty-six voted against. From the public at large, there was a resigned silence. After the royal assent had been given on 1 August, Cornwallis recorded that 'there was not a murmur heard in the street, nor, I believe an expression of ill-humour throughout the whole city of Dublin'.[12]

Delighted that her overworked husband had at least achieved his aim, Lady Castlereagh gave a masked ball in Phoenix Park.

4

Troublesome Times

With the Act of Union Ireland's parliament no longer existed: from now on her representatives would sit in Westminster. These included one hundred Irish Members for the Commons, and thirty-two representative peers* for the Lords. Among the latter was Lord Longford, elected for life. And a richer Longford he was too, since each patron of the disenfranchised boroughs had been compensated with £7,500 per seat, including those whose Members had voted against the Union.†

For nearly another year, Cornwallis continued on as Lord Lieutenant, with Castlereagh his Secretary, until they both resigned with Pitt in February 1801. The Prime Minister's resignation was provoked by his failure to carry Catholic Emancipation – 'without which all we have done will be of no avail',[1] as Cornwallis wrote sadly. It had finally been abandoned by the British Cabinet when the King proved obdurate. For some in Ireland this was no excuse. 'The Catholic Emancipation', fumed Sarah Napier's husband George, 'is now admitted on all hands to have been one of [Pitt's] rascally juggles. He has been a blasted Juggler throughout his whole political Life, without having once shown himself a conjuror.'[2] Pitt's failure to carry the measure was to smoulder on, undermining the Union.

---

* Twenty-eight temporal, and four spiritual.
† The government paid out £1,250,000 in total compensation to the owners of disenfranchised boroughs. See Edith Johnston-Liik, *History of the Irish Parliament*, Vol. II, p. 202.

With Irish MPs no longer meeting in Dublin, the city changed. The elegant town houses of so many of the gentry were not a requirement any more – in some cases they were quickly sold, before there was a glut in the market. The old parliament building itself was transformed into the Bank of Ireland; fifteen years later, the Duke of Leinster sold his enormous town house off Stephen's Green to the Royal Dublin Society. For a while, however, social life continued in much the same way; after all, the Lord Lieutenant still lived in Ireland. In 1802, according to one report, there was a concerted campaign to keep people in the country: 'Dublin was uncommonly gay this spring. All the unionists strove to prevent people from going to live in England by giving Balls and Masquerades.'[3] The Conollys, for example, felt it their duty to give a summer ball, where Lady Louisa persuaded Louisa Pakenham to dance – 'merrily when once she began', although 'at first ashamed because of her *Ten* children'.[4]

In the meantime, Thomas Pakenham, whom Cornwallis had recommended as deserving 'every attention', continued at the Ordnance under the new Lord Lieutenant. The Government had made him a Rear-Admiral in 1799, but all too soon the Admiral had new problems on his plate. Tom Conolly, his uncle by marriage, died on 27 April 1803. It was Admiral Pakenham's eldest son Edward who was due to inherit Castletown under Conolly's will.* When Thomas and his brother-in-law Lord Dunlo,† who had been 'bred to the law', began unravelling Castletown affairs, they found a horrible mess.

Tom Conolly had bequeathed a shameful legacy. Although Lady Louisa had been left Castletown and a good provision for the remainder of her life, the estate itself was verging on bankrupt. His debts in England alone amounted to £100,000. Now the Admiral thought there would not be 'a chance of [Dunlo's] legacies being ever paid or of Edward having one farthing from the property or of Castletown, and everything else escaping the creditors'.[5] Henry

---

* Since the death in 1798 of William Conolly Staples, the brother of Louisa and Harriet Staples.

† Richard Le Poer Trench was married to Henrietta Staples, Louisa Pakenham's sister, and was styled Viscount Dunlo from 1803. He inherited the title Earl Clancarty in 1805.

Stewart was also owed a considerable sum, even young Emily Napier's legacy was in doubt. There was also the matter of a generous gift to be paid to a Mrs Jennet – Conolly's long-hidden mistress.

Both the Admiral and Dunlo did their best to hide the extent of the damage, and the existence of Mrs Jennet, from Lady Louisa. The poor Admiral, tough as he was, was deeply affected by the effects of the bankruptcy on Conolly's tenants. Back and forth he rode, between Castletown and County Donegal, unearthing more and more commitments that could not be honoured. 'I crave your pity,' he wrote to Dunlo from Ballyshannon,

> for all the miseries heaped on me at this damned place, where Conolly has been picking up money by every expedient of Promising Renewals which we have not now the power of fulfilling – the Distress arising to many poor People who have borrowed Money for those Purposes is not to be described; it is heartbreaking to witness it . . .[6]

Conolly's angelic widow, Lady Louisa, however, did not wish for anything except that the debts should be honourably paid. 'What may be deemed in the world sacrifices cost me nothing absolutely nothing', she confessed to her brother Richmond. 'Admiral Pakenham's generous Heart, I am forced to fight against, his gratitude will not permit him to see anything but my advantage (and comfort if he could procure it for me) in every transaction, and I naturally wish to see his family in future benefited so that it becomes necessary for me to take a part.'[7]

Naturally the Pakenhams, who had always been close to the Conollys, became closer still during this process. By the September following Conolly's death, Lady Louisa had invited the Admiral and his family to leave the house he had leased nearby and live with her 'entirely'. Louisa was pleased, seeing immediately that it would be a comfort to her aunt to have the bustle of the large family around her; for them, it could only be an 'advantage . . . having my Girls brought up under her Eye'. Luckily the other important female at Castletown also appeared to approve. Emily Napier, Lady Sarah's daughter, had been adopted by Lady Louisa and Tom Connolly when she was a baby and had lived there ever since. Louisa Pakenham could only say positive things about her:

> Dear Emily who improves every day in looks, spirits and every amiable quality seems also to enjoy this (plan) which I trust will make the approaching winter less dull to all parties & in these troublesome times Mr P. thinks he shall consider us all as in more safety at Castletown which can be better defended against any attack than this Small house,* for these troublesome times makes it necessary to consider one's house as a Fortification. We never go to bed without preparing the Arms and setting the Guard as if in an Enemy's country [.] If this lasts much longer, every Gentleman's house will become like the Barons Fortified Castle in old times, but if the age of Chivalry were returned it might improve the manners of our poor CountryMen . . .[8]

By October 1803 the Pakenhams had moved in, bag and baggage.

The 'troublesome times' to which Louisa twice refers were the fresh outbreak of rebellion. Robert Emmet, whose elder brother Thomas Addis had been in the Executive of the United Irishman, led a new rising against the Government but it proved a mere fiasco. It began in Dublin on 23 July, with the murder of Lord Kilwarden, the Chief Justice. His carriage was attacked by an armed mob who had attempted to take the Castle; Kilwarden, his nephew and a Colonel Brown were dragged out and piked to death. More might have come of it if Kilwarden's daughter had not escaped and raised the alarm. In fact, Emmet was caught just a month later, and executed that September. At Castletown, even in the midst of her own sorrows, the ever-thoughtful Lady Louisa invited poor Brown's widow to seek refuge with her, away from the 'dreadful scene of misery' to the tranquil 'house of Mourning'.[9] In such a state of affairs, it was no wonder Admiral Pakenham wanted his wife there too.

Also on the 23rd, a band of fifty men ransacked Colonel and Lady Sarah Napier's empty house in nearby Celbridge, looking for arms. Admiral Pakenham, who had taken on Conolly's militia, was

---

* 'Rockfield' in Celbridge.

commissioned to round up the insurgents. Throughout that summer and autumn he went after those who had been involved in the rebellion, hunting them across north Kildare. Still as fit and stubborn as ever at nearly fifty, Pakenham continued his pursuit over the next two years. He chased one man named Tindall, who had escaped his prison ship, for miles on horseback. Cornered in a lane, the fugitive charged at Pakenham, with 'the fury of a Devil and the fleetness of a Dromedary with a very Pretty Pitchfork . . . Unluckily', Pakenham related in his report, 'the only Implement in my Possession was an old Mourning sword of Parson Ask's'.[10] After two hours of jockeying, Tindall jumped through a thick ditch and escaped.

Sarah Napier was widowed in October 1804. Her house at Celbridge was sold, but she had ceased to see Castletown as her refuge and second home. From London she wrote to her cousin Susan that 'considering my 5 sons will be settled in England, it will be advisable for me *ultimately* to settle here also. In the mean time we must be at Castletown, where I shall feel the unpleasant sensation of knowing that it is not my dear Mr Conolly I live with, but Adl Pakenham, a very sincere friend, but *still* only a friend.'[11]

Lady Louisa Conolly had not foreseen one consequence of the Pakenhams' removal to Castletown. Nineteen-year-old Edward – son of the Admiral – was soon smitten. What could have been more natural than to fall in love with this favourite sister of the Napier boys? Emily, clever, unattached and adored by Lady Louisa, was his ideal of a wife. Marriage to Emily would also mean that the Napiers would have a future connection to Castletown. By August 1805 it was an open secret that he was going to propose. Her mother Sarah, though, laughed at the idea:

> [It is] so completely ridiculous to us all, that of course if you hear it you may safely contradict it; for you may guess Emily will make a more refined choice than a very tiresome little P., for even if he is improved it is *but* a Pakenham at best! But my dread is her showing her dislike, so I hope he will turn out as I expect, an amiable well-disposed lad and no more.[12]

Such withering comments by Sarah Napier seem surprising. Did she still feel a residual bitterness towards Admiral Thomas's family after the horrible events of 1798? If Sarah's views were continually blowing hot and cold, the Lennox pride remained as strong as ever. There is no more mention of how Emily treated Edward when they did meet, but a letter written a year later from Holland House suggests that being the Admiral's son was enough to make him unpalatable to her. She had just received a description of life at Coolure from Anne Staples, Louisa's widowed sister-in-law.* Her reply cast a damning light on the family that would have astonished poor Louisa Pakenham:

> What a true picture of Coolure you have drawn! *Je le reconnais à chaque ligne* . . . When I read your description of the P's I could not help thinking of how necessary it is to consult similarity of taste and character in marriage, for they are the picture of what the ménage of a Rake and a Notable Woman, must always be: she has, as she deserves far the advantage over him, but *quelle triste avantage*! To see the man you have chosen as your companion for life, with a mind worn out thro' abuse of its powers and obliged to be content with the vapid dregs of his society! Happily she don't see her situation in its true light, but for you or me Anne, would not death be better? As to him I think you have exactly described him, he is blasé in the fullest extent of the expression, and those spirits which once contributed so much to his success, now only serve to add restlessness to indolence and languor; dearest Anne does not this a little abate your admiration for a Wit? When you see how little it contributes to real pleasure or comfort.[13]

The 'Notable Woman', however, left nothing but kind thoughts behind in her own letters. Her much adored eldest son, the 'tiresome' Edward Pakenham, eventually married one of his second cousins in 1819. It took Emily Napier nearly thirty more years to find a husband who met her criteria.

Lady Louisa Conolly went on living chiefly at Castletown until

---

* Née Stewart, the widow of William Conolly Staples.

the end of her long, industrious life. She adored Louisa Pakenham and her increasing family with an uncritical love that would not be moved by the less flattering opinions of her Lennox relations. Often the Admiral's wife and eldest son stayed for long periods. 'Edward Pak is a ferrit to your heart's content in making me walk out', Lady Louisa wrote to Emily Napier in 1808, so clearly there was no awkwardness in mentioning his name.

The security of the country was a constant anxiety – even three years after the Emmet rising. Just to the north, in County Longford, gangs of masked men calling themselves 'Thrashers' attacked and robbed houses for any arms they could find. The root cause of this new disorder was the burden placed on the Catholic peasantry to pay tithes to the Protestant Church – an old injustice that those in Government freely admitted, but did not yet undo.* Richard Lovell Edgeworth sent reports to Dublin Castle that houses in Edgeworths-town were being set ablaze by ejected tenants.

Across the bog at Pakenham Hall, Lord Longford drilled the local cavalry regiment. An English visitor described with amazement how dangerous the country seemed. 'People of immense property in this country all *absentees* let their lands as high as they can to people who let them to poor undertenants who are *ground* so terribly that they may well wish a change of masters.' She naturally excluded her host:

> Lord Longford does a world of good, but no one man can do enough among such numbers. It is the policy & has been so long as I can remember to suppress all knowledge of evil & not to suppress the evil itself from the Govt of England that the Lord Lieut. may *seem* to govern well, therefore you will be told that the insurrections here are *nothing*, but I happen to be on the spot where a *week* ago within *seven* miles of this house it was necessary to call out a considerable military force to disperse the numbers that had collected . . . Several were killed & many taken prisoners who are to be tried for their

* The Tithe Commutation Act was passed 1836. The tithe was converted into a rent-charge, paid by the head landlord and added by him to the charges made on his tenants.

lives. Lord L & his Yeomanry are out almost every night for some hours . . . [The] great massy gates shut every night & many other precautions taken.[14]

Faulkner's Dublin Journal of 4 December 1806 reported that Lord Longford had even placed guards on the bridges that crossed the Longford bog-rivers, to prevent the passage of the Thrashers into Westmeath. Longford's yeomanry were not dissolved until 1814.

5

Private Lives and Private Sorrows

If the men of the family were defending their property, the women were busy acquiring some of their own. A well-made marriage was the natural end in view for all the Pakenham daughters. Even in the turbulent year of 1798, courtships progressed. Bess Stewart, the confidante of all her siblings, was eager that her three younger sisters should find the independence and happiness that she had gained. She had them to stay with her in Dublin whenever she could, and, with her mother, chaperoned them at the assemblies. That year her nearest sister Kitty was twenty-six, and still much admired, five years after Arthur Wesley's proposal. But though, according to Bess, many offers came her way, Kitty remained adamantly single. Bess turned to the next of the three, twenty-five-year-old Helen.

Helen, from her picture, seems to have been a beauty. She was also musical, and captivated Mr Edgeworth with her harp-playing when he came to see them all:

> Shepherds beware & timely fly
> For if you dare come near
> She's sure to catch you by the eye,
> And hold you by the ear.[1]

Yet Helen's large, soulful eyes have a touch of tragedy about them. Serious, bookish, deeply perceptive, she had no taste for the fashionable new dandies of post-Union Dublin. Fortunately, the Stewarts' house at Tyrcallen was not far from another estate in Donegal – the pretty demesne of Brown Hall. This house, standing in the vast tract of the beautiful but poor land of the west of Ireland, was the seat of a handsome, eligible cousin of Henry's: Mr James Hamilton. An eldest son and a modest man, the match was easily made; James married Helen in the spring of 1799. After the wedding, Lady Longford and her other daughters went with the couple to London where Lovell Edgeworth found them all happily ensconced. He had come with engravings of Kitty's drawings for a new edition of Maria's book: *Parent's Assistant or Stories for Children.** 'She means to have plain C.P [Catherine Pakenham] at the corner of the print' reported Lovell, impressed at the modesty of the artist.

As for the new Mrs James Hamilton, marriage had made her more agreeable than ever, according to the Edgeworths. It was a relief for Helen to have her own establishment. She was an introspective but determined character, perhaps rather too serious for some of the more light-hearted members of her family. She was also very deeply in love with her 'Jemmy'. Like-minded in their distaste for high society, the Hamiltons lived quite contentedly in Donegal, where they were good and popular landlords. Before the end of 1800 their first son, John, was born.

In the midlands, the new Mrs Edgeworth revived the regular visits of the Edgeworth family to Pakenham Hall. Frances Edgeworth saw the house as an 'island' in the vast Longford-Westmeath bog, where musical evenings and literary conversation could cheer up the winter gloom. Always interested in the domestic lives of others, she and Maria became increasingly fond of the Pakenham clan. From 1802 another link was forged between the families, by Anna-Maria Fortescue, the orphaned niece of Captain Lord Longford, who had spent much of her life under her cousin Longford's roof. When she married Mr Parkinson Ruxton of Red House in County Louth, she had neatly tied herself to a relation of Maria's favourite cousin Sophy. It was to Sophy that Maria frequently reported the goings-on at Pakenham Hall.

The widowed Lady Longford herself now only visited Westmeath for a few weeks a year, living mainly in Dublin or Langford Lodge, the house in County Antrim she had inherited on her brother's death

---

* First published in 1796, following *Letters to Literary Ladies*.

in 1796. With her second youngest son Henry away at school, and William, Hercules and Ned in the military, Catherine Longford moved with the ebb and flow of polite society, chaperoning her two unmarried daughters. At the same time, she was trying to find a cure for Robert.

Robert had always lived quietly at home in the country. Langford Lodge on the shores of beautiful Lough Neagh was the perfect refuge for the crippled boy. A large, ramshackle house which the architect John Nash had plans to improve, it was surrounded by valuable land with a good estate income. Ultimately Langford Lodge was to go to Ned, the second son. In the meantime, Catherine spent the summers there.

Later, when Helen Hamilton's sons were old enough to be sent to the Royal College in Armagh, just as their uncles had been, Langford Lodge was the natural place for them to spend their holidays. The unmarried Kitty and Caroline stayed with their mother, and helped with the children, and all were frequent visitors of the kindly Lord Enniskillen at Florence Court in nearby Fermanagh. Kitty's particular friend was Enniskillen's sister Florence, married to Blayney Balfour of Townley Hall, not too far away in Louth. But it was another of the Cole family who played a more important role.

Enniskillen's younger brother, Lowry Galbraith Cole, a gallant and successful soldier, found himself in love with Kitty. The kind and gentle Colonel was almost as shy and retiring as Kitty herself, and by 1802 she seemed to return his feelings. Sometime in that year he was encouraged, proposed, but was then suddenly declined by Kitty. Nobody in the Cole family could understand why, but perhaps several in the Pakenham family guessed. In any case, the friendship between the two families continued largely unaffected.

When it appeared that peace had returned to Europe in 1802, with the Truce of Amiens, Longford and Hercules went on a brief excursion to Paris with two of the Cole brothers, Lowry and William. Their time was spent 'amusing ourselves in the public places', and seeing all the wonderful treasures 'plundered from the different conquered countries'.[2] In London, William Cole's only complaint against the Longford family was Longford's 'stinginess': 'going about in a hackney coach even to the Queen's Ball, it is really a shame for him to appear so shabbily'.[3] Only Kitty herself came in for any criticism, for appearing to 'bring on the subject again' with Lowry once at Cheltenham. It was cruel of her, his brother complained, but would do no good, for Lowry was now behaving 'like a burnt child, to fear the flame'.[4] But whatever Kitty or her mother's feelings, Lady Longford and her daughters continued uninterrupted the round of visits in Ireland and travels to the English spas of Harrogate and Cheltenham. The years passed quietly.

Every Christmas the extended family met up at Pakenham Hall. If the memories of 'former happier days' for Lady Longford were painful, only her daughter Bess was able to tell. She believed in cheerfulness and stoicism. As for Longford, he was hospitable almost to a fault: there was nothing he enjoyed more than a large family party. It seemed to him of no consequence that from 1801 the old house was being turned upside down by builders.

Pregnant Helen Hamilton, staying for the Christmas of 1802, began a journal. She found her old home noisy and disturbed, her beloved mother confined upstairs with 'erysipelas',* and tempers fraying in the cramped conditions. 'No pleasure is to be expected perfectly unmixed', she reminded herself, clearly disappointed by the less than harmonious family atmosphere. Certain 'misunderstandings' are not elucidated, sadly, apart from a hint that somebody's behaviour has shown a lack of sincerity – that 'First of Virtues'. She quotes a line from the enlightened Scottish writer John Moore which seemed to echo her thoughts: 'people who are naturally ill humoured shew it more at breakfast than at any other time'.† She resolved to control her own feelings, drawing a fine line between 'firmness' and obstinacy. She also read Maria's book on the teaching of children – and was impressed:

---

* A painful inflammation of the skin or joints.
† *Mordaunt* (1800), a novel satirising the manners of fashionable London society, set against the horrors of revolutionary France. John Moore was father to the famous Peninsular War hero, General Sir John Moore.

I am more of the opinion than I ever was before that Severity towards Children ought most particularly to be avoided. Miss E thinks it has not the desired effect, but hurts the child, so I think & not only the child but the parent. I think it gives an imperious manner & as we cannot always throw aside those Habits when we have no longer any use for them, I think it better not to indulge this one, we all wish our Children to be in time our Friends.[5]

Lady Longford, too, was concerned with education. She wanted to do something for the poor female children on the estate, and set about it in the practical manner that governed all her actions. A small stone and thatch house was built near the farm, just beyond the walled garden of Pakenham Hall. This 'neat' little school took

about twenty Scholars who came after their breakfast & rec.d at noon potatoes and milk – and stayed till half past three in Winter and 6 in Summer, being of different persuasions mostly Romanist taught Writing & arithmetic . . . all the protestants well instructed in catechism & psalm singing & taken to church by the mistress – Some parents had sense to value this good, but many not & they seemed to think it a gain when they could keep their children at home at any ordinary work, this my Dear Mother by encouragement & reproof as she judged most effectual endeavoured to prevent & her patience was not Wearied . . .[6]

One of the Edgeworth girls drew a small sketch of the school that still survives; Maria provided copies of some of her stories for the children. It was a success for several years, and Catherine Longford built a similar institution on the estate in Antrim.

Soon after the New Year holiday Helen Hamilton went to Dublin to give birth, this time to a frail little girl. Lady Longford stayed with her daughter throughout and left nothing to the nurses, sitting up all day and night with the sick child on her knees. A solemn line ends this section of Helen's journal: 'We are now going to have another War'. This was April 1803; the fragile Peace of Amiens was coming to an end. By 18 May, France and Britain were indeed again at war.

Death was never far away. By August 1803, Helen's 'dearest Friend', her 'best good Jemmy', had begun to show symptoms of the lingering disease that had killed so many in Ireland. This was tuberculosis, whose infectious nature was not yet understood.* On the advice of doctors, the Hamiltons went to Exeter, for the mild climate and 'good air', leaving their three children behind. Her brother Longford did what he could to comfort his sister, taking her little boys to Pakenham Hall, 'to care for them as if they were his own'. Even the new baby, Kate, was left with Bess in Donegal, a trial that made the melancholy exile worse than ever for Helen. Her mother, Caroline and Kitty soon joined her in England. But Helen moved as if in a dream.

In Exeter, Helen continued her journal. Month after month passed in a horrid state of limbo, with nothing to do in a neighbourhood where the ladies had little acquaintance, except to read aloud volumes of classical history and philosophy from the circulating library. By November they had heard that their soldier brother Ned – 'dearest Edward' – was now on his return from the West Indies. One of Helen's books made her ponder on his experiences of soldiering. 'One chapter brought him much in to my mind, in which he [Porteus]† condemns the illiberal Idea that Soldiers are & must be cruel, he puts their Character in a very fair & amiable point of view.' And about this time the family met the friendly Serena Holroyd, the unmarried sister of Lord Sheffield. With no family of her own close by, 'Mrs' Holroyd was soon adopted by the Longfords. She found them delightful. 'I verily think it is the happiest family I ever met, were it not for the state of health of Lady L's son in law Hamilton . . . They *hope* & that keeps up their spirits',[7] but the

---

* Otherwise known as 'consumption' or 'decline', or in Irish 'Seirglighe' which literally means 'shrinking of oneself'. Although there are no firm statistics for the early nineteenth century in Ireland, the (1843) report by Sir William Wilde (father of Oscar) show that *c*.16,000 people a year died of tuberculosis in the 1831–41 period, and it was the most common cause of death. Females outnumbered males by 5:4, and the disease was most prevalent in the 15–35 age group.

† Beilby Porteus was an evangelical Church of England Bishop whose lectures were frequently published.

cheerfulness of the family could not obscure the dismal truth: Jemmy was dying.

In private, Helen revealed an overwhelming depression. As she withdrew further and further into herself, all her thoughts were centred around Jemmy's recovery. The crowning of Napoleon Bonaparte as Emperor in France barely stirred her emotions; the progress of the war passed without comment. Finally, in January 1805, James Hamilton died. On the surface Helen showed the Christian calm expected of her, but in reality her grief for Jemmy made her lose all interest in life. Kitty, too, was quite broken down. In the doctor's opinion, the sisters 'would have been Victims of their attention to [James]' if the patient had lasted any longer. Their brother Ned wrote anxiously to Henry (also referred to as Harry) Stewart:

> As to the Conduct of my Sister Helen, and also Kitty, even the language of a brother is too weak to describe it. On Reflection, it appears the loss of this valuable fellow has been but a release to himself, and that providence took advantage of the occasion to show in the instance of his admirable wife, the perfect compatibility of feeling without affectation, sorrow with Remarkable firmness. This last display of their amiable Qualities has been dreadfully dearly purchased . . .[8]

Two years later the disease began to show its cruel signs in Helen Hamilton herself. She had no doubt of the result, and with a last purposeful resignation she made plans for her children's future. Ned, the idol of the boys, was named their guardian. She was to die on Easter morning of 1807, 'a superior order of spirits . . . a bright example & an irreparable loss to her children'.[9] Lady Longford, ever maternal, gathered the three orphans under her wing. 'My dear good grandmother . . . took us as her own, and her house was our own and her heart a mother's heart to us.'[10] Catherine's friends worried that she would fatally tax her strength; she was now in her sixties, and already worn out by the hopeless search for a cure for Robert. 'Poor Ldy Longford', reported Lady Louisa Conolly sadly,

I see is devoting herself to [the Hamiltons], there are two Boys and a Girl, & one sees how it will all be, that new anxieties are beginning to belong to her, but I hope they will be mixed with pleasure, for she is a most excellent woman, & very like her charming mother in firmness of character, & everything that is essentially good . . .[11]

Olivia Sparrow, an old friend of the family's, set about arranging for a governess. As for poor Robert, 'a most sweet and gentle boy', he continued to suffer 'heavy strong & nauseous medicines but bore it like a hero if passive courage can entitle to such praise'.[12] But there was little or no improvement. His shadowy life came to an end at the age of eighteen, in late summer of 1808, his death quiet and long expected. His name does not even feature on the family tree.*

The third and last of the Pakenham daughters, cheerful, musical Caroline, was to marry in the summer of 1809. But in the meantime a domestic event had taken place that outshone all others – in terms of pure romance. To the ever-literary Edgeworths, it made up 'one of those tales of real life in which the romance is far superior to the generality of fictions'.[13] Sadly, this 'tale' was to become little more than a footnote in another more famous story.

---

* A week before his death, Serena Holroyd had written: 'He is *gay* & keeping his mother from grieving for him . . . & tho' she doats upon her dying child she *really* sees his happy prospects & forgets her own loss.' Serena Holroyd to Maria Josepha Stanley, 13 August 1808. Cheshire Record Office, Stanley of Alderley papers, DSA/ 39/Part 4.

6

Romantic Fiction

❧

Tom Longford, standing in his blue velvet coat a few yards from
the clergyman, was conscious that sweat had begun to trickle
down his forehead. He hoped nobody had noticed, but in the still,
clear light of the drawing room it was hard to conceal. In the double
role of 'father' and brother to the bride, he was prickling with nerves.
The small gathering of a dozen people stood in a silent order in front
of the ranked chairs. Outside, the spring sunshine filled Rutland
Square, and the noise of horses, carriages and hawkers occasionally
drifted through the draped windows. But the bride, her thin white
hand now clasped in the hard brown one of the groom, did not
tremble. As for the groom, his hawk-nosed profile remained absolutely still. 'In the name of the Father . . . Amen', pronounced the
Reverend Gerald Wellesley. The private wedding ceremony swiftly
came to a close. Kitty Pakenham was now the wife of the man she
had loved for thirteen years, Sir Arthur Wellesley.

But Dublin was a city where one could have no private affairs. A
friend of the Longfords had compared it unfavourably with London:
'Small towns after great ones are insipid things,' she complained, '& I
feel it in nothing so much as in the quick circulation of lies, a much
greater degree of curiosity & a more minute observation of what
everybody says or does.'[1] Certainly, for Kitty Pakenham it cannot
have been easy to keep secret Arthur Wellesley's first proposal. But
although it had been declined, neither she nor her closest friends had
forgotten it.

Arthur had left Ireland and Kitty in June 1794, once he had
received the letter of refusal from Lord Longford. That the match

was declined through 'prudential motives' suggested to Arthur that it could be remedied – if he was to increase his financial standing. With this determination, he had written to Kitty once more before he went to India two years later, to promise that 'my mind will still remain the same'.[2] As for Kitty, romantic Maria Edgeworth later saw her friend's behaviour in turning down 'that amiable hero General Cole who was desperately in love with her',[3] together with her refusal of 'innumerable' others during 'her reign as a beauty in Dublin' as evidence of an admirable and blameless constancy. Like the heroine of *Persuasion*, Kitty appeared to go on loving without hope. Maria did not know that hope – or fate – had stepped in, in the form of Olivia Sparrow.

Mrs Olivia Sparrow herself bore a strong resemblance to another Austen heroine, Emma Wodehouse. She wanted nothing more than for her friend Kitty to find happiness. She had taken the bull by the horns when it appeared in front of her, and had been covertly corresponding with Wellesley since 1801. Her subject was Arthur's heart; his 'disappointment' was to be remedied if she could help it. Sometime in that autumn, Mrs Olivia Sparrow had received a letter from India. 'You may recollect a disappointment that I met with about 8 years ago, in an object in which I was most interested', Sir Arthur had written. 'Notwithstanding my good fortune, and the perpetual activity of the life which I have led, that disappointment, the object of it, and all the circumstances are as fresh upon my mind, as if they had passed only yesterday.' Wellesley went on to say that he was anxious to return home, once peace had been declared and that he wanted to be remembered to their 'friend . . . in the kindest manner'.[4]

The contents of this vital letter were soon passed on to Kitty. It sent her into a spin of agitation: 'I am afraid of saying a word ever since your letter arrived for fear it should be his name'. It had come at the very moment she might have been tempted to think of Lowry Cole, and had even encouraged Cole to believe she would accept him. But the cruelty was, it would take six months before another letter could be expected from Arthur in India. In the meantime,

Kitty's doubts continued; it seemed to her that Arthur's letter was not as warm as it could have been. Ironically for Cole, his younger brother – another Arthur – was working in India, and part of the Wellesley 'family'. But neither brother may have known how attached Kitty still remained to the rising star of the Army.

Over the next three years, as further letters arrived from India to Olivia, only Olivia knew with what agitation Kitty thought of Arthur. Kitty's greatest anxiety was that he should not be misled into renewing a pursuit out of obligation. She didn't dare send any message about her own feelings, but the message was clear enough. When Arthur finally returned from India in the autumn of 1805, Olivia Sparrow chased him to Cheltenham. Through her thorough powers of persuasion and charm she convinced the General that he was still the only man Kitty could love.

As for Arthur himself, there is no doubt that he had continued to cherish a romantic ideal of the girl he had last seen in 1794. He wrote nostalgically to Olivia on the subject. 'Every time that I have heard of her since I left Europe has tended to confirm the impression which had been made on my mind by the former knowledge of her and I am convinced that the enthusiasm of an admirer and the partiality of a friend cannot find words to describe all her good qualities.'

After leaving Cheltenham he made a brief visit to Stowe, to see his old master, the ex-Lord Lieutenant, Lord Buckingham. According to one witness, he showed no desire to discuss his Indian experiences but wanted to reminisce. 'I wonder if he will now renew his flirtation with Kitty Pakenham!' scribbled Buckingham's curious young cousin Miss Nugent in her diary, adding later, 'I think he still retains his old feelings.'[5] Wellesley was by now a highly regarded General whose successful command in India had left him with a dazzling reputation. His only anxiety appeared to be that Kitty might believe the 'scandal and calumny'* with which some jealous characters in society had marked him since he had last seen her. Again, Olivia reassured. Finally, in late October 1805 Arthur wrote Lord Longford a formal

---

* Presumably the slanderous public accusations of one James Paull that both Wellesley brothers had lined their pockets whilst in India.

letter proposing himself as Kitty's husband, and when this had been favourably answered, wrote to Kitty herself.

Strangely, Kitty's sister Bess was in Cheltenham at the same time and met Wellesley, but afterwards declared 'we knew nothing of [Wellesley's] overtures to my Dear Kitty'. The whole drama was a secret between the three of them.

Up till then, no one had considered Kitty still in the marriage market. She was now an old maid of thirty-three. Of course her close friends and family thought of her as highly as ever, one of the Edgeworths reporting the general view that Kitty was: 'all gentleness & spirit, sensibility & sense, cultivated & accomplished & quite unaffected. Ld Longford seems to adore her, indeed so do all the rest.'[6] Mr Edgeworth, according to Maria, loved her as deeply as any father or brother would. Nevertheless, even Kitty's favourite brother Ned assumed she would simply become a 'companion' to the widowed Helen.

Kitty had been overpowered with apprehension. 'I am very much changed and you know it', she appealed to Olivia, 'so much that I doubt whether it would now be in my power to contribute [to] the comfort or happiness of any body who has not been in habit of loving me for years like my Brother or you or my Mother.'[7] She was wise enough to know that the years of strain in helping her mother look after Robert, and in keeping up her spirits, had taken their toll. Then the nursing of James Hamilton had cost her yet more; now she was thin, faded and coughing, possibly even consumptive: the very opposite from the blooming girl Arthur had last seen. Kitty's doubts continued throughout the winter of 1805; after all, shouldn't Arthur at least see her again before renewing his offer? Once again she gave him the chance to withdraw. They still hadn't met, since almost immediately after his return from India the General had been sent to Germany. But Olivia Sparrow would have none of it; all would be well, Kitty would see. Arthur, to his credit, agreed. It was Kitty's mind, he declared, that he was in love with, and that could not alter.[8]

When Arthur finally arrived in Dublin in April 1806, the news of the engagement had only been made public a few days. Naturally, the ladies of her circle were almost as much on tenterhooks as the bride-to-be herself. 'And now my dearest, about Kitty Pakenham', wrote Mary Balfour to her sister-in-law, Florence Cole:

> I did not hear anything of Sir A. Wellesley till your letter, nor did I know that all was settled till 2 days ago . . . It seems it has been fixed these six months but kept a profound secret . . . They have not met for above 12 years & some little agitation She suffers at the idea of being altered since, but not much, as she seems to have the most perfect reliance on him both in affection & all other things & to think him the very first of human creatures. I do think she is and will be I trust very happy & certainly an affection that has subsisted for 12 or 15 years promises very well . . .[9]

In fact, Mary Balfour had not been told quite how badly Kitty had suffered. As her aunt old Lady Eliza revealed to Maria Edgeworth, Kitty 'had not once closed her eyes' for a whole fortnight, whilst Arthur was being tossed about at sea.

On 1 April Arthur, his brother Henry and his clergyman brother Gerald arrived in Ireland. Longford was delighted to see him. He and Ned were there to meet him at the docks, and assure them the bride was well. Then they rode on ahead to Rutland Square, to let Kitty know Arthur had come. For two terrible hours, Kitty's 'isolation' was kept up;

> when however [Kitty] heard his voice at the hall door her agitation became so excessive that she was obliged to retire to her sitting room which was w[ith]in the d[rawing]room. Sir A was there received by her family, after some conversation Ld L opened the door of the adjoining apart. Led in Sir A and left him and Kitty to recognize each other. What passed at this interview has not transpired except that Sir A could not discover that his beloved had lost any of her personal charms.[10]

So the story was reported to the Edgeworths, by their cousin Sophy Ruxton.

The wedding date was fixed for the following Thursday; the lovers had less than a week to talk through more than a decade.

'Does he not deserve that I shd allow of this haste?' explained Kitty, with feeling. According to the romantic Sophy, the time was passed fittingly in

> reciprocal confession of past and present thoughts and opinions and in increasing conviction of that they were formed to make each other happy. Lady Longford told me that she happened the day but one after they were married to be standing at the landing place of the stairs when Sir Arthur and Lady W[ellesley] met by chance, he coming up she going down 'Well met', said she giving him her hand. 'It would have been a sad pity if we two had not met' was his answer, and never, I believe, did lovers speak with greater truth.[11]

A single cloud over the happy reunion was the inevitable pain of Helen Hamilton. Too ill to come to the wedding ceremony, worried about one of her children's health, and thinking always of poor Jemmy's death, she was urged to retreat to her aunt Bective's. She refused. Her room was directly above the drawing room where the ceremony took place. 'She heard everything that passed,' reported the sympathetic Sophy.[12] How well the Edgeworths could imagine the melancholy scene.

But on a positive note, the family liked Arthur 'vastly', and 'think him but little altered by his Indian absence'. After all, the victor of Assaye now had a large fortune, which was 'rather a recommendation'. Old Lady Eliza Pakenham, whose spinster fate had so nearly been Kitty's, was proud and fond of him, particularly as he showed the lack of affectation that she valued most in people. Lady Longford quietly added a further £2,000 to Kitty's dowry of £4,000. Caroline was cheerful, beaming and delighted; Ned, Hercules and the younger boys saw everything good in a military hero. Even in India, when the news finally reached Arthur Cole, he declared himself 'very glad to hear of Kitty Pakenham's marriage to Sir A. Wellesley who is a fine fellow though I like him least of his family'.[13] Yet the sober Mrs Edgeworth, who had compared the romance to a tale of fiction, struck a sombre note in a letter to her cousin: 'I hope the imaginations of this hero and heroine have not been too much exalted, and that they may not find the enjoyment of a happiness so long wished for, inferior to what they expected.'[14]

The wedding celebrations were brief, for General Wellesley was in the power of the Government, and the Government was on a war footing. If it was all rather rushed, that was the nature of Army life. On 16 April Arthur re-embarked for England, leaving Kitty to be brought over a few days later by his brother Gerald. That gave Sophy the chance to see the bride in person.

> I thought myself a fortunate creature to pass one evening with this charming woman. Her whole conduct – her air – her manner have afforded me a study for all that is dignified – for all that is peculiarly suited to the female sex. Having once consented to unite herself for life to the man who had won her esteem and love all the absurdity of decorum vanished before the single idea of convenience.[15]

The ripples of reportage continued; the Edgeworth family was alive with gossip. Mrs Edgeworth wanted to know still more:

> Pray when you have leisure gratify an ardent and I may say affectionate curiosity & pray tell dear good Lady Elizabeth we are so delighted with the news, and so engrossed with it that waking or sleeping, the image of Miss Pakenham swims before our eyes. To make the romance perfect we want . . . a description of the person of Sir Arthur . . .[16]

The description turned out to be quite simple: 'handsome, very brown, quite bald, and a hooked nose'.[17]

There was one more anecdote for the Edgeworths on the subject of the Wellesley romance. Soon after her arrival in London, Lady Wellesley was presented to Queen Charlotte.

> Her Majesty said, 'I am happy to see at my court so bright an example of constancy. If anybody in this world deserves to be happy, you do.' Then Her Majesty enquired, 'But did you really never write *one* letter to Sir Arthur Wellesley during his long absence?' 'No,

never, madam.' 'And did you never think of him?' 'Yes, madam, very often.'[18]

As Maria herself had said, 'Who dares now to say that merit & virtue & constancy are not rewarded in this world.'[19]

7

Fun, Folly & Frolic –
The Bachelor Lord of the Castle

❧

And Longford himself, why was he not husband, father by this time? The Union passed, Ireland now relatively peaceful, Longford was free to settle down to the life of a country squire. His European tour had left him with a desire to improve the old family home – and with the £15,000 in Union compensation in his pocket, it could not have been a better moment. The taste he had formed for landscape made him wish to spend more time in an idyll of his own making. Like his father, he strongly disapproved of Irish landowners living in England, neglecting – or at least leaving to their agents – the care of their estates. He too was interested in improving the land, draining bogs, sowing flax and hemp, raising bullocks and, above all, planting trees – fifteen species of oak alone. But he differed from his pragmatic, cautious father in that he was a romantic.

Even with a net income of about £4,000 a year, prudence dictated he didn't do too much. Back in 1801 there were still more than half a dozen claimants on his income: his mother, his spinster aunt Lady Eliza, his two then unmarried sisters Kitty and Caroline, his brothers Ned and William, still early in their military careers, Hercules a student at Cambridge, not to mention Henry, who had yet to finish school. Expenses! Expenses! But with the price of grain high, and the demand for meat to feed the British Army as great as ever, he seized the chance of creating a more beautiful, as well as a more profitable, estate.

Who could resist imposing their own identity on a building which, though comfortable and homely, had none of the grandeur or drama about it that the fashionable world prescribed? Longford wanted a castle. After all, he was now one of a select band – an Irish peer in the English House of Lords, a man of dignity and position. Moreover, as one historian has pointed out, the rebuilding of his home would add to his status in the county – and his authority in the county elections.[1]

The greatest influence on his ideas had come from a surprising source. Eight years previously, just before he had set off to the Continent, Longford had spent a few months in Scotland, touring the Highlands. On the whole he had been impressed, but the Duke of Argyll's castle on the banks of Loch Fyne had overwhelmed him: 'I should prefer Inveraray to any place I ever saw', he enthused in his journal. The gothic battlements and windows were in a style that could not have been better suited to their surroundings, set off as they were by the dramatic coastline of west Scotland. Inside, the furnishing and decor was quite the contrary, being light and classical: 'yet even this seemed rather an improvement than a fault, for the house is so contrived that in the inside it is not possible to imagine that the building is in the least Gothic, the windows are large the rooms large, well-proportioned and most superbly fitted up'.

The only criticism he had was that the grandeur of the furnishings was quite impractical; the worry of their being 'damaged or dirtied' would have 'set me distracted'. In every other way, though, this was Longford's ideal of a castle. But the chief architect of Inveraray, Roger Morris, was long since dead. To whom could Longford trust such a plan?

Longford's intimacy with one family in Ireland may have given him an idea. Castle Upton, the Templetown family seat, was a Robert Adam creation which had inspired the architect Francis Johnston. Johnston was also the chief architect for Townley Hall, the home of Longford's friends Florence and Blayney Balfour. Above all, Johnston's hand had shown the same skill with the gothic style at Charleville Castle in Offaly that Longford had so admired at Inveraray – in fact, the precedent for Charleville's tall central tower had been the Scottish castle. Johnston's love of classical regularity, light and space chimed perfectly with what Longford looked for.

Johnston certainly knew the Pakenham family before he was

commissioned. A note in the architects's journal of 1796 mentioned a visit to 'Captain Pakenham' in Portsmouth: this was Longford's uncle Thomas. Moreover, Johnston was building a new church just around the corner from their Dublin house: St George's, Rutland Square. Accordingly, by 1801 Johnston had come up with some grand designs. He proposed two round towers to project from the southern corners of the house, and battlements all around the lead flats of the roof. A new gothic porch giving onto the old hall would bring grandeur and gravitas. More practically, an improved stable block was to be built to the north of the house, behind battlemented walls. Longford applauded the plans, and building works slowly began.

Internally, the lack of 'luxuries' Longford's father's guests had met with came to a timely end. Along with the round towers and battlements a particular concession was made to modern convenience. This was a four-storey lavatory tower erected in the kitchen courtyard, in which pairs of water closets sat sedately on each floor, with a luxury single one on the ground floor. They were served by the rainwater tank on the tower's roof. There was still only one bathroom, but every bedroom contained a tin hipbath, to be filled by hand by one of the many servants.

For over five years, the work continued. Longford delighted in the building; it met all his ideals of modernisation and culture. He found a great shared enthusiasm with his inventive neighbour, Mr Edgeworth. In fact he was so busy with it that even Ned, away at war, was quite anxious, demanding of his mother, 'What is Longford about? – he sends me high accounts of the alteration of the house, it much perplexes my knowledge box to imagine how that happy old house can be altered; it never was a good one, and seldom other than a cheerful one.'[2]

By April 1806 Longford had already spent £1,172 on the works. At Christmas the following year, the whole Edgeworth family came to see it. Naturally, Maria was more interested in the domestic arrangements than the new battlements:

Lord Longford has finished and furnished his castle which is now really a mansion fit for a nobleman of his fortune. The furniture is neither gothic nor chinese nor gaudy nor frail but substantially handsome and suitable in all its parts, – the library scarlet and black with some red morocco cushioned chairs and some this shape [tiny picture] very handsome, plain black with white medusa heads in front of back inside (very clear!) I was desired to estimate these chairs, and Oh shameful chance! guessed them at a guinea and a half when their price was 9 guineas . . . The furniture in the drawing room a kind of old china pattern like an old gown of Aunt Mary's – a delightful abundance of sofas and cushions and chairs and tables of all sorts and sizes – the immense Hall so well warmed that the children play in it from morn till night. Lord L. seemed to take great pleasure in repeating 20 times that he was to thank Mr Edgeworth for this, the whole house and every bedchamber, every passage so thoroughly warmed that we never felt any reluctance in going upstairs or from one room to another and yet every room is so comfortable that where you are there you wish to be always . . .[3]

Mr Edgeworth had certainly repaid his cousin for all the youthful hospitality he had received. His system of hot air rising through elegant floor gratings was a triumph; Pakenham Hall became the first private house with central heating in Ireland. It was so efficient, in fact, that later one of the two great fireplaces in the hall was replaced with a gothic organ, which Henry Hamilton* played remarkably well. The Edgeworth system remained in place for nearly sixty years, until a Victorian Pakenham installed hot pipes in 1861.

It was Longford's sister Caroline who had chosen the new furniture – 'she does everything', boasted Longford to his guests – 'she is my slave'. Still unmarried, Caroline acted as mistress of the house, choosing the furnishings with economy and taste. She entertained them all with her charming voice, so much so that Maria was not surprised to hear Lady Longford comment that 'always when she is at a disagreeable inn or any place where she wants amusement Caroline is sure to sing unbidden all her favourite songs'. At this point in her long letter, Maria's imagination took another leap:

* He was to marry Caroline Pakenham in 1809.

I hope you anticipate what I am going to say that now Lord L has made such a comfortable nest he must certainly get some bird with pretty plumage and a sweet voice to fill it – . . . we see no signs of it except that his house is so ready for a bride & another sign indeed is as admiral P with his usual sagacity pointed out – Lord L. – has put his clock now upon a footing with other people's & his guests are not forced to get up (like the devil) at break of day – . . . I have a notion it will be Miss Crewe* – but he keeps himself in his 'snugs' & all his family say he is afraid to marry lest he should not meet with a woman who is as happy in her family as he is in his own – He has been much disgusted by a near view of the domestic lives of some fine ladies.

Of whom this 'near view' was, Maria did not say.

The paeons of praise continued to flow from other members of the Edgeworth clan. 'The whole family is so well united & so happy in each other that it is most delightful to be amongst them', declared Honora to Sophy Ruxton. Mr Johnston's improvements were deemed a total success, the house pronounced 'most agreeable', with 'all the comfort . . . which can be necessary, without any of the pomp or parade of magnificence'.[4] But Longford was far from finished. He still had no bird for his pretty nest. Nor, it seemed, was he actively seeking one.

In fact Longford was already a father. In 1793 or 1794 a little girl was handed over to the care of a respectable middle-aged spinster, Miss Lucretia Pakenham of Little Burstead, in Essex. She may have been conceived whilst Longford was abroad on the 'Grand Tour'; or perhaps even earlier, durng his sojourn at Glasgow University. Blonde with large blue eyes, the child was named Catherine, and her surname was given as 'Weekes'. For the next forty years she lived a secluded, provincial life in the southern counties of England with this cousin of the Pakenhams. From Longford, she received a handsome annuity of £60, and was left quite a fortune when her adopted

---

* Elizabeth Emma Crewe, granddaughter of Mrs Greville, and only daughter of Frances Crewe.

mother died (see Epilogue). Whether she knew the identity of her father we cannot be sure, but it seems likely that she guessed at it. In her portrait she looks remarkably like the 2nd Earl.

And Lord Longford was far from ready to settle down. About this time he began to keep his private accounts in a small brown leather notebook. It records the everyday expenses of a philandering playboy. Dashed across the front in a thick black pen is: 'Fun, Folly & Frolic – A Full & True Account of Life & Adventures &c &c in London Town'.

When Caroline Pakenham married Mr Henry Hamilton, her usefulness as a decorator came to an end. But the marriage brought a colourful figure into the family, as well as confusing family historians, by adding another branch of the Hamilton family to the Pakenham family tree. Henry Hamilton had exciting genes, as the grandnephew[5] of Bishop Berkeley, the radical philosopher, and author of *The Querist*. His father, Sackville Hamilton, declared by the celebrated Mrs Delany to be 'by much the prettiest gentleman in Ireland', had been one of the most highly respected civil servants there. He had been made one of the three commissioners assessing compensation for the disenfranchised boroughs and offices after the Union. His son Henry, though poor in capital, had a good Government job in the Customs House. Although Maria Edgeworth, who had long adored the literary Caroline's quick wits, had not been sure she liked Henry, she found marriage improved his manners. 'He does not snuffle half as much as he did; & I like his conversation much better; for more of his knowledge now comes through his mouth and less through his nose.'[6] Soon Caroline was as 'happy as a lark, and plump as a partridge',[7] and living in a charming house in Fitzwilliam Square in Dublin. Later her adoring husband had a villa built for her in County Down, looking over the beautiful Carlingford Lough. He immortalised her in its name: Carpenham – Caroline, Penelope, Hamilton.

8

The Secretary's Wife

In April 1807, Lady Longford celebrated with quiet joy the return of the Wellesleys to Ireland. Sir Arthur had been appointed Chief Secretary to the new Lord Lieutenant, the Duke of Richmond, the nephew of Lady Louisa Conolly. It was a vital job that involved liaising between Dublin Castle and the Government in England. And bundled up in the carriage beside the new Secretary were two others: Kitty was returning to Ireland as a mother.[1]

Catherine Longford had been with Kitty for the birth of baby Arthur, in early February; now Kitty was there to support her through the first traumatic weeks after Helen Hamilton's death. The Wellesleys were to live in the Secretary's Lodge in Phoenix Park, the great forested estate on the outskirts of Dublin.

Kitty was delighted. The Duke of Richmond and his wife were genial and friendly, sincerely interested in her family's happiness. The society of her childhood friends surrounded her; it was no hardship to give a welcoming ball, even though she was already in the first months of her second pregnancy. The Coolure cousins were delighted too. Louisa Pakenham immediately wrote to beg General Wellesley to let her have Kitty and the children* to stay whilst he went to sit in Parliament. She cajoled him playfully that he must 'make amends' for having taken the Admiral so much away from her to his Dublin duties at the Ordnance. Arthur responded shortly that it was quite up to his wife. He was up to his eyes in Castle business, and in no mood for domestic arrangements.

* Kitty also had little Arthur Freese, Arthur's godson, living with her.

The fact that two months after her sister Helen's death Kitty was still in mourning irritated Arthur. What he needed was the cheerful support of a social hostess, not a fragile dependant. He was working extremely hard, rallying support from the Irish contingent for the new Conservative Prime Minster, the Duke of Portland, now that Lord Grenville and the coalition 'Ministry of all the Talents'* had been ousted. Moreover, the depressed and anxious state of Arthur's brother Richard, Marquess Wellesley, charged with corruption in India by a troublesome MP,† was worrying him. And the Pakenhams were not entirely playing his game.

The Admiral – although a Castle man to the letter – wrote crossly that Wellesley had chosen quite the wrong place to install a new barracks for the defence of the country, since Mullingar's canal 'does not lead and probably never will lead anywhere else'. Mullingar being the local market town to Coolure and Pakenham Hall, the Admiral felt he knew more about the matter than the Chief Secretary. He had not forgotten that some years previously the Wellesley brothers had tried to poach his job at the Ordnance from him.

As for Tom Longford, he turned out not to be the compliant brother-in-law that Arthur might have expected. In Ireland politics had always been a thorny subject, as Lady Longford's friend Mrs Holroyd explained to her niece: 'conversation existed not in Ireland at the dinner parties, for to avoid splitting on the Scylla rock of political differences [the Irish] moved into the Charybdis whirlpool of the most determined and deliberate trifling'.[2] The reason politics was so controversial was twofold: Catholic Emancipation and patronage. The Chief Secretary of Ireland was inevitably embroiled in both.

In May 1807 there was a general election. Each Irish county now returned two Members for Westminster, even if most of the borough seats had been erased at the Union. (This was the case with Longford borough, whose electorate was too small to be allowed to return a

---

* Grenville's Cabinet that had been brought in by the King after Pitt's death on 23 January 1806. Portland, a former Whig, was appointed Prime Minister on 31 March 1807.
† James Paull.

borough Member. Longford county, however, sent two Members to Westminster.) The hundred Irish MPs were a desirable force for Portland's shaky Government to keep its hands on. As a landowner in both Longford and Westmeath, Tom Longford could still be expected to exert a good influence in those counties – for the Government side.

For Longford, however, friendship meant more than party. With regard to the Longford seats, he had previously given his support to Lord Granard's son, George Forbes, although Forbes was a Whig and Granard one of the Irish peers who had voted against the Union. When asked by Wellesley to help 'kick out' Lord Forbes, Longford responded hotly that 'no difference of politics should ever induce him to withdraw his support from George'. 'This', Lord Granard repeated, 'I can never forget.'

Longford's support did not waver: Forbes held his seat in Longford until his death in 1836. As a *quid pro quo* Granard declined to put his second son in as a candidate for Westmeath when a by-election was held there the following year.[3] This time Longford successfully put up his own man, his brother Hercules.

Left to her own devices in Phoenix Park, Kitty Wellesley did go for a May visit to Coolure. Maria Edgeworth went to inspect her old friend but made no comment, except to say that the children were 'beauteous'. Lady Eliza Pakenham immediately used the family connection with the Chief Secretary to try and secure a position in the Church for one of her orphaned nephews. Sir Arthur's reply showed just what pressure he was under from all sides – both from the Pakenhams and his own numerous family – on the tricky subject of patronage:

> Nothing can give me greater pleasure than to have an opportunity of doing anything for Mr Sherlock . . . But you must be aware that I am in a very delicate situation in this country: and being connected with it myself, it is my duty and it is expected from me to avoid pressing upon the government objects which may be referable only to my own views in favour of my own friends and connections . . .[4]

But Arthur could also be kind. He was fond of children, and his wife's many little nephews and nieces took happily to him. When the three Hamilton orphans were recovering from measles a few months after their mother Helen's death, the Wellesleys had them to stay in Secretary's Lodge. John Hamilton described it forty years later:

> One evening a curious circumstance occurred, considering who one of the persons concerned came afterwards to be. Sir Arthur and my uncle Henry Pakenham . . . took my brother and me out to walk – evening came on – dinner-time drew near, and the boys were weakly and could not run fast, so Sir Arthur took me on his back, and my uncle Henry took Edward and set off running. Soon it became a race. I was a good deal the heavier and my uncle Henry, then about twenty-two, was very active and left us far behind for the first couple of hundred yards. But Sir Arthur had bottom and began to regain his lost ground, and at last came up close to his antagonist, shouting, and both put out their utmost speed and both shouted with all their lungs. The gate was to be the winning post and with a wild Hollah! Sir Arthur passed to the front and won by a few yards, but in half a minute was a prisoner in the custody of the guard mounted at the gate, and who in the dusk did not perceive who the disturbers of the peace were.[5]

Sadly, cracks were already beginning to show in this domestic peace. Arthur was constantly away, and Kitty was constantly making blunders. Her trouble was her tender heart, and lack of domestic economy: she lent a large sum of money to her insolvent brother Henry, paid out guineas to every charitable cause that came her way, and left household bills in arrears. It infuriated Arthur. 'My dearest Kitty,' he wrote from London in July,

> I am much concerned that you should have thought of concealing from me any want of money . . . Once for all you require no permission to talk to me upon any subject you please; all that I request is that a piece of work may not be made about trifles . . . & that you may not go into tears because I don't think them deserving of an uncommon degree of attention.[6]

Elizabeth Countess of Longford

Thomas Pakenham, *above left*, painted at the time of his marriage to the heiress Elizabeth Cuffe, *above right*, in 1740. In 1756 he was made 1st Baron Longford, a re-creation of her great-great-uncle's title, in view of his accession to her estates and control of two parliamentary seats. *Below*: His younger brother, George Edward Pakenham. Both male portraits are probably by the fashionable Irish painter, James Latham.

G. E. PAKENHAM
OBIT 1768

'They hunt as they do in England and drink as hard.' An illustration from George Edward Pakenham's journal of 1737–8. It shows his brother's house, Pakenham Hall, as a tiny sketch in the background and also its elaborate formal gardens of canals and basins, which were to be swept away later in the century. The fox is escaping off to the right.

It's 1781 and Captain Tom Pakenham, *right*, younger brother of Captain 2nd Baron Longford, is about to lose his ship, the *Crescent*. In scene one, *left*, two Dutch frigates attack the *Crescent*; in scene two, *below left*, the *Crescent* loses her main mast in the ferocious engagement, while her companion ship, the *Flora*, abandons her to go after the other Dutch prize. In the last scene, *below*, 'Without a Gun to fire or a Sail to set', Captain Pakenham is rowed away from his crippled ship. Lord Longford commissioned the first two pictures of the battle from Dominic Serres and the third from Thomas Whitcombe, after the subsequent court martial exonerated his brother of all blame.

'(With) 30 Men killed and 70 wounded, my Brother was under the necessity of Striking his Colours.' Detail of the stricken ship. A sailor tries to cut away the damaged mast with an axe.

Above left: Captain Edward Michael, 2nd Baron Longford, 'a man of strong practical sense and decided temper'. He was also deeply humane and was reported to have wept when commanding a naval press gang. *Above right*: His wife, Catherine 2nd Baroness Longford, daughter of Hercules Langford Rowley. The only surviving picture shows her as a girl. She was left a widow in her forties with ten children, but lived on to 1816 to become, in Maria Edgeworth's phrase, the 'mother of heroes'. *Below*: Summerhill, the Rowley mansion in Co. Meath, described as '487 feet wide & built of hewn stone most indeed like a Palace'. Captain Lord Longford found it 'lugubrious'. It was burnt down in the Troubles of 1919–22.

There is no doubt that they were not temperamentally suited. Arthur was a man of resolve. Kitty, wilful in her own way, loathed making decisions and didn't yet trust her own judgement. She was more than a little overawed by Arthur. Much to her husband's annoyance, she looked to the reassurance of her mother and sisters and not to him. The delicate state of her health did not help matters; even the usually fearless Lady Longford awaited Kitty's second confinement with anxiety. From abroad Ned, optimistic as ever, treated the matter as lightly as he politely could, teasing his mother that '– what ever [Kitty] is most anxious to add to our strength, either King or Queen, God send that safety and good fortune may attend, – with my remembrance, say I shall only object to anything of lower Rank than the above'.[7]

Thankfully, on 16 January 1808, the baby arrived safely. A second boy, he was christened Charles – perhaps in honour of the Duke of Richmond. With less than a year between the boys, they were baptised together that June, Lord Longford standing godfather to little Arthur, and Kitty's mother to Charley. The family was only briefly together, for the Continental war had now called Wellesley away.

Two months before, Napoleon's General Junot and his army had invaded Lisbon to punish the Portuguese for refusing to join the Continental blockade of British ships. Spain was already a puppet state in the hands of the French. By the spring of 1808, General Wellesley's preparations to take command of the army in the Iberian Peninsula were completed. On 12 July he sailed from Cork for Portugal, and Kitty was left alone. The gossip soon began.

'July 1808. We only spent 2 days in Dublin. The town was empty, however, and we only heard of all the Castle proceedings of the last season; among which, the disagreement between Sir A. and Lady Wellesley made the most prominent feature', Miss Maria Nugent recorded in her diary, still following the progress of that affair. The quarrels may have been over money, or Pakenham friends and relations oppressing him with their demands.* But Kitty tried to

---

* Rather unfairly, Wellesley assumed that Longford would even pester him to be made a Knight of St Patrick. There is no evidence that this occurred.

remain cheerful, writing to thank her brother-in-law Marquess Wellesley for sending her the war news:

> The Hopes with which the newspapers are filled, are too agitating
> not to give great uneasiness but I am a soldier's wife and the husband
> of whom it is the pride of my life to think, shall find that he has no
> reason to be ashamed of me. All promises well, the Cause is a
> glorious one, and Please God we shall see our friends return safe and
> successful . . .

she scribbled untidily, adding 'My Boys are well and lovely.'[8]

By the first week in September, the reports of victory against the
French General Junot had reached Ireland. At first, there was only
delight; the strange and exciting names of 'Roliça' and 'Vimiero'
were on everyone's lips.[*] Maria noted the happy timing with her
usual zeal. 'What glorious news from Spain and Portugal . . . Don't
you envy Lady Wellesley her feelings at this moment! What exquisite pleasure to see the man she loves, the hero of his country,
applauded by all ranks – And Lady Longford! How fortunate that this
news comes just to balance, or at least divide her feelings about Poor
Robert P.'[†][9] The Duke of Richmond wrote to Arthur that he was
expecting him back at his Dublin post, now that the 'business' was
over. 'Lady Wellesley is quite well, and highly delighted, as you may
suppose. Louisa and Charlotte [Richmond's daughters] say, as you
have killed all the French, you must now come back.' But, unfortunately, a furore was about to break over Arthur's head.

After winning his two victories in Portugal, General Wellesley
had been superseded in command by his military superiors, Generals
Burrard and Dalrymple. Their decision was to pursue Junot no
further, but to come to terms. With little choice, and perhaps
reluctance, Wellesley then signed an armistice with the French,
which was quickly ratified at Cintra, near Lisbon. Its terms included
the evacuation of Junot's army from Portugal to France aboard
British transports. It caused outrage in all patriotic quarters; the

---

[*] Fought on 17 and 21 August respectively.
[†] Robert Pakenham had died in August.

erstwhile hero of Roliça and Vimiero was made the scapegoat.[10] A Court of Inquiry was ordered. In fact, Wellesley was entirely blameless, since it was Burrard and Dalrymple who had drawn up the document; Wellesley's only fault had been to sign it without thought to the consequences. Nevertheless, whilst disgrace hung over Arthur's name, he temporarily lost the adoration of his new supporters. From North America, Ned Pakenham wrote anxiously: 'How is Kitty? I should like to write but I think it better not, – the case is so singular that silence is best, though perhaps at the expense of being considered negligent'.[11]

Maria Edgeworth tried to prise some Pakenham opinions from old Lady Eliza, but she loyally demurred. Longford, however, did not: 'he wished Sir Hugh D hanged & Sir A. W hanging be[side] him *if he could not justify himself*'.[12] Perhaps it wasn't just patriotism that provoked the outburst, but an unconscious reflection of his feelings of loyalty to Kitty. As Miss Nugent's journal shows, it was hardly a secret that the marriage was under strain.

By 14 December the Court of Inquiry was over, and Wellesley had justified himself. He was exonerated of all responsibility for drawing up a faulty armistice with the French, and returned to Ireland with a clean slate, even if the 'shame' was never quite erased from all minds.[13] But the appointment in Ireland was rapidly coming to a close. In early January 1809, Kitty was making preparations for a parting ball at Secretary's Lodge; by the middle of the month the Wellesley family had removed to London for the parliamentary season.

Napoleon's armies, meanwhile, were as much on the offensive as ever. In November 1808 they had reinvaded Spain, and Joseph Bonaparte now sat in the palace at Madrid. Brave General Sir John Moore – who had come to Pakenham Hall the day after Ballinamuck – had been killed on 16 January 1809 at the Battle of Corunna while embarking British troops from Spain. Moore had predicted with his dying breath that Portugal could not hold if Spain fell. Only Wellesley believed that something could be done. Both the people of Portugal and Spain had risen up against their imposed dictator, and would provide troops for the British army. Lord Castlereagh, by now the Secretary of State for War, had faith in Wellesley, and offered him the command of the forces. The proper campaign against Napoleon's marshals on the Iberian Peninsula could begin.

Arthur did not hesitate for a moment. He wrote a parting letter to the Duke of Richmond, resigned his seat in Parliament and took a cool leave of Kitty, whose household bills had again come rushing out at him. By 12 April 1809, Wellesley was once again on his way to Portugal. This time, he wouldn't return for five years.

9

Brothers at War

For all younger sons, a profession was essential. For Edward, Hercules and William Pakenham, marriage was not a consideration they could yet afford to entertain. Theirs was a career in the Services begun early. For the youngest two particularly, with the prospect only of a small inheritance from their mother to supplement the £4,000 left to each of them on their father's death, it was essential to do well. By 1808, the eldest of the three was already well on his way.

Edward Michael Pakenham, 'Ned', was born at Pakenham Hall on 19 April 1778. 'I have got another son', noted Captain Lord Longford in his naval journal, though he himself was cruising the Channel with the fleet. With his four elder sisters and his brother Tom, baby Ned had arrived into a cheerful family home that he remembered with affection throughout his life. Like Tom, he was sent to the Royal School in Armagh, where the strict teachings of Dr Carpendale gave him a belief in duty and strong discipline.

Ned showed a natural bent for the Army. 'Reading is not Edward's forte', wrote Longford in 1793 as he viewed the military academy at Stuttgart with approval, soldiering was a vastly better route for him to take than 'pouring over Latin and Greek which he does not understand'. By the time Ned was fifteen, with Britain embarking on war against France, he had his first commission. At eighteen, his elder brother was delighting in tales of his brother's improvement. 'Such a young man so tall so handsome so genteel is rare to be seen', purred Longford with satisfaction. He was not in the least surprised at Ned's success, since Ned had always 'promised to be so'. Promotion – through a mixture of influence and purchase – came fast. At twenty, Ned was riding as a Major of the 23rd Light Dragoons in General Lake's army against the French; at twenty-two he was Lieutenant-Colonel of the 64th Foot, with 1,000 men under his care.

But Ned wanted to be off campaigning. In February 1801, to his delight, he was sent out to the heat of the West Indies, to capture the Danish and Swedish islands.* These countries had just joined Russia in the Baltic League of Armed Neutrality against Britain, and now were to pay the price. The voyage took fifty-three days, and was rather a trial. 'My party consisted of nine gentlemen, two ladies . . . two children and Betty the maid. At meals all was delightfully formal and immediately after, exactly the reverse.' Even in such a confined space, the ladies had their charms: 'The lady opened the day by a tune on the lute which stole on our waking through the chinks of the little cabin . . . and what the burden do you suppose? Why "Nobody coming to marry me". I cursed my unmusical soul which did not enable me instantly to reply.'

Neither Sweden nor Denmark were traditional enemies of Britain, nor were they in a strong position to defend their Caribbean possessions. As Ned had anticipated, the conquest of the islands was quick, and bloodless. By mid-summer 1801 he was peacefully installed on the Danish island of St Croix and delighted with his house, his horse, and the excellent, un-potholed roads. Here he remained for two years, moving between St Croix, Barbados and St Kitts, happy amongst the plantation owners and their eager wives, who took to the charming Irishman at once. He was amused by the narrow society, which seemed innocent and provincial even to a young man from Westmeath. He read Edwards on the West Indies, danced at the evening parties, and reflected cheerfully that Dr Pangloss'[1] dictum was his own. As for the slaves on the plantations, he thought them surprisingly well treated – though man-trade *ought* to be abolished – and the whole place incorrigibly lazy. There was time

* Before he left Ireland, Ned ordered 1,358 pairs of socks to be sent to the Foundling Hospital in Armagh.

enough indeed between his regimental duties for some light flirtation. At twenty-two, his heart lay wide open to the smiles of beautiful
girls. Before long he found himself attached to one girl in particular,
in a dalliance that was to last three years (see p. 104).

But Ned also missed home. Even as he had left Ireland, he had
confessed to his mother that 'With my home I have my inmost
affections, and a larger proportion rests with you. If I let out all I felt
by you, my sea store would be diminished too much'.[2] He wrote
frequently to her – 'in the very act of writing to you, I find
happiness!' – and cherished her replies:

> Your letters to me are worth millions! Don't tell me too much of the
> best mother's thoughts and wishes for the son, me, I myself am as
> liable to build castles as anyone, and hang me if vanity is not always
> near the foundation of these fabricks; – occupation however brings
> the best recollection, – just sufficient of that turns the D[e]v[i]l off,
> and affords content though absent from all friends.[3]

To make his stay more cheerful, packages arrived from home to
the great excitement of all:

> Some good Western Folks who all know the value of a Dollar,
> were present when I opened this Chest; out came Books, boots,
> Hats, shoes, followed by little snuggeries; all said, such things were
> never seen; – and who sent them out? 'Some body named Ld
> Longford'; 'who is Lord Longford?' Said the curious. Answering
> 'My Brother,' I tugged up my shirt neck, for I found what I said was
> true . . .

Longford's affection was a powerful remedy to reassure Ned that
all was well at home. Although only four years older than Ned, he
acted as friendly advisor and cheerful newssheet. Helen Hamilton
had always believed Longford the best brother possible – 'Longford I
must say is the most constantly kind & one of the most affectionate
of brothers, as to Edward he seems to me to regard him more as a
tender Father than a brother. All who know Longford both love &
esteem him, but very few know his real value.'[4] The news that
domestic tranquillity continued ensured Ned's own letters remained

sunny. In fact, his only minor anxiety was that the European peace looked like putting him out of work.*

But by May 1803 the Treaty of Amiens had broken down. Even in the faraway West Indies, battle recommenced as the British forces fought to take St Lucia and Tobago from the French. This time Ned was not so lucky. An assault on the fort of St Lucia left him wounded in the neck, and lying unconscious on the glacis. No doubt he would have bled to death if he had not been found by a French family who had gone out on purpose to search for him when they heard his regiment had borne the brunt of the fighting. Ned had saved the women from the brutality of the English troops in an earlier assault; in gratitude they took him into their home and nursed him back to health. His mother was horrified to hear of the wound, and Ned hurried to reassure her.

Barbadoes, July 20th 1803

My good and Dearest Mother,

   That care and affection which I have ever had from you since my Recollection, I apprehend you have suffered to pass bounds on my account lately; let this letter put you perfectly at ease, neither have I any hesitation in saying that you have suffered much more than I have done.

He was soon 'quite made good again' and able to 'despise the doctor as much as usual'. His optimistic nature boosted her spirits, as he assured her that his one wish was that 'amongst the list of your children [I] may add to your ease and comfort when much older'.[5] Catherine Longford's devotion to all her ten children was great. But Ned, the baby born so soon after her husband had set sail for the war, was her favourite.

By the autumn of 1803 the convalescent Colonel was on his way home. At Exeter, his mother and sisters waited in hope for his arrival. Finally, on Christmas Eve, a horse was heard on the cobbles outside

---

* Peace of Amiens, 27 March 1802.

the rented house. There he was. 'I could not find a moment to write', one of his devoted sisters recorded in her journal. 'Yesterday we had the happiness of seeing our dear Edward . . . and most surprised I was to find him so very little changed, the Dear boy was quite overcome by meeting his friends. I look upon him as one saved from death & most sincerely I hope he may never again visit those fatal Islands.'[6]

The happy family circle was made complete by the arrival of Hercules, just graduated from Cambridge. Although Ned considered him far more intelligent than himself, and suited for the Church, Hercules soon followed his brother into the Army. By April he had been commissioned a Lieutenant in a regiment of light infantry, the 95th Rifles – the 'green-jackets'. The presence of 'these dear young men' cheered the family gathering. The only blight on the gay family reunion was the news that their cousin, Tom Vandeleur, had been killed fighting at Laswari in India.*

Ned spent the next four years drilling his new regiment, the 7th Royal Fusiliers. He was in Ireland to witness the marriage of his sister Kitty to Arthur Wellesley in the spring of 1806; he even toyed with the idea of standing for Parliament, since his mother's family estate in County Antrim brought with it the chance of a county seat. In the event he stood down, having realised perhaps that a political career didn't suit his modest character. The London world of the *ton* was not his; in fact he was deeply shocked by their easy morality. He confessed it all to Maria Edgeworth when she caught sight of him:

> We were fortunate in seeing something of the mirror of Colonels whilst we were at Coolure. Col. Edward P. burnt his instep *by* falling asleep before the fire out of which a turf fell; so he was luckily detained in the country a few days longer than he had intended & dined & breakfasted &c with us – He is very unaffected & agreeable – wonderfully modest considering all the flattery he has met with – He says the women of rank & ton in England are growing

---

* He was a nephew of Captain Lord Longford.

abominably like Frenchwomen in their morals – of the Dutchess of Gordon's freedom of conversation he spoke in particular with horror – He said that one night at the opera he was in her Grace's box with a *young* lady when the Dutchess said something which confounded him to such a degree that he would have given the world to have been out of the box or to have known what to say next – a woman of the town he thinks *could* not have made the speech . . .[7]

In fact Maria was delighted with Ned's modesty for a particular reason. She was keeping the Colonel up her sleeve for a pet project – marriage to her favourite cousin, Sophy Ruxton. She was convinced that Sophy – who lived in neighbouring County Meath – would make the perfect wife for Ned. Kitty may have given her some encouragement in this fantasy, for she also loved Sophy, and spoke to Maria about her with great animation. Sadly we have no mention of Sophy on Ned's side. In any case, he suffered the women around him to make their plans.

In August 1807 Ned and Hercules accompanied General Wellesley to Denmark. The besieging of Copenhagen was meant as a pointed reminder to the Danes that Britain, not France, was their friend. Although glad to be back in service, Ned disliked what he saw as unnecessary destruction, innocent as he still was of how a conquering army behaved to civilians. In fact, after three days of bombardment and harassment, the Danish fleet delivered itself up to the British, and the affair was over. Some months later Hercules was on leave.

'A little while after we arrived,' Honora Edgeworth wrote to her cousin from Pakenham Hall at Christmas,

we heard some bustle in the house . . . Lady Longford, who had not yet seen us, rushed into the room, took no notice of any of us, but pushed forward to Lady Elizabeth and exclaimed, 'Here is a gentleman that wants to speak to you.' At this instant there entered the room a young gentleman like Lord Longford, and very like Miss Pakenham, who ran up to Lady Elizabeth and embraced her . . . you may imagine what delight his coming gave rise to, and how eagerly his friends looked at him from head to foot, to see what alterations had taken place in him, & whether it really was him whom they saw before them.[8]

Hercules gave an account of the siege that thrilled the Edgeworths. 'My father has scarcely quitted his elbow since he came, and has been all ear and no tongue', commented Maria, amazed that anyone could silence the garrulous Mr Edgeworth.[9] Her sister Honora was not so impressed, and thought the Captain's language rather coarse, too full of the 'expressions of a soldier' and he 'too fond of abusing all of whom he speaks', insisting that she liked 'Ld L's [wit] a thousand times better'.[10] There was quite a jostle in the family as to which Pakenham brother was to be preferred. Ned was Edgeworth's favourite hero, but that 'mirror of Colonels' was soon sent off again, this time to North America. Maria declared that 'Lord L. I always like the best of all the gentleman of his family', then reported that her father made her scratch it out, since for him it was 'high treason to prefer anything or any body to the immaculate colonel'.[11]

It was Ned who was made godfather of baby Michael Pakenham Edgeworth, Mr Edgeworth's last child.

For Maria, the Pakenham brothers continued to be the pattern for military heroics. Her own romantic life had been short and sad: a proposal by a Swedish diplomat* in 1802 had been turned down largely because she could not bear the thought of leaving her home. (Maria was moved to tears for years afterwards whenever Sweden was mentioned.) Now in her early forties, Maria enjoyed making matches for others. She was convinced that Lady Longford had the same idea of her sons' marriage potential as she did. Maria had always liked Catherine, and admired her refreshing frankness, once saying of her 'I have never seen a woman so little spoiled by the world.'[12] She was therefore delighted when Lady Longford and old Lady Eliza frequently praised Sophy. Sophy was 'the first young woman in the world . . . I am sure that if they had 40 sons to dispose of in marriage they would put them all at Sophy's feet & leave her to

---

* Abraham Edelcrantz. He died in 1821, having never married.

settle which was most deserving of the praise – in my opinion – but that opinion sink or swim I will keep to myself.'[13]

When Arthur Wellesley had made his first landing in Portugal in August 1808, Hercules had been with him. The 95th Rifles running ahead of the main body of the army, 'every man using his own wits to make the most of cover', Hercules had been slightly wounded in a skirmish outside the small village of Obidos. Wellesley had sent to Richmond in Ireland a cautious note not to let Kitty hear of it except from him or the family, for she was sure to overreact. And in a typical instance of thoughtfulness for his officers, even in the middle of the Cintra controversy, Wellesley had asked the War Office to give Hercules a promotion, admitting 'he is really one of the best officers of riflemen that I have seen'.[14] (Hercules was appointed Major in August 1810.)

During the long retreat from Spain that had ended with Sir John Moore's tragic death at Corunna, Hercules had ridden over the frozen mountains with the famously irascible Major-General Craufurd. Private Benjamin Harris, a fellow rifleman, and Dorset 'sheep-boy', remembered it in his memoirs. On Christmas Eve,

> Suddenly a shout arose in front that the French were upon us. In an instant, every man was on the alert, and we were rushing forward, in extended order, to oppose them . . . The honorable Captain Pakenham . . . on the first sound of the enemy being in sight, made a dash to get to the front, at the same moment I myself was scrambling up a bank on the road side. In the darkness and hurry the mule the captain was mounted on bore me to the ground, and, getting his forefeet fast fixed somehow between my neck and my pack, we were fairly hampered for some moments. The captain swore, the mule floundered, and I bellowed with alarm lest the animal should dig his feet into my back, and quite disable me.[15]

Eventually the over-zealous Hercules got himself and his mule clear of poor Harris, and 'spurred over the bank'. It was to no avail, however, for a few hours later Craufurd received the orders to about-turn and the nightmarish retreat south to Vigo began, the exhausted men marching with few or no provisions. There, on the

coast, the ships waited to repatriate the British army. Only Craufurd's iron will and bullying determination had saved his men. It was
an example that Hercules never forgot.

Meanwhile Ned, wounded again during the successful attack on the
French island of Martinique in February 1809, knew that the Iberian
Peninsula was where the real fight lay. By the time he had recovered,
he was desperate to join his brother-in-law. 'What a degree of fame
that man has arrived at! I still hope it may ultimately produce as
much comfort to his family as honour to his country.'[16] He saw Kitty
briefly in Broadstairs on his way to London, and found her 'vastly
well', in spite of the absence of her husband, 'quite stout in comparison to my expectation'. In London, good luck and the hard
pressing by Longford of Lord Castlereagh, Secretary of State for
War, gave him the chance for which he had been waiting. By the
end of August, Ned was on his way to Portugal as bearer of the
Government dispatches.

'Edward is the happiest fellow,' wrote Longford to their sister
Bess, 'except myself who feel that I have been instrumental in
making him so.'[17]

10

Good Old Pakenham Hall

⌒

At Pakenham Hall, Tom Longford continued as gay and hospitable as ever. Whenever they had leave from the Army, Ned and Hercules were welcome to stay; Kitty too, with her delightful babies in tow. His youngest brother Henry, now ordained, was often there. Neighbours came and borrowed books from the excellent library his grandmother had created, plays were put on in the great hall. Longford loved company; nothing suited him better than the noise and bustle of a full house.

He was also still averse to taking orders. When it had been suggested to Longford by Chief Secretary Wellesley that he must come over to England, as his presence was needed in the Lords, he refused to budge with playful regret. 'That I should most unwillingly leave a party of most pleasant ladies . . . to present myself to a pack of dull pompous Lords in Battle array, on such an occasion as moving or seconding the address, can (to you at least) be in no way surprising'.[1]

Wellesley might have been the name on everyone's lips, but Longford was still holding his own.

In the icy New Year of 1809, the Edgeworths were staying again, for the Pollard ball. The Pollards, neighbours and sometime rivals to the Pakenhams, lived at Kinturk House, just the other side of Castlepollard. Maria found the arrangements quite wonderful. She was still on the lookout for a partner to join Longford in his nest.

Lord Longford acted his part of Earl Marshal in the great hall, sending off carriage after carriage, in due precedence, and with its

94

proper complement of beaux and belles. I was much entertained: had Mrs Tuite, and mamma, and Mrs Pakenham, and the Admiral to talk and laugh with: saw abundance of comedy. There were three Miss X, from the County of Tipperary, three degrees of comparison, the positive, the comparative, and the superlative; excellent figures with white feathers as long as my two arms joined together, stuck in the front of what were meant for Spanish hats. Oh how they towered above their sex, divinely vulgar, with brogues of true Milesian race – talking of saates for seats. &c . . . Supper so crowded that Miss Pakenham and I agreed to use one arm by turns, and thus with difficulty found means to reach our own mouths. Miss Caroline P. grows upon me every time I see her. Indeed she loves Sophy & talks of her so much that there is one never failing agreeable subject of conversation & sympathy between us – Then she is as quick as lightning, understands with half a word – has literary allusions as well as humour, and follows and leads in conversation with that playfulness and good breeding which delight the more because they are so seldom found together. We stayed till between three and four in the morning . . . the postillion had, it seems, amused himself at a club in Castle Pollard while we were at the ball, and he amused himself so much that he did not know the ditch from the road: he was ambitious of passing Mr Dease's carriage – passed it – attempted to pass Mr Tuite's – failed – ran the wheels on a drift of snow which overhung the ditch & laid the coach fairly down on its side . . . we were none of us hurt – The us were Mrs E – Mr Henry P. & myself – Mrs E fell undermost; I never fell at all for I clung like a bat to the hand strings at my side determined that I would not fall upon my mother and break her arm . . . The gentlemen hauled us out immediately . . . Admiral P lifted me up from the dirt and carried me in his arms as if I had been a little doll set me down actually on the step of Mr Tuite's carriage & I never wet foot or shoe – And now my dear aunt I have established a character for courage in overturns for the rest of my life . . . All the Gosfords Lady Olivia Sparrow & many other fine birds were to come the day after we left P. Hall viz Monday . . .²

Longford, certainly, was no snob.

His eldest sister, Bess, was not at the house party. Eight-year-old Kitty, her only daughter, had died on 26 December 1808 at Summerhill. Paralysed with grief, Bess could not face sociable Pakenham Hall, choosing to remain in huge, empty Summerhill with only her mother and Harry for comfort. Maria was touched, reporting that the Stewarts with their quiverful of sons had looked to their daughter as a future 'companion in retired life'. Even Arthur Wellesley was sympathetic, and sent Kitty straight away from Dublin to be with her sister, telling her to stay as long as she wished.

By 1809 Catherine Longford had ten grandchildren, including the three orphaned children of Helen Hamilton. When not at school, the little Hamilton boys sometimes spent their holidays with their uncle Longford in Westmeath, accompanied by their grandmother. There they found their doting great-aunt Eliza[3] busy with the harvest, or a visiting Emily Napier, or syllabub specially prepared for dinner when the Coolure Pakenhams – and their 'happy unpolished but agreeable urchins'[4] – came over to dine. The system laid down for their education was the same as Catherine had dictated two decades before for their uncles. It chimed perfectly with Richard Lovell Edgeworth's view that the best learning could be put to practical use. As an adult, John Hamilton looked back with admiration on his grandmother's liberal views:

> My grandmother knew no fear and used to say she had no nerves . . . She allowed us the utmost licence in climbing trees, digging pits, building piers in the lake, only the rule, unchanging as that of the Medes and Persians, was: 'Give no extra trouble; if you make a mess, clean it up yourselves; if you dirty a second pair of shoes, clean them yourselves. If you want a garden, dig and plant, – a summer-house, build it.'[5]

It was a doctrine of self-help that he never forgot.

When Maria, a favourite guest, came to stay at Pakenham Hall again in the winter of 1811, she found a 'whole tribe of merry children

– Stewarts and Hamiltons' busily entertaining themselves. This time there was a new craze.

> . . . the card playing passion rose to such an alarming pitch that the children were found playing at cards before breakfast (*private* in the water-closet) and Mrs Stewart with great good sense & address instead of issuing prohibitions turned the cards into a greater source of pleasure by cutting them into pantines* which she painted & strung so well that they charmed the young folk . . . In the evening the six children in a row seated themselves each with a pantin before them pinned to the carpet a yard & 1/2 distance – candles on the floor – & *orders* for no one to come across the gossamer strings – indeed this order was quite necessary for they were quite invisible to mortal eyes & the first thing Lady Elizabeth did was to sweep full across them & to get entangled in all the chords of harmony – Exclamation in all tones! The puppets swept off the face of the carpet! Some round her ladyship's ankles some mounted to her pocket-holes! – Legs arms & heads however were at length set to rights & the dancing began with excellent music – one of the footmen playing on the fiddle – none more charmed with the performance than my father, who as usual was the *soul* of the dance & the joy of the children . . .[6]

Other children too had not been forgotten; Lady Longford took Edgeworth and Maria aside to show them a picture of her 'beautiful' Wellesley grandsons. As for Kitty, Edgeworth snorted with irritation that an attempt should even be made to draw his favourite: 'it is absurd of anyone to attempt to draw Lady Wellington's face because she has no face, it is all countenance'.[7] Longford himself, 'dear, (yes, *dear*) Ld L.', as Maria put it, was on one of his 'flying visits'.

Longford's frolics continued. It is true that in Ireland he galloped about the countryside in all weathers, seeking advice on how he might improve his estate, staying frequently with his serious friend George Knox in Dungannon or the great farming improver, Owen Wynne of Hazelwood. Wynne was something of a mentor to

---

* 'Pantines' were cut-out puppets.

Longford, twenty years his senior and married to his friend Lowry Cole's sister Sarah. Wynne had even inspired one traveller to describe him as 'just the sort of person of whom, could one put down one at every thirty miles throughout Ireland, it would in forty years time become as much civilized as England'.[8] Avuncular Wynne encouraged Longford's serious leanings. Yet when in London, another side to Longford re-emerged. He drank and gambled at White's club, and dined and danced at the famous Almack's ballroom, controlled by a formidable group of noble hostesses.* Naturally, Longford did his duty in the Lords, and voted for the Government, but he also made as much as he could of the glittering social scene.

Longford never mentions the girl who Maria had once had a 'notion' would be his bride. Miss Crewe, the granddaughter of old Lady Longford's friend Mrs Greville, married a Mr Cunliffe in 1809. Instead Longford was charmed by the widowed Mrs Apreece, much to Maria's concern, since the society hostess was notorious for setting her cap at all eligible bachelors. Longford confessed he particularly liked the way Mrs Apreece decided in favour of Irish gentlemen, in a discussion of the merits of the two races. His aunt, Lady Eliza, was horrified. 'I declare if [Mrs Apreece] comes to storm Longford in his castle I wont let her in . . . I would not have him fall in love with her for the world.'

Maria sat listening enchanted to Longford's traveller's tales. One of these described sharing a coach with a convict, whose overalls concealed his irons and whose slow movements Longford had mistaken for gout. When Longford mentioned he regretted not travelling further with this interesting character, '– This excited Lady Longford's indignation – "Longford! Would you have gone in the coach with this man?" "Aye Ma'am to be sure I would. Such an opportunity I would not lose." "Then I tell you, you deserve to have had the fetters on yourself" '[9] exclaimed his mother, throwing up her hands, and delighting Maria, who liked to think of Lady Longford

---

* Almack's assembly rooms, established in 1765. In 1814 the committee was listed as Lady Sarah Jersey, Lady Emily Cowper, Lady Sefton, Princess Esterhazy, Countess Lieven, and Mrs Drummond-Burrell.

having 'more principle & more virtuous indignation' than anyone she knew. The authoress was equally pleased to be supplied with 'a great many excellent anecdotes of gaming, eating & extravagant men', many of which she would 'tell' in her novels. For Maria was by now a famous writer, whose first volume of *Tales of Fashionable Life*[10] had been a tremendous success in England and Ireland.

Longford remained a regular visitor to the Edgeworths. Kind and agreeable, he never failed to cheer them up. 'What I admire in his whole conversation is, its being without effort, and always to entertain the company & not to show himself off – or by implication or otherwise to boast of his fine acquaintance or his grandeur.'[11] Perhaps Maria was even a little bit in love with him herself, sighing over the memory of a visit 'you know the various charms both for the head and heart at P.H.'. Longford entered into Mr Edgeworth's progressive schemes with enthusiasm, helping Edgeworth to erect his 'collapsible spire' on the church at Edgeworthstown as eagerly 'as though he was their own brother'. But most of all the Edgeworth family looked to the bachelor Lord to pass on to them the war news.

By 1811, two of his younger brothers were veterans in fighting the French.

11

Mother of Heroes

Colonel Edward Pakenham had finally caught up with the Peninsular army just after the battle of Talavera,* in early August 1809. His brother-in-law, made Viscount Wellington on 4 September, immediately put him on the staff. By November he was Deputy Adjutant-General, in the absence of Sir Charles Stewart – Lord Castlereagh's half-brother – who was on sick leave. Although it was to prove the turning point in Ned's career, it was not a position he came to relish.

In theory the Adjutant-General's office was the most important staff office in the Army, responsible for co-ordination with the Horse Guards in London; but in practice Wellington was not the character to tolerate independent authorities. The essential paperwork of war for a man of action was particularly irksome, and Ned soon complained to Longford of his distaste for 'this damned clerking business'. He was itching to get out into the thick of it. Perhaps Wellington was protecting him; perhaps he was relieved to replace a man he regarded with suspicion – Stewart – with one he could rely on absolutely. In any case, the 'wild Irishman' was not pleased. But Ned recognised that there was someone who would be:

> Kitty, to whom I mentioned Lord Wellington's kindness both to my brother and to me, has I hope mentioned the fact to you; for besides the gratification it would afford to you, I wished her both to have the satisfaction of relating it, and by that relation to have impressed on

---

* 27–8 July 1809.

her that the kindness we receive has been much caused by our having such a sister.[1]

The job on the staff, however, had one enormous advantage for him: it meant almost daily contact with the Commander-in-Chief. Here he could absorb the thinking behind Wellington's strategy, and the process by which he was transforming an amateurish, poorly administered army into a masterful fighting machine.

This machine naturally included soldiers from the Allied armies of Portugal and Spain. For the moment, however, Wellington intended only to support Portugal; as Lord Castlereagh had instructed, it was his 'first and immediate object'.[2] Suspicions of the Spanish Junta were high in London, since they seemed better at obstructing the line of supply than contributing to it. But Ned was impressed by the skill of the Spanish troops, if not their mendacious leaders.

'If there was but Ten honest men of talent in this country it might yet be saved, – but even as it is, depend on it, Bony has more occupation destined for him in this country than He is yet aware.'[3] An overly optimistic judgement, perhaps, at the moment when Napoleon, having beaten the Austrian army at Wagram at the beginning of July, was free to turn the whole of his strength against Spain. After the casualties at Talavera,[4] Wellington's force in the Peninsula was scarcely 18,000 men, while the French army under Marshal Soult alone was 30,000-strong. But Ned, unlike Napoleon's generals, knew that his chief had a secret weapon up his sleeve.

Wellington's 'defensive system' – the great Lines of Torres Vedras – was being constructed at that very moment. Using the natural contours of the landscape outside Lisbon, Wellington arranged twenty-nine miles of fortified outposts, in three lines, behind which his troops could protect Lisbon and, if necessary, retreat to the Atlantic. They came as a complete surprise to Soult when he encountered them a year later.

For Ned, relief from pen and ink came in August of 1810, when to his joy he found himself once more in command of a brigade. His old battalion of the 7th Fusiliers had arrived from Nova Scotia, and formed part of it; with them he rode the retreat through the barren

Portuguese mountains and turned to fight at the city of Busaco on 27 September. He described the battle to his mother as a 'vastly glorious and advantageous occurrence to the Common Cause'. Five thousand French had been killed, the Allied losses numbered 1,200. Three old friends from his boyhood had also been fighting in the Peninsula: the Napier brothers, Charles, William and George. Charles Napier, Lady Sarah's favourite son, was wounded again: his jaw completely smashed. This did not stop Napier from trying to return to the front almost immediately, only Ned's intervention preventing it. But by mid-October, the whole of Wellington's army was secure behind the Lines, whilst the French General Massena's troops were forced to retire to the scorched and barren fields of northern Portugal.

> To give you an instance of the comprehensive mind of Wellington, I must tell you, we had a grand Ball, previous dinner, and concluding supper, at the Palace of Mafra, on the occasion of Beresford's being created Knight of Bath. The facts of a General having invited the officers of his Army to an amusement, distant from the nearest point of from three to four leagues, and an opposing Army of Fifty thousand strong close to our Lines, appears like madness. But look to the result. All Lisbon were invited to Meet us. The Portuguese like spectacle and were pleased by the installation; – the General assemblage of the Staff and other officers has placed the Natives at ease as to the situation of the Army: The Portuguese Officers have been pleased by witnessing the distinction granted their immediate Commander [Beresford], and which honor is in a measure attribut-able to their own good Conduct! – in short, by this simple or apparently mad act of amusement, Confidence has been transmitted to the Capital, – pride and self consequence instilled into the National Troops of Portugal. Viva!!!

Ned appreciated strategy. He was even prepared to forgive Wellington's private failings, although they so closely concerned his own sister.

> I hear constantly from Kitty, who seems in reasonable spirits, and indeed so far as relating to her husband's public Duties, she ought to

be most proud, – for no Man under similar circumstances ever did such justice to the Charge reposed in him. For my part I should rather be a Man with his acknowledged failings, than a Minister with all his supposed accomplishments; – those now in office – for to speak of power would be laughable – I pity almost as much as I commiserate the country they are bound to serve.[5]

Kitty herself was keeping her head down. Moving between the various spa resorts of Broadstairs, Ramsgate and Cheltenham, she avoided London and the searchlight that would inevitably descend on her – hardly surprising when she was alternately an object of pity and fascination to the public. For Wellington was rumoured to be following the typical pattern of a soldier's life, in his domestic habits. Sarah Napier vented her spleen after the near-death of her son Charles at Corunna: 'a Commander-in-Chief, who publickly keeps a mistress at head-quarters, does not give all the attention to the care of his army & disgusts his army, who lose all confidence in him'.[6] But if she was keeping quiet, Kitty was also fiercely loyal, writing to Bess after the news of the Battle of Talavera that 'He is safe and well and has been blessed with success thank God of Heaven[;] this has been a most hard fought, desperate Battle, but our success is complete . . . the consequences of this dear bought Victory will be the safety of Millions . . . Adieu my Bess I hardly can hold my pen.'[7] But in Ireland, even Maria Edgeworth was not sure that it was worth such a sacrifice to be married to a hero:

> I fear Ld W will not come home a popular hero but he has his good 2000 per annum[*] secure & I do not believe he has heroism enough to be sorry for that – Poor Lady Wellesley! The price of victory, the price of marrying a hero is terrible! I think Mrs H. Hamilton is a thousand times more happily tho' less grandly married.[8]

Out in Portugal, unlike many of his fellows, Ned did not petition for leave. Christmas 1810 was spent with Hercules drinking the fine

---

[*] This was the pension allowed to Wellington after Talavera.

Lisbon port they had bought with their pay. As another winter of stalemate between the two sides passed, Ned had leisure to think of another matter altogether.

At the time of his happy life amongst the planters of St Croix, a certain girl had caught his eye. This was Ellen Gwynn.[9] In due course she had three children by him, only one of whom survived. This little girl, Helen – named after Ned's favourite sister – was now ten and Ned wanted her removed from the unhealthy climate of the West Indies (and presumably her mother's low origins). The man he asked to carry the child back to Ireland was Captain John Armstrong of the Fusiliers.

Armstrong was the one man, outside his own family, whom Ned trusted with everything. Back in 1803, at the near-disastrous attack on St Lucia, Armstrong had rallied the troops; they had been firm friends ever since. When Ned had transferred from the 64th to the 7th Fusiliers, he had brought Armstrong with him as Paymaster; when Armstrong's second son was born in 1808, he was christened Edward Pakenham. By February 1811, Ned was writing to his mother asking her to take the Captain on as her agent at Langford Lodge. Soon after, he repeated the appeal to Longford, declaring that 'a home he shall have whilst I live, and attention to this man's worth and distress is perhaps the only request I shall have to make to my friends in the event of accidents . . . I have taken him as a friend, and I shall never let go my grasp.'

There is no mention of the child in his letter. But Captain John Armstrong was successfully installed as the agent at Langford Lodge and made a considerable success of it: 'I think he does great justice to the charge he has undertaken,' reported Longford. Later clues suggest that Armstrong and Ned's brother Hercules were made legal guardians of the child, and that Helen Pakenham was brought up under her own name – which was rather unusual.*

Behind the Lines, the weeks of waiting for the French to make their move continued all through the spring. The long campaign had

---

* The three 'natural' children of Longford were given alternative surnames. See Chapter Seventeen.

taken its toll on Ned's equipage: 'I beg you will have sent out by the first safe opportunity', he wrote to Longford, 'cloth for Regimental coat, blue cloth sufficient for facings, cuff and collar-trimmings', boots, buttons and above all horses 'for I am in very great distress'.[10] In March the war recommenced, this time with the now starving French army on the defensive, harried out of Portugal by the Allied troops.

Wellington's 'scorched earth' policy may have been successful, but resulted in the torture and murder of the poor peasants in the retreating army's path. Mothers and their children were strung up above fires in an attempt to get information about food they might have hidden, villages were razed to the ground.

> The debased ingenuity of man, when converted to human torment, could hardly be supposed capable of suggesting the acts of horror actually committed by these fiends of hell; – every Village and Town has been set fire to, all peasants taken have been killed in the most crewel manner, the women, nay even females from childhood violated . . .'[11] *

Thirty years later, Hercules too could still not forget the scenes he witnessed, and described the blood that had been streaked across the walls of the houses like stripes of the most obscene decoration.†

Nevertheless, by 10 April the French had been pushed to the

---

* Charles Napier was driven to write a furious comment in his diary of the period by what he saw as the indifference at home to the real situation abroad. 'England, how little you know of war!'

† 'Colonel Hercules P told Caroline that when they were in pursuit of the French in Spain they once came to a small town from which they had but half an hour before fled after committing indescribable cruelties – There was literally dead silence – not a human creature left alive – not an animal alive – In one room where there were mangled bodies and a horrid quantity of bloodshed there was an instance of the sort of playfulness or cruelty which Hercules P said shocked him more than all the rest – and was before his eyes when he tried to sleep nights afterwards – All round the chimney piece & all round the room over the walls there was a regular border made of a bloody hand fresh dipped – scarce dry – This is indeed the tiger & monkey character mixed.' Maria Edgeworth to Fanny Wilson, 23 November 1834. BOD MS Eng. lett. c.708, fol.33.

Spanish border, and the inhabitants of Portugal were able to return to their homes. Hercules was amongst many who reported the buoyancy of morale, and above all the adoration all felt for their Chief: 'even in Retreat the Spirit of the Army was integer [unbroken] . . . [its sentiments] in respect of Lord W. cannot be expressed'.[12]

Wellington's strategy, now that Portugal was secure, was to march on the offensive into Spain. He planned to capture two old fortresses that guarded the two main routes into that country, Ciudad Rodrigo in the north, and Badajoz in the south. On 16 April 1811, Wellington rode south to inspect the part of the army who, under General Beresford, were besieging the walled city of Badajoz, still occupied by the French. Ned doubted the skill of the men Wellington had left in command. 'Sir Brent Spencer has charge of this corps,'* he wrote to Longford, 'and is as good a fellow as possible to meet at a County Club, but as to succeeding Wellington it is quite Dam . . . n to him'. As for General Beresford, Ned was even more inclined to pessimism. '[Beresford] is a clever man but no General; his Anxiety is too great, and he cannot allow an Operation to go through by its first impulse without interference, which generally on such occasions mars every thing.'

He detailed the lost opportunities that resulted from dithering. But Wellington could not be everywhere. By 2 May, thankfully for Ned, he was back in the north. There Wellington quickly determined to put paid to General Massena's last designs on Portugal.

As a first step, the taking of the small Spanish border village of Fuentes de Oñoro was the key. Here, where a maze of narrow winding streets made death traps for the unwary, the two armies played a game of cat and mouse. By midday on 3 May, it seemed that the Allies had nearly succumbed to the continuous waves of French attack. Then, on Wellington's command, Ned and his friend Colonel Wallace led the last hope against the enemy, the 'wild Irishmen' of the Connaught Rangers. In a ferocious charge, the French were driven out of the town 'at the point of the bayonet'. Even after it was free of the French, their guns were still bombarding the town;

---

* 6th Division.

'nevertheless', wrote Sir William Grattan of the 'Rangers', 'Sir Edward Pakenham remained on horseback, riding through the streets with that daring bravery for which he was remarkable. If he stood still for a moment, the ground about him was ploughed up with round shot.'[13] Grattan rode up to Ned soon afterwards: 'He was in a violent perspiration and covered with dust, his left hand bound round with his pocket handkerchief as if he had been wounded – he was ever in the hottest of the fire, and if the whole fate of the battle depended upon his own personal exertions, he could not have fought with more devotion.'

In his letters home Ned did not mention such details, only reporting how the 'Chief's' fine control of his forces had brought the Allies victory again. Sadly, this victory was considerably undermined by the secret escape of the French garrison from the besieged fortress of Almeida,* just over the border in Portugal. In the middle of the night of 10 May, the trapped French troops swept across the bridge of Barba de Puerco and rejoined General Massena at Ciudad Rodrigo, blowing up Almeida behind them. The blunder could patently have been avoided: two officers had failed to read their orders and stop the breakout. Wellington was furious; it confirmed his belief that he was 'obliged to be everywhere and if absent from any operation something goes wrong'.[14] Unfortunately, a far worse 'something' was to come.

In Longford, Maria Edgeworth was closely following events in the Peninsula. After she heard the reports of the battle at Fuentes de Oñoro, she couldn't help her excitement. 'Huzzah for the glorious Colonel Pakenham!' she scribbled to her cousin Sophy, 'but if anybody dares to think he's too grand for you, I will hate him or them! And you know it is impossible to hate Lady L – therefore you know it is impossible she should think so.'[15] It seems Maria was still holding on dearly to her pet project.

---

* Although the French had retreated from Portugal in March, French troops continued to occupy Almeida. Massena intended to relieve the garrison and regroup his army.

Longford too was gleaning every piece of news he could, and over the coming months sharing it with the Edgeworths. 'He was extremely entertaining & told us such horrible stories of the French cruelties as would make your hair stand straight up on your head', Mrs Edgeworth relayed to Fanny, adding with pain that 'General and Colonel Pakenham saw these things or I would ease my mind by not believing them'.[16] At Pakenham Hall, Lady Eliza joined in the excited chatter about the 'dear boys'. She reported to Bess that Catherine had received a 'most satisfactory account from them . . . You may judge of my sister Longford's Happiness she is quite young today'.[17]

In the south of Spain, General Beresford turned from the failed siege of Badajoz to fight the French at the battle of Albuera. Wellington, delayed by the commotion at Almeida, had not yet arrived at his side. Ned's low opinion of Beresford's abilities was proved only too right. A victory was gained – or at least a French retreat – but at a terrible price. Ned's own regiment were decimated on that 'glorious field of grief':[18] the Allied losses numbered 4,000 out of a total of 10,000; the French 7,000 out of 24,000. It was only due to the swift and unauthorised action of Kitty's old suitor, Lowry Cole, who moved up the 4th Division without orders when Beresford was dallying, that the battle was turned in their favour. Ned himself had not been there, having been ordered by Wellington to stay with Spencer in the north. For Ned it was an agony to have been away from his men when he was most needed.

For some days he was too overcome to write to Longford. As for Beresford, his written account of the battle made Ned even more convinced that the General was not fit to command. 'In truth there never was an official detail which more completely failed to put the Authorities . . . in possession of both the circumstances and fact of the Affair.' He did not know that Wellington had ordered the original dispatch to be rewritten.[19]

Initially, the public had only the published version of events to go by. Even so, Ned's mother was brimming with relief that he had escaped the carnage. 'My dearest Bess,' she wrote to her daughter in Ireland, 'at last the sad yet Glorious account of Marshal Beresford came in last night in the inclosed Gazette you will see with satisfaction the unamity that exists between the Spaniards & British. It increases my Gratitude for dear Edward not being with his Regiment which suffer'd so very much.'[20]

But by August Ned had at last got his wish to be back in full command: 'I am to go to a Brigade. Wellington, though quite the commander of the Forces is positively my brother in all our dealings.'[21] He had still not got the horses he had asked Longford to procure. 'The fact is, my dear Tom, you have been seated on your broad A[rse] in London whilst I have been astride a pigskin on the very worst animals, and nothing but destiny has prevented my being taken.' Pigskin saddle or otherwise, the excitement of a return to action was short-lived, for the malarial fever that had struck him intermittently since his stay in the West Indies returned in force. Although he was taking 'quantities of bark',* it seemed he nearly died from the effects. 'Wellington on finding that I was in for it, not only came over himself, but in the kindest manner, sent Hercules to me, the best Medical Men and everything I could possibly want – there was never such a fellow when it comes to the point.' He was sent home on leave, to stay with Kitty once again.

He arrived in London just in time to hear the news of an appalling naval disaster in Ireland. The Captain of the ship was William Pakenham, his brother.

---

* It had been known since the time of Cromwell that the cure for malaria was quinine, made from the bitter red bark of the cinchona tree, which grows in the Andes.

12

Dreadful Games

Captain William Pakenham of the British Navy had come out to the Peninsula just before the Battle of Busaco in 1810. He had returned from India earlier that year – leaving enormous debts of 4,000 rupees* in Calcutta – and was waiting for news of an available ship. His rise in the naval service had been slow compared with his soldier brothers, although he had been at sea since the age of fourteen. Many captains had been left unemployed after Trafalgar, with the fight against Napoleon no longer concentrated at sea. At a loose end, William Pakenham decided to come and see Wellington's army in action.

After the battle, he lodged with the Napiers in Lisbon whilst they were recovering from their various wounds. 'A gayer or more kind-hearted fellow never wore a blue coat', as George Napier put it, William threw himself into enjoying the delights of the city. They were a cheerful crowd in spite of their injuries, using the opportunity to befriend the prettiest Portuguese ladies. But a few weeks into William's stay the news came through that a ship had been found for him, the 36-gun frigate HMS *Saldanha*. He was to return immediately to Portsmouth. William left George Napier with an unusually mournful comment that his friend couldn't forget. 'I care not where I am sent so that it is not to cruise Lough-Swilly Bay on the Irish Coast, for if I go there I am sure I shall be lost.' Laughing off such a melancholy thought, his brothers and the Napiers wished him luck. By March 1811 William was at sea, cruising that very coast.

The story of the *Saldanha*'s shipwreck can be found in many of the

---

* Approximately £5,500 in today's money.

romantic histories of Donegal. She had been on the lookout for French ships for some months. The conditions on this coast were famously dangerous, and William was rightly wary of the place, writing to his mother on 25 November: 'Here we are again [in Lough Swilly], but I hope not for long.' It seems that the storm which had been growing increasingly violent over the previous days 'blew a perfect hurricane'[1] by the morning of 3 December. The *Saldanha*'s companion ship, the smaller HMS *Talbot*, managed to turn about to avoid the rocks at the entrance to Lough Swilly, but the *Saldanha*, to the leeward of them, was not so lucky. On 4 December watchmen in the towers at Lough Swilly saw a light rapidly entering the lough, which must have been the *Saldanha*. She was blown onto the notorious Swilly Beg rock, lost her masts and rudder, and was swept on into the lough quite beyond the control of her captain. She smashed in two on the lee shore of Ballymastoker Bay; all 274 souls on board were drowned.[*]

William's body was recovered two days later. 'The poor fellow must have attempted to save himself by swimming as he was found on the strand without any other dress than his shirt and trousers,' wrote Captain Hill, the commanding officer at Derry and a friend of William's, 'it is altogether the most heartbreaking event I ever heard of.'[2] The body was 'not in the least disfigured'.[3] They buried William in the old Priory church at Rathmullan, overlooking the lough, and Longford later had a monument erected and charmingly inscribed.[†] Only one more sailor's grave is known. Any other poor smashed bodies that washed up were interred in a mass grave somewhere in the dunes of that wild shore.

---

[*] In fact the only survivor was the Captain's parrot. Sadly a gardener shot this pet a year later, when it was mistaken for a hawk. It was found to have a gold ring around its neck inscribed Captain Pakenham, HMS *Saldanha*.

[†] 'Here lieth till the hour of Blessed Resurrection the Body of the Hon. William Pakenham, Captain of the Saldanha Frigate, who, with his whole crew, perished by Shipwreck in Ballymastoker Bay on the 4th December 1811, aged 29 years. Vigorous in mind, Benevolent in disposition, His friendship was truly valuable and justly valued. Daring in enterprise, Firm under every trial he stood forth Beloved & respected, a gallant officer, an honest man. He feared his God, no other fear was known to his intrepid soul.' The tomb was repaired a hundred years later by another Captain William Pakenham.

This blow, coming amid the relief that her Ned was safely home, was a fresh shock to Lady Longford. 'My Mother my dear excellent mother is the person to pity!' wrote Kitty to Marquess Wellesley. 'Most earnestly most ardently do I pray that the God who has afflicted her will mercifully support her for her loss is dreadful.'[4] Only Ned's presence was any comfort to her. But according to other witnesses, it was he who suffered the most; still weak and ill from fever, he was 'very much affected'.[5] 'Bill' had been his protégé, the charming but perhaps reckless young man whose career he had been most concerned with. It was Ned who had begged Longford to 'find Bill a ship'.

Over the London winter, Ned slowly recovered. Adored by his sisters and treated with a devoted tenderness by his mother, by the spring he was well enough to taste some of the delights of society. For the first time in his life, he thought seriously about his future in peacetime. There was a particular reason for this, although he denied it. At some point in the early weeks of spring he had fallen very seriously in love.

Miss Annabella Milbanke, nineteen and an heiress, was clever, attract-ive, and – most importantly for young ladies – 'holds up her head', according to Maria Edgeworth.[6] She had been out two seasons, had sat for the portraitist George Hayter, and had already rejected several marriage offers – which perhaps explains why the Duchess of Devon-shire found her 'odd' and rather an 'icicle'. Her London set were connected with the Pakenhams, through the Hamiltons and Kitty; Ned found himself constantly at her side, entertaining her with anecdotes of Wellington. Impulsive as ever, he proposed to her on Saint Patrick's Day 1812. Unfortunately, his gallantry and good looks did not appeal to her: she found his manners 'too silken', his opinions 'not founded on the same principles' as her own, and, most damning of all, she was put off by 'the strong tendency to insanity in all the Pakenhams'.* She

---

* Many large families tended to have a few skeletons of this sort in their cupboards. Probably she had heard about some of the more dubious members of the Rowley family, Ned's maternal cousins, who had intermarried. One of these was confined to an asylum in Kensington. Or she may have been misled about the nature of poor Robert Pakenham's illness.

turned him down politely. A few days after the rejection, Ned came to say goodbye, assuring Annabella's aunt that he had 'submitted to reason' and would 'never again [think] of his presumptious hopes':

> I met him with cordiality. He said: 'I am grateful for your friendship – be assured you shall never repent it.' I replied, 'I have perfect confidence in you;' and we then talked as if nothing of this nature had ever passed between us . . . My purpose was to prevent his encreasing his malady by a conduct that could only proceed from his unconsciously cherishing a remain of hope. I am quite satisfied with the part I have acted in regard to him – I meant it for his good, and I am sure that it has proved so.[7]

Annabella, it seems, always knew she was right.

But such a strong dose of disappointment made Ned itch to get away. The urge was clear enough to the family for his sister Kitty to comment that she was 'glad' he was to go back to his regiment, 'for he has become so anxious to join you all, now that you have been moving, that a longer delay in this country would but vex and irritate his nerves and probably retard his recovery'.[8] By 14 April, he was again en route to the Peninsula.

Three years later Miss Milbanke finally agreed to marry someone whose manners were far from silken. On the other hand, the man in question had a much richer seam of insanity in his genes. When they first met, however, he was the darling of society, with *Childe Harold's Pilgrimage* published on 10 March 1812, just days before Ned's proposal. Annabella, captivated by the poem, was introduced to the author the following month. After a couple of false starts, she became Lord Byron's wife in 1815, and was duly miserable.*

Hercules did not hear the news of William's death until 6 January 1812. His Chief consoled him in a typical fashion. 'I think however that you will bear your misfortune like a Man', directed Wellington,

---

* Byron and Miss Milbanke were married on 2 January 1815, just a few days before the Battle of New Orleans. Her preference of Byron to Ned Pakenham was 'unaccountable' to Mr Edgeworth (*Romilly–Edgeworth Letters*, p. 137).

'and will seek to divert your Mind from reflecting upon it, by attending to your duty in the new scene which is opening before us.'[9]

The storming of the Moorish fortress of Ciudad Rodrigo certainly proved a diversion. Charging with the Light Division, Hercules was lucky and survived, but his ferocious commander, General Craufurd,[10] who had so determinedly led his men to safety in 1809, was hit in the spine and died a week later. Moreover, Hercules' great friend Colonel Henry Mackinnon was blown up on the ramparts, while directing his men.[11] Both had inspired Hercules with their bravery at the forefront of the siege.

George Napier too was hit, his arm smashed so badly that it had to be amputated.* This was only the latest wound in a long series to afflict the Napier brothers. As Hercules had once remarked to Longford, 'the fact is, they cannot see, and acting independently as Light Troops, their Zeal gets them into scrapes'.[12] But even Ciudad Rodrigo was nothing to the next assault.

The storming of Badajoz, less than two months later, began in earnest on Easter Sunday. It was one of the hardest and most desperately fought assaults of the whole Peninsular campaign. After its conclusion, Wellington remarked that the battle had showed 'as strong an instance of gallantry as has ever been displayed. But', he added, 'I greatly hope that I shall never again be the instrument of putting them to such a test.'[13]

As the British infantry were forced back from the city walls by the flying fireballs of red-hot shot, Hercules was ordered to take the fortified castle under General Picton.[14] He could do no less than his friend Mackinnon, and threw himself into what was a forlorn hope. Some years later, the awful assault was described in detail by his nephew John Hamilton:

> The walls of Badajoz were unbroken on that side, forty feet high, and a fosse full of pointed stakes between them and the wall. As they

---

* In an instance of typical kindness, Ned arranged for George Napier to be put on the staff after the loss of his arm, but George was adamant that he preferred to stay with his division. Ned was highly vexed at first, but then forgave him – probably understanding the desire all too well.

marched the artillery fired over into the fosse, which in a great degree cut up the stakes,* and then, with the help of fascines that the men carried, they got over and rushed with the ladders to the wall. Sir Hercules was hit when half way up the ladder by a ball that had glanced off the wall, and, though it did not penetrate his person, it knocked him off into the ditch, and he had to begin again.

This time he succeeded in gaining a parapet, leaped in upon the wall, gathered a half score who had also been successful in getting in, and charged the enemy with such impetuosity that they fled round a corner, but soon returned with recruited numbers and charged at our men, first firing a volley and then dashing forward. One man rushed with his bayonet at my uncle who raised his sword to cut at him, but when a few paces distant the man whose musket my uncle supposed had been discharged, fired from the position of the charge. The ball struck the sword arm between the elbow and wrist, passed along to the wrist and through it slanting, came out in the palm of the hand and took off the top of a finger. Of course the arm fell, he put out his left arm to parry the bayonet thrust, and just as the point reached his hand a volley from both sides roared, and he and his assailant fell together. How long after he revived he knew not, – opened his eyes, recalled the state of affairs and remembered having been hit. He resolved to get up and seek for aid, but on trying fell, and fainted.

On recovering he tried again, but now found one side incapacitated, and passing down his left hand he found a hole in the groin; he then gave himself up for lost. However, after a time our victorious troops came to look after the wounded, found him and carried him away. It was found that besides a horrible smash of his arm, wrist-joint and the bones of his right hand, a bullet had entered the groin, split his hip bone and stuck in the cleft. They dressed his wounds and left him, and soon a retreat being ordered, he and the other wounded were put in ox carts and removed, following the army. The torture was dreadful, and many stronger men and less severely

* An awful line of *chevaux de frise* made of bayonets, which the French troops had had time to dig in when there was a delay in the attack.

wounded died in agony. He said he attributed his holding out to the habit by education of employing his mind, and so not being the victim of a constant contemplation of his sad state, or of ennui, when the physical pain left room for another species of suffering . . .[15]

It seemed that his mother's training in positive thinking had saved his life.

Meanwhile, Ned arrived back in Spain too late to do anything except ensure that Hercules got the best medical care, and to arrange his passage back to England. His gangrenous hand was saved, even on the verge of amputation, by a 'camp-follower', an uneducated surgeon who 'anointed it with *unguentum Angelicum* which with exquisite torture burnt off all the moribund flesh'. When Hercules was well enough to travel, Ned had him carried on men's shoulders to Abrantes, and from there embarked for England. His gallantry was rewarded with promotion to Lieutenant-Colonel, although he would never see active service again. Kitty wrote from London how much the news had cheered her: 'I have of late been both Idle and Sad, and will be so no more. Heaven bless you and your dear Excellent Chief.'[16]

Ned continued in Lisbon, writing his bulletins home, and sending with them old Madeira to comfort the invalid. He was still far from well himself, living off quinine as much as ever. His impotence made him miserable. It was all very well following the Pakenham motto, doing what the General ordered and running the staff, but Ned was in need of distraction. Employment, he reminded Longford, is the only cure for disappointment. He was impatient to be off and rejoin his shattered Fusiliers.

Just over three months later, Ned got his chance. As luck would have it, Hercules' old commander, General Picton, had also been invalided home after Badajoz. He recommended Pakenham for his brigade – and Wellington for once agreed. 'I am glad,' Picton said when he heard of it, '[Pakenham] has to lead my brave fellows; they will have plenty of their favourite amusement with him at their head.'[17]

The Battle of Salamanca that followed, described afterwards as the 'best manoeuvred' battle of the war,[18] brought the chance for glory Ned had been longing for. It was 22 July. After weeks of stalemate, and three days of marching in a line nearly parallel to the French, the opportunity came very suddenly. General Marmont, eager to cut off Wellington's retreat to Portugal, failed to notice that he had let a gap of about a mile open up between two of his divisions. 'By God, that will do,' cried Wellington as he spied the mistake through his eyeglass, threw down his half-eaten chicken leg[19] and galloped off to his brother-in-law's side. 'Ned, d'ye see those fellows over there?' he cried, pointing to the French left. 'Throw your division into the column; at them! and drive them to the devil.' Ned's reply was 'I will, my lord, if you will give me your hand', or something like it.[20] Within half an hour Ned was leading his men up the crest of the ridge in a ferocious charge of the French lines. Napier describes him with great flourish, as shooting 'like a meteor' across Thornière's path, breaking the lines into 'fragments' with the 'might of a giant'.[21] One of his sergeants recorded the giant's words: 'There they are my lads, just let them feel the temper of your bayonets!'[22]

In two hours it was all over. Captain Johnny Kincaid said later that the victory was never in doubt for a moment, and the retreating enemy left behind 'seven thousand prisoners, two eagles* and eleven pieces of Artillery'.[23] Generous William Napier wrote to his wife that Ned 'has particularly distinguished himself'. Most importantly, Wellington reported in his dispatches that he was 'very glad' he had given Ned the command of the 3rd Division, as 'he made the movement with a celerity and accuracy of which I doubt many are capable and without both, it would not have answered'. He also added a rather more ambivalent note of praise. 'Pakenham may not be the greatest genius but my partiality for him does not lead me astray when I tell you he is one of the best we have.' Moreover, according to Ned's brother Henry, the General was so impressed that he took the Star of the Bath off his own breast and fixed it on Ned's.[24]

* The 'eagles' were bronze sculptures carried at the head of every regiment, and their capture brought shame to the regiment in the same way that the capture of British 'colours' would.

Less than three weeks later, Wellington and Pakenham were both in Madrid, magnificently billeted in the homes of Spanish grandees. Yet again Ned was struck down with a fever, and his brother-in-law moved him into his own quarters. It was here that news reached him that Lady Longford, already shaken by William's drowning and Hercules' nearly fatal wounding, had lost her nerve. He didn't hesitate in reprimanding her.

My Dearest Mother, Permit me to give you a very good Rating. I have heard from very good authority that you have allowed yourself to be over anxious for the fate of your Kin in the Peninsula. I am pleased in the assurance that the official dispatch has long since put you at Ease, but why don't you recollect, Woman, that you are the Mother of Soldiers, and you must meet our Circumstances with good countenance as they come.[25] *

He kept the detail quiet that he was lying wretchedly ill at the time, only mentioning two months later to Longford that 'to say Truth, I have suffered vastly, and since the 12th August have been confined'. The cold of winter proved to be the only cure.

---

* Ned was not the only soldier son cajoling his mother at the time. Charles Napier wrote in a similar vein to Sarah Napier after he had been wounded at Busaco. 'Such as your children are, they are your work . . . You must have fortitude in common with thirty thousand English mothers, whose anxious hearts are fixed in Portugal, and who have not the pride of saying that their three sons had been wounded and were all alive!' (*Life and Opinions of Sir Charles Napier* by General Sir William Napier, p. 144).

13

A Little Quiet

❦

In England, news arrived of the great victory at Salamanca on 17 August 1812. The nationwide celebrations which followed topped new heights. In Tunbridge Wells, where the hero's wife, Kitty, was quietly spending the summer, the Pantiles* were illuminated. Naturally, her reaction to the victory was closely examined: 'She appeared to have suffered a great deal from the uncertainty which everybody had been in, for more than a fortnight,' the lady of letters Miss Berry confided to her journal, 'and she spoke with an enthusiasm and a worship of her hero which was truly edifying . . . She goes to London to-day to be present when the Te Deum is sung in the Portuguese ambassador's chapel in honour of the victory.'[1]

But the years that Sir Arthur had remained abroad were difficult, often depressing ones for his wife. Constantly thrown between jubilation and despair, she could hardly bear the emotional turmoil. She retreated further and further out of society, just when it was most expected of her to shine. Her Wellesley in-laws could not understand this behaviour, and cajoled her to play her part. The celebrations for the Salamanca victory came at one of Kitty's lowest points. 'Found Mrs Pole† very angry with me for not having gone to the Ball last night. It was given in honour of Ld W's victory . . . I could not go.'[2] She was determined 'not to be held up *en spectacle* and finding myself totally unequal to attending the ceremony of putting up the Eagles [captured at Salamanca], I thought my best plan was to leave town'.

---

* A parade which had been paved during the reign of Queen Anne.
† The wife of William Wellesley-Pole, the second Wellesley brother.

A month later Kitty was still in Tunbridge Wells. Lady Liverpool, whose husband had been Prime Minister since June,* was furious. 'I cannot help it' Kitty wrote stubbornly in her diary. Only kindly Lord Bathurst, who had replaced Castlereagh as Secretary of War, sounded a note of understanding, praising the 'modest & retiring conduct of Lady Wellington during the exaltation of this city'.[3]

To her own family, Kitty tried to explain herself. It was not just shyness that persuaded her that a low profile was the best tactic, but fear that she might be used as a political weapon when party factions – and royal favour – were more highly coloured than ever. A few months later, when the Prince Regent appeared to slight her, Kitty would not rise in indignation. As ever, Bess was her confidante.

> February 27th 1813. I assure you my dear Bess I am a most admirable politician, so deep a one that I never on any account expose my opinion. Indeed I cannot find a single human being with whom I could communicate on political subjects without either some near relation or some warm friend of Lord Wellingtons, or the Prince who does all that man or Prince can do to prove his sense of Lord Wellington's service, being abused to me in the most violent language. I take refuge in the school room, mind my work and bless Pakenham Hall where I learned anything but to meddle in politics.
>
> Really dear Bess one would sometimes imagine we had in this world no causes of anxiety and that it was our bounden duty to be unhappy by the pains that are taken and trifling subjects that are magnified into causes of offence. Ex: the Prince [Regent] having confer'd on the Lord W every honor in his power to bestow, gave a ball and by some accidental omission I was not invited to sup at his table. The omission was not known till my vacant place exposed it, I received every apology such a mistake called for all however to no purpose the Prince is not to be forgiven, I am called on by my regard for my husband to resent with proper spirit this intentional affront to Lord Wellington in the person of his Wife. Fools! My dear Bess, old

---

* 1812, after the assassination of Spencer Perceval on 11 May.

Pole* is the only one who will allow me to think well of [the Prince]; there is no mischievous ill nature in his mistakes.

Here was Kitty in a positive frame of mind. Soon after she made an optimistic assessment of her understanding of Arthur:

... my Husband is blessed whenever his name is heard, he may possibly soon return to a Wife who will no longer worry him because he is soft as well as strong, complying as well as firm, every thing that is gentle & domestic, being obliged to live a Soldiers hard and wandering life. I am grown wise my Bess and rejoice that I have lived to be 7 years a Wife![4]

Yet wisely or not, she hated playing a public role in the fashionable world, replete with busybodies and social climbers. Even at home in Harley Street, she saw few of the *bon ton*. Her mother and brother Longford visited frequently, and later Hercules, but most of the time she only saw those who knew her best, like Olivia Sparrow or the Poles.

When Maria Edgeworth and several of the Edgeworth family made a long visit to England in the spring of 1813, Kitty was filled with horror at the thought of introducing them:

... I cannot express with what consternation I heard of the intended visit ... my Mother has written to desire me to be of use to them, what does that mean? I cannot unless they desire me to introduce them to the very few people of high rank with whom I am here acquainted and strange to tell, I have no other society living as much at home and alone as I have thought it best to do, I have in fact little or no society. I have no box at the opera or play thinking that if I had it to spare £250 a year may be spent in a more satisfactory way and my dear Bess I really cannot think of attaching them to myself ...[5]

Kitty need not have worried. Oblivious to these concerns, the Edgeworths continued to be loyal. Two weeks after their arrival in London, Maria sought out Kitty with no hesitation:

* Kitty's nickname for William Wellesley-Pole.

Charming! Amiable Lady Wellington! As she truly said of herself 'She is always Kitty Pakenham to her friends'. She received us just as she would have done at Pakenham Hall. After comparison with crowds of others, beaux esprits, fine ladies and fashionable scramblers for notoriety her dignified graceful simplicity rises in ones opinion and we feel it with more conviction of its superiority. She let us in in the morning, talked about her children . . . Delightful children! I could go on but I must not fill this letter with Lady Wellington because I can tell you nothing of her but what you know.[6]

And with her own charming manners, witty and erudite conversation, and endless interest in people, Maria was a great success – without any help from Lady Wellington. Her reputation was high, with the second volume of *Tales of Fashionable Life* just published the previous autumn. She was invited everywhere, and the great Sir James Mackintosh – the eminent political writer – pronounced that the authoress was 'a most agreeable person, very natural, clever, and well informed, without the least pretensions of authorship', who 'remained perfectly unspoiled by the homage of the great . . . Upon the whole, the party make a great acquisition to London'.[7] This was quite an achievement, in the midst of such a 'sneering town' as London.

For the whole of that summer the cheerful Edgeworths continued their English tour. When in London, it became a habit with them to pay morning calls on Kitty and her boys, and again and again mentions of her were included in letters home. 'I must just say that half an hour we spent with Lady Wellington yesterday was by far the most agreeable part of the day', wrote Maria, and repeated all Kitty's anecdotes with relish:

'My dear Lady Wellington', said one lady, 'How many times a day do you think of your dress?'

'Why three times – Morning, evening, and night besides casualties.'

'But this won't do you must think of it seriously – at other times and when you go into the country always dress to keep the habit my dear Lady Wellington.'

Mrs Edgeworth, who shared her stepdaughter's interest in whether society had affected her Irish friend, declared her: 'the same creature here as at P. Hall. Unchanged by place or time or rank or fame – she looks as pretty, and is still more interesting'.

We spent another fortnight in London in the midst of the beau monde . . . none appeared more charming than Lady Wellington who maintains the most perfect freedom from affectation the most complete kindness of manner and the most charming mixture of sense & sensibility & *humour* that I ever saw combined – she looks better than she did some years ago – and if Ld W. neglects or *appears* to neglect her when he returns – his laurels will fade as rapidly in my eyes as he has won them.[8]

The letters make no mention of Kitty appearing anxious about what was happening in Spain. In early 1813, Hercules had said to Henry Stewart that Kitty's 'strength of mind' was 'daily improving'. In fact, Kitty swung between complete conviction that her husband would be spared by God, and the old pessimism that fate would deal her a hard blow. By December 1813, she was certainly convinced of the former. Just after the news came through of the victorious battle of the Nivelle (10 November), Bess Nugent received a letter from her cousin Kitty and immediately brought it to show another old Pakenham family friend, Serena Holroyd. Serena found it

written with such spirit and hope as quite surprised me, for no glory can prevent her anxiety at such a critical period; so much at stake! Her darling brother too, Sir Edward Pakenham, with Lord Wellington in all the engagements and several times wounded. She lives with the greatest propriety quite retired at Tunbridge with her two fine boys . . . If any one seems to *look at her* she goes away directly.[9]

But whether Kitty was cheerful or otherwise, Mrs Edgeworth had put her finger on the real anxiety for their friend. What would the hero make of this retiring, domestic creature when he did finally return?

By May 1813 Colonel Edward Pakenham had been made Adjutant-General on Wellington's staff. ('Everyone speaks very highly of Pakenham', reported another staff officer, Larpent, to his step-mother.) But what pleased Ned most was the order to move out, commanding the 6th Division. After the long months of winter in Portugal – where there was little to do but refit the army and hunt wolves, or tramp up to Oporto to order pipes of port for his brother Longford – he was delighted to be marching north again towards the final frontier of the Pyrenees.

After the decisive victory against Joseph Bonaparte, Napoleon's brother, at the Spanish town of Vitoria in June, Wellington had shown himself to be on the attack. By 25 July Marshal Soult's counter-offensive across the Pyrenees had begun. Soult was hoping to break through to Pamplona, but was beaten back by Wellington's troops at the battle of Sorauren on the 28th. Other ferocious engagements followed, but Soult was unable to stop the British advance onto French soil. The year ended in the defeat of Soult on the banks of the River Nive on 13 December. By now Wellington's forces were firmly established in France.

Much to his embarrassment, Ned had heard from England that he was to be a made a Knight of the Bath. His old teacher and mentor, Dr Carpendale at Armagh, couldn't resist congratulating Ned's brother-in-law, Henry Stewart:

> I have always perceived in General Pakenham the seeds of high and exalted character & looked forward to their maturity with a kind of prophetic satisfaction. All that his most sanguine friends could hope for, I think, now has been realized, if not surpassed and his country feels & ought to feel a lively interest in his health and preservation.[10]

Ned's modesty made him unusually rude: when the Royal College of Arms begged to put 'some Emblem of Victory in the Armorial Bearings', he civilly informed them that he would 'see them Dam–d first'. He felt quite the opposite about his friends receiving honours, telling anyone who had influence that Lowry Cole should get a peerage after his heroics at the battle of Vitoria.* Still, the family letters resounded with pride when Ned, amongst others, received a unanimous vote of thanks from Parliament on 8 November.

By the New Year of 1814, hopes for peace were high. Ned, with an unaccustomed note of exhaustion, took the view that although Napoleon would require a few more stiff lessons, all would soon be over. He couldn't help admitting that more than anything he would like 'to try the Experiment of a little quiet'.[11] In London, Hercules concurred: 'I trust quiet times are returning, how strange we shall all feel without the stimulus of these dreadful Games to interest us.'[12]

For two more months the games continued, the two armies fighting over the high passes of the Alps and into France. Ned remained in combat on the front lines, although still not in full health but at least 'high in the opinion & favour of Lord Wellington'.[13] By the end of March the Allies† had entered Paris, and Soult had been forced back as far as Toulouse. There, on 10 April, Wellington fought the last victorious battle of the Peninsular War, which was to give him the ducal title. He was not yet aware of Napoleon's abdication four days before, which finally brought about the French surrender and led to Napoleon's exile to Elba. On 30 May the (First) Treaty of Paris was signed between France and the coalition armies and peace was officially concluded. This eventful news came six weeks after Ned's thirty-seventh birthday; he had been a soldier for over twenty years.

As the long trail of soldiers began returning to Ireland and England, Ned stayed on in France to 'see everything home'. He helped his friend George Napier circumvent some of the red tape involved in leaving France ahead of his regiment, to be with his sick wife. By August it was time for Ned himself to pack up his worn-out regimentals and return. At the forefront of his mind was tremendous

---

* Ned had been on sick leave during this famous battle on 21 June 1813.
† At this time the Allied armies consisted of the Russian, Prussian and Austrian troops.

relief, because it seemed that the current war in America* would fizzle out, or at least not require his presence. 'I shall consider myself vastly fortunate', he wrote to Longford, 'to escape such a service.' By September he was back in Ireland.

In County Antrim, Ned was welcomed by his mother at Langford Lodge. ('Had you a peep of Sir Edward?' Maria asked Sophy,[14] whose home was en route.) By Lady Longford's side were the two shy little Hamilton boys Ned had last seen six years before. He promised young John a hunter if he could jump over a gate on his pony, but when the moment came, the horse and rider came apart. 'Uncle Edward said I should, nevertheless, have the hunter, for we (horse and I) had gone over, though not together.' In ten days he had 'won' their 'boy hearts', and then the awful moment came when they had to return to school. John's attempt to be manly failed, he suffered a nervous collapse. He became so convinced that he never would see his idol again that he was put in the school infirmary. 'When I came out my brother proposed that we should order two suits of new clothes which our uncle had directed us to get, but I said: "It is no use for we shall have to get new black clothes before the vacation." '[15] He did not share the morbid thought with his grandmother.

As for Maria Edgeworth, she was disappointed not to have seen Sir Edward when he made a flying visit to the Pakenhams at Coolure, but he had been called over to London to attend a court martial. It was here that Ned saw another friend from the old Irish set, Lord Castlereagh, by now the Foreign Secretary. For some reason Castlereagh asked Ned to introduce him to his doctor, Doctor Howell, and all three breakfasted together in St James's Square. In the middle of a conversation about anatomy, Castlereagh asked exactly where the jugular vein was found. After explaining, Howell added that if it were pierced, death would be instantaneous. 'Indeed?' rejoined Castlereagh carelessly. 'You must think me very ignorant, but I am rather curious in such matters.'[16] As the doctor then expanded further, Ned noticed a rather odd look on Castlereagh's face, which he later

* War had been declared on 18 June 1812, after the Royal Navy blockade on the east coast of America. After Napoleon's defeat, treaty negotiations were begun.

mentioned to his companion. 'I am afraid, Doctor, you were too explicit about the jugular artery . . . for I observed Castlereagh to be in a strange mood when you had finished your anatomical lecture.' The incident was peculiar considering Lord Castlereagh was to cut his own throat seven years later.

Back in Ireland, Catherine Longford was alone again. After Ned's brief visit, her friends had begun to speculate on how Ned should improve the Langford Lodge estate once he was properly returned. The mother of heroes declined to join in. 'I have learned', she said quietly, 'only to reckon on the present.' Perhaps something of poor young John Hamilton's feelings affected her too. The short 'experiment of a little quiet' was about to end.

14

New Orleans

The United States of America had declared war on Britain on 18 June 1812. Two years later the war still dragged on, only by then American morale was low. The failure of their invasion of Canada, and the success of the British General Robert Ross's capture and burning of the public buildings of Washington that August, had led to divisions in the American Senate and a desire for peace. It was well known that the victorious veterans of the Peninsular War were on their way across the Atlantic. The rich prize of New Orleans – the great trading port for sugar and cotton – seemed the obvious target.

By October 1814, news reached England that General Ross had been killed outside Baltimore. Although the negotiations for peace had already begun,[*] the British Government's view was that nothing should be settled until a military force was in a position to press for the best possible terms. In London, the Ministers at the War Office began urgently conferring as to who should be sent to take command. Wellington made it very clear that he had no desire to take it on, although of course he would go if ordered. Picton and Hill were considered, both tried veterans. But in the end it was Major-General Pakenham who was chosen, perhaps because of his experience in the West Indies and Nova Scotia. By 24 October he had been given his orders. Major-General Samuel Gibbs was to go as his second-in-command.

Far from 'escaping America', Ned found himself suddenly ordered across the Atlantic. He arranged his affairs in a hurry, leaving

[*] Under the mediation of the Russian Tsar Alexander I, at Ghent.

Above: The opening scene in the 1798 rebellion illustrated by George Cruikshank. The stopping of the mail coaches from Dublin on 23 May was planned to precipitate the rising.
Below: A gently satirical picture by Caroline Hamilton shows the occupants of a Wicklow mansion awaiting attack by a band of United Irishmen.

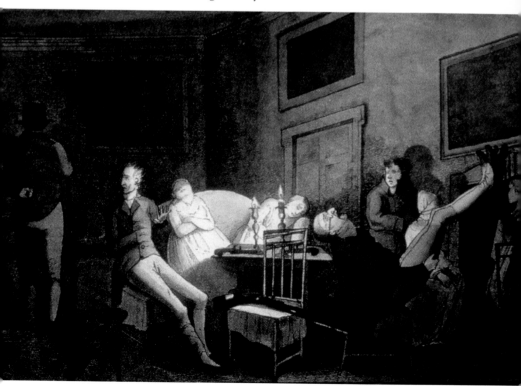

Above: Catherine Lady Longford's schoolhouse-and-gatehouse drawn by Richard Lovell Edgeworth's daughter Charlotte. The cottage was used to give lessons to the children living on the estate. *Below*: The Edgeworth family painted by Adam Buck in 1789. Richard Lovell Edgeworth, *centre*, wrote enthusiastically to a neighbour, 'We have lately had a man of genius in the art of painting upon a visit . . . He has taken a group of my family (nine children) in Swiss crayons . . . and has given a striking likeness of every one of them.' Maria, the eldest daughter, is on the left facing her father. His third wife, Elizabeth, sits immediately behind him.

Above: A 'Perspective View' of Pakenham Hall drawn by Robert Sandys, probably in 1783, when Lord Longford paid him £6 16s 6d. It shows the house was still a plain classical box as in 1738, although an extra floor had been added. Twenty years later Captain Lord Longford's son was to begin transforming it into a gothic castle to the designs of Francis Johnston.

Below: The Gothic Revival castle of the 1820s. James Shiel continued Johnston's gothicisation by adding a bay window on the east front and an elegant curve to conceal the offices.

'Society, 1801' by Caroline Hamilton. The abolition of the Irish parliament after the Union led to decided *ennui* in Dublin circles. *Inset*: A portrait of Tom, 2nd Earl of Longford, painted in Rome by the German Philipp Friedrich von Hetsch, while he was making the Grand Tour in 1793–5.

Two of the Pakenham sisters, Helen
Hamilton, *above,* and Bess Stewart, *right,*
as young girls. Helen was to die aged
thirty-two of tuberculosis.

Kitty Pakenham, eight years after her marriage to Sir Arthur Wellesley. The artist, Sir Thomas Lawrence, has captured the sweetness of countenance so often described by Maria Edgeworth.

The storming of the Castle of Badajoz,
6 April 1812, which nearly cost Hercules
Pakenham, *left*, his life.

instructions with his fellow guardian[1] that his Hamilton nephews were to be given the best system of education possible, which meant Cambridge. If the cost of this could not be met, he would 'turn American bear and live on my paws to give such boys the means of gentleman's life in gentleman's education'. He knew his mother would be heartbroken. He trusted to Caroline to 'calm' her before he should manage to write, admitting sadly that he himself was 'not fit to express my feelings on this occasion, so should I seem to you like Iron, allow for the Circumstances of the case'. In fact his last letter to Lady Longford is written with such promised self-control: 'It was my expectation when I left you to have Returned to your little party at the Lodge. Public events have otherwise determined my private movements . . . I confess to you there is nothing that makes this employment desirable – but under the circumstances of my improved health, I cannot resist a National call'.[2]

The fact was, as Hercules wrote to Longford, that the officers in North America were in sore need of good generals. 'Before the American war broke out, that quarter was esteemed as a good place to provide for well-meaning inefficient officers . . . hence a string of names known only in the Service as unequal to command.'

Ned sailed for America on 1 November 1814. As always, his brother Longford came to see him off. The ship was uncomfortably crowded; Ned shared a cabin with five other officers and the ship's Captain. Like Wellington, Ned made use of the voyage to prepare himself as well as he could, studying a collection of maps of New Orleans borrowed from the Spanish archives. But although he appeared cheerful and busy, 'one of the most amusing persons imaginable . . . and, to our astonishment, very devoutly inclined',[3] he was also anxious. Like his father the Captain, he saw the Americans as Britain's natural allies, not their enemies.

It took the frigate *Statira* nearly two months to arrive at the mouth of the Mississippi, frustrated by contrary winds and an over-cautious Captain. Pakenham's troops finally joined the first contingent of the army outside New Orleans on Christmas Day. To his dismay, Ned found that the naval commanding officer, Admiral Alexander Cochrane, and his advance party had already begun the campaign, with Cochrane determined to win the valuable prize of New Orleans.* Two days before, 2,000 troops under General Keane had captured the plantation estate of Major Villeré, only half a mile from the town. But before Keane had pressed home his advantage, an American schooner and gunboat had crept silently along the Mississippi River and opened fire, taking the troops completely by surprise. It was a bad beginning.

High up in the branches of a crooked pine tree, a young British Lieutenant called Wright tried again to make out some weakness in the breastworks before him. The objective, the city of New Orleans, seemed unobtainable. The American General Andrew Jackson had everything on his side. (He even had the French General Humbert, who had tried so hard to defeat the British in Ireland in 1798.) The British forces, on the contrary, were dug into an impossible position, on a narrow isthmus of marshy ground, only 1,000 yards wide, between the Mississippi and an impregnable cypress swamp. The men were already exhausted after days of nerve-racking shelling from the American boats anchored in the river. All they wanted was to move against the enemy. The arrival of their new commander – whose reputation as one of Wellington's best had preceded him – had lifted their morale. Yet Edward Pakenham could not see an immediate way forward. For once, even his buoyant spirits failed. He had no way of knowing that the day before, 5,000 miles away, the Treaty of Ghent had been signed, though not ratified.† War with America was all but over.

Many years later, Ned's friend Sir Harry Smith wrote that the General was full of suppressed anger to find the army so committed. For here, on the narrow swampy fields immediately below the city, the army would be forced to fight in the sort of narrow column that made them easy targets, and had ruined the French in the Peninsula.‡

* The 'first' Battle of New Orleans was fought on 23 December.
† The Treaty of Ghent was signed on 24 December. Orders were that hostilities were not to cease until the Treaty was ratified.
‡ That is, forty men wide and ten deep, tactically inferior to Wellington's lines of two men deep and 400 long.

Not only that but the essential line of supply both of ammunition for the artillery and provisions for the troops was hopelessly stretched. The British ships, anchored in the deep water of Lake Borgne, were nearly eighty miles from headquarters and could not get any nearer. It took three days to land the heavy cannons and ammunition from the fleet, dragging them through the mud when the Villeré canal came to an end. It was impossible to supply even these guns with enough ammunition – several of the transports that were carrying stores from England had never even arrived. Meanwhile, the heaviest guns, the 18-pounders, had to be supplied from the Navy, and their carriages soon sank into the soft ground, making firing all but useless.

American artillery strength was very different. Behind their breastworks were 6s, long 12s, 24s and even a pair of 32-pounders. These had the ready supply of powder that the British lacked, stored carefully in the city's magazine. As for their batteries, the Americans had stacked bales of cotton, which not only absorbed the shot but also acted as solid foundations for the guns. In front of these, what was usually a dry canal had been filled by letting in the Mississippi, which meant that any musket shot fired was quenched as soon as it fell from the slanting stockade of timbers behind it. The British batteries were made only of what scanty materials were to hand, largely wooden sugar casks packed with earth, whose inadequate height left the gunners exposed. It was no wonder, then, that the first attempt (on 1 January) to disable Jackson's guns failed.

Ned realised that his only hope of success lay in a two-pronged attack. The weak point of Jackson's defences was the west bank of the Mississippi, where only a small force under the American General Morgan protected the city. If, Pakenham and Cochrane agreed, Morgan's own guns could be captured and turned on the city itself, well in advance of the main attack, the whole line of the enemy would be quickly enfiladed. Colonel Thornton was given the order to make the attack on the west bank, which would mean crossing the Mississippi with his men under the essential cover of darkness. When this had been achieved, the infantry would attack the city breastworks directly, under Generals Gibbs and Keane. A third party was to lead a diversion into the cypress swamps, whilst General Lambert was to keep his two regiments in reserve. All the manoeuvres had to take place just before daylight; everything depended on surprise.

One by one a series of disasters crippled the plan. The engineer charged with widening the Villeré canal miscalculated: as soon as Thornton tried to launch his boats from the canal into the Mississippi, he found an impassable mud-bar blocking his way. There was no choice but to haul each heavy boat over by hand. By dawn on 8 January only a handful of the boats had reached the opposite shore, and even those had drifted too far downstream. Thornton's force was now only 340 men when he had expected to have 1,400.

Woken out of his exhausted sleep by Smith, Ned took in the British position with horror. Daylight was creeping up on their surprise attack with alarming rapidity. Nobody had dared wake him earlier to give him the bad news; perhaps because, as Smith confessed on an earlier occasion, to fail in his orders 'was as bad as the loss of a leg'.[4] Ned could hardly believe that so much of the plan had gone awry. 'Smith, most commanders-in-chief have many difficulties to contend with, but surely none like mine.' He ordered the rocket to be fired. Smith, who was against going ahead with the plan, begged him to reconsider. But Ned was adamant: he was sure all would be lost if they did not press forward. 'It is now too late; the columns would be visible to the enemy before they could move out of fire, and would lose more men than it is hoped they will in an attack. Fire the rocket, I say, and go to Lambert.'[5]

As the columns rushed forward they soon came under the full power of the American artillery. 'That's a terrific fire, Lambert' Ned shouted as he galloped past Smith and Lambert. Worse was to come. As the 44th Regiment under Gibbs ran forward to within 100 feet of the American breastworks, panic set in. Where were the ladders and fascines to help them breach the canals and breastworks? Somehow, they had been left behind. Exposed to the American ranks, General Gibbs' troops began to fire from where they stood, making themselves easy targets.[6] Almost at the same moment Gibbs was mortally hit. Ned galloped forward, waving his hat to urge the 44th onwards; he had just succeeded in getting the troops moving again when a ball shattered his knee, and killed his horse. As he tried to remount, another hit him in the spine. His aide MacDougall[7] carried him to the rear, but there was nothing to be done. Bending down close to his chief's dear face, MacDougall heard Ned whisper his last recorded words: 'Lost through lack of courage'. His mother's bible was found in his breast pocket.

On the far side of the Mississippi Thornton, meanwhile, had finally succeeded. Ironically, the riverbank attack had routed Morgan's troops at their post, and the Kentuckians had fled. Even Jackson admitted that it would have been calamitous for the Americans if that advantage had been pressed. But it was too late to help the main body of men against the artillery fire. Seeing two of their leaders fallen, the columns wavered, 'which in such a situation became irreparable'.[8] With 2,500 men dead or wounded, the next in command, General Lambert, sounded the retreat.

In the aftermath of such a terrible defeat, Lambert felt a truce was all he had left to him. The surviving troops never renewed their attack on New Orleans. Ned's body was sent back to Ireland in a cask of rum;* his heart was buried under a pecan tree on the Villeré plantation. (For years after, the slaves refused to eat the pecans, claiming they were streaked in blood.) Colonel Mullins of the 44th was found guilty of failing to bring up the ladders and fascines in the opening charge, and was cashiered at the Royal Barracks in Dublin. Lady Longford, generous as ever, 'was pleased his life was spared'. She told Bess that she thanked God she felt no resentment. For the Hamilton orphans, it was 'A loss to us unspeakable'.

Harry Smith, who met Wellington a year later in France, found himself so overcome with emotion as he told the story of the battle that he didn't dare bring up Pakenham's name. To his credit, Wellington admitted how much the death of Ned had cost him in a letter to his brother-in-law, just days before his own greatest battle:

---

* There is an improbable story that the cask was mistaken for another and went to Barbados, where it was only discovered to contain a man's body after the contents had been drunk. The beverage became known as the 'Pakenham cocktail'. Officially Edward Pakenham is buried in the family vault in Killucan, Westmeath.

May 22nd, 1815 (Bruxelles)

My dear Longford

I have received your letter of the 18th and I am very much obliged to you & highly gratified by your poor brother's recollection of me.

Neither time nor the interesting concerns which have had to transact can efface the impression which the account of his loss made upon me, almost by the last shot of a contest in which he so frequently distinguished himself; and received at the very moment at which I was about to enter on a new scene in which his assistance would have been so useful to me. We have one consolation, that he fell as he lived in the Honourable discharge of his Duty; and distinguished as a soldier and as a man. I cannot but regret however that he was ever employed on such a Service or with such a Colleague. The expedition to New Orleans originated with that Colleague and plunder was its object. I knew and stated in July that the transports could not approach within leagues of the landing place; and enquired what means were provided, to enable a sufficient body of troops with their Artillery provisions and stores to land, and afterwards communicate with them.

Then as plunder was the object the Admiral took care to be attended by a sufficient number of *Sharks* to carry the plunder off from a place at which he knew well that he could not remain. The Secret of the expedition was thus communicated, and in this manner this evil design defeated its own end. The Americans were prepared with an Army in a fortified position which still would have been carried if the duties of others, that is of the Admiral, had been as well performed as that of him whom we lament.

But Providence ordained otherwise and we must submit![9]

Was it rash of Ned to have charged forward into the artillery fire? Wellington may have thought so, since when questioned on the subject in general he declared it 'very wrong' for a commander to 'expose himself unnecessarily'.[10] But perhaps it was necessary. Ned may have decided before he even arrived in America that he would have to lead from the front. In his memoirs, George Napier recalls the last conversation he had with the departing soldier:

I could not help begging him to recollect that as commander-in-chief of an army he ought not to expose himself as much as he was accustomed to do in action, for he was remarkable for always being in front, and generally wounded. I shall never forget either his reply or the look with which it was accompanied. He said, fixing his expressive eyes upon me, 'George, my good friend, I promise you that I will not unnecessarily expose myself to the fire of the enemy, but you are too old and good a soldier not to be aware that a case may arise in which the commander-in-chief may find it absolutely necessary to place himself at the head of his troops in the hottest fire and by his own personal conduct encourage them to victory. If this happens I must not flinch, though certain death be my lot!'[11]

To anyone who reads Ned's letters, his behaviour at New Orleans could not be mistaken for vainglory. His personal philosophy is quite clear. Courage, honour, duty, modesty and cheerfulness were much more important than anything else. He was an old-fashioned soul, whose sentimental nature made him popular with officers and men alike. In St Croix, the 'conquered' inhabitants had taken him so much to their hearts that he was presented with a long and wordy eulogy on his departure, together with a magnificent sabre mounted in gold and enamel. When he had left the 67th Fusiliers to become a staff officer, the officers there gave him a two-hundred-guinea sword, and placed his portrait in their mess.

He was embarrassed when praise came his way. William Napier, whose long experience of military brutality made him cynical, wrote to his wife in 1813 that 'General Pakenham makes me now and then think there are some good men in this world'.* His modest character would not have approved of Lord Castlereagh's proposal that a monument be raised of Pakenham and Gibbs in St Paul's. It was, as Longford noted, a particular mark of Ned's 'Country's approbation'

---

* William Napier had nothing but good to speak of Ned. After Ned's death he wrote: 'That amiable man's character was composed of as much gentleness, as much generosity, as much frankness, and as much spirit as ever commingled in a noble mind. Alas! That he should have fallen so soon and so sadly!' *History of the War in the Peninsula*, Vol. V, p. xxii.

since 'the effort in which he fell was not successful'.[12] The double statue by Sir Richard Westmacott stands in a corner there today.

Back in Dublin, the Whig press greeted the news of the New Orleans disaster with satisfied gloom. 'The American War has closed with unmitigated dishonour for England', declared the *Dublin Evening Post*, although it generously described Ned as a soldier of 'the most romantic and chivalrous daring'.[13] The official dispatch reported that 2,454 of the British forces had been killed or wounded at New Orleans; the Americans declared that they had only lost 265 in casualties. The great tragedy was that the battle should have been fought at all: the Treaty of Ghent was ratified by the American Senate on 16 February 1815. Yet the affair did not linger long in the public mind, eclipsed entirely by events three months later on the field of Waterloo.

There is a mysterious postscript to Ned's story. In 1823, the Duke of Wellington received a request from one Dr Hunter of Yorkshire, asking his help on a delicate matter. Hunter, it seems, had fallen in love with a Miss Helen Pakenham,* the natural daughter of General Sir Edward. She appeared to be under the guardianship of Ned's friend Captain Armstrong and his brother Hercules. Now Helen's guardians were, in Hunter's view, unfairly refusing to hand over Helen's full inheritance as a marriage portion. Was Hunter a gold-digger? There is no record of what Wellington replied, aside from a scrawled pencil note of 'keep amongst my papers'.[14] It seems that the marriage did go ahead, however, since by June of that year Captain Armstrong was asking Hercules about the best way to ensure that Dr Hunter should gain a promotion, since he has 'no very high opinion of the Doctor's management or exertion'. He proposed to send money to the couple 'once they have arrived in Bombay'. Perhaps

---

* This is the first news of Helen since 1815, when a sad letter from Ellen Gwynn appears in the family papers addressed to Lord Longford, begging for news of her child and to be allowed to write to her. In the margin of the letter, Longford has scribbled his reply: 'Assured her that the child should not be neglected, that she might occasionally write to me to enquire about her child, but that no correspondence with the child could be permitted. L.'

India was the best solution for a daughter born on the wrong side of the blanket. Perhaps even now there is a descendant of Ned's living there, and those fine 'expressive eyes' still shine in our time.

15

French Affairs

W hat, all this time, had been happening to Kitty? In the years of
fighting that came to an end at the Treaty of Paris in 1814,
Arthur Wellesley, now Duke of Wellington,* had had little time to
think about his wife. Kitty, on the other hand, had had all too much
time to think, to imagine, and to believe the worst. When a victory
was reported she was all excitement, enthusiasm, 'running as fast as
she could to Lord Bury at Lord Bathurst's . . . to learn the first news
of her husband',[1] Maria reported. But all too often there were no
letters, just rumours. She was left with a morbid inclination to self-
chastisement, promising in her diary that she would 'at last keep
resolutions so often repeated, so often broken'.

She had spent much of her time living a retired life in Broadstairs
or Tunbridge Wells, taking long walks and borrowing books from
the circulating libraries, and teaching her two little boys. Her children were her greatest pleasure, her 'first earthly consolation' and
her greatest distraction from depression. After the Duke's return
from the Peninsula, even these were denied to her. In 1814 both little
Arthur – now known as 'Douro', the courtesy title given to Wellington – and Charles had been sent off to boarding school, since Kitty
was due to follow the Duke out to Paris.

Wellington had been made Ambassador – and the prospect of
such a public role as Ambassadress was quite horrible to Kitty. The
Duke had given her the chance of refusing, but of course she couldn't
refuse. 'I have no hesitation in deciding to go, no other wish than to

---

* He was created a Duke on 3 May 1814.

go . . . your task is a most arduous one . . . but to an ambassador's Wife there are no difficulties which I do not feel myself equal to overcome, no duties which I am not willing to perform.' Kitty had written Maria a carefully light-hearted account of her parting from the boys, quoting Douro's sweet words of advice which so clearly echoed her own, 'get up early . . . read books of improvingness, and do your duty and that will make the time seem short!'. Maria was deeply touched; 'how few ladies . . . would have their heads & hearts so full of their children, or would think of taking such good advice'.[2]

According to contemporary gossip, Kitty must have found a miserable reception in Paris, for the Duke's name was linked with all the great beauties of the day. Lady Bessborough, who made constant visits to the Embassy, condemned the Duke's cruelty to 'that poor little woman' for the public way in which he gave his 'attentions' to the famous Milanese contralto Grassini: 'he is found great fault with for it, not on account of making her miserable or of the immorality of the fact, but the want of *procédé*'.[3] Mr Edgeworth exclaimed that such 'public want of decency' would shock 'all the ancient nobility'; nevertheless the Duke later hung a portrait of the singer in his study at Château Reynière. Fanny Burney, on the other hand, claimed it was another singer, Catalani, who charmed the Duke the most.

Some held Kitty's modest, unsophisticated looks against her. One visitor to the Embassy, Lady Elizabeth Yorke, concluded that the Duchess's 'appearance, unfortunately, does not correspond with one's notion of an ambassadress or the wife of a hero', but added sweetly that 'she succeeds uncommonly well in her part, and takes all proper pains to make herself and her parties agreeable'. This was tactfully put by a woman who was to be Ambassadress herself, as the future wife of Wellington's successor, Sir Charles Stuart. If Kitty did not attempt to play the grande dame, it was perhaps from a sense that there was something immoral in dressing up when so many in Europe were starving. When Maria congratulated her on a newspaper's description of her appearance at the French opera covered in feathers and jewels, Kitty laughingly denied it:

I believe had all the humming-birds which have been hatched since the flood been plucked for me they would hardly have been enough to have made the tippet with which the Lady's Magazine has decked me . . . my diamonds are yet in the mine and my humming birds yet wear their own feathers – for the first of these facts the poor of Spain and Portugal ruined by the French Marshals and relieved by the English can account.[4]

And the poor little woman wrote a surprisingly cheerful letter to her sister Caroline, describing the grand yet comfortless house in the rue du Faubourg St Honoré, the Hôtel Charost, which had once been the home of Napoleon's sister, Pauline Borghese.

Paris, Oct 27th 1814.

I have now been above a fortnight in la bonne Ville de Paris and find it much as it had been described very dirty . . . our House is splendid and comfortless not a table within for work or writing not a shelf for a book, by degrees I am succeeding in making it comfortable. I have myself had a great deal of ceremonial to go thro'! The presentation of an Ambassadrice is no joke I can assure you. It was written out for me to get by heart and if I can find it I will send it to you. I am sure you will pity me when you fancy me making a *compliment* to the Duchess of Angoulême* in French and then seated on a Tabouret in the middle of her Salle d'Audience opposite to her and all Duchesses & Marechales of France making a circle round us. Oh it was horrid. With respect to society here, I am sure it will be much better than it has as yet been, by degrees people grow less afraid of speaking to each other and there is a natural willingness to speak in the people of this country that meets you half way. I have made more way here in one fortnight that I had made in England in 3 years. As far as their sincerity as I do not want to make friends of them, that is their affair, but nothing can be more obliging more *amiable* than their manner.[5]

It seems Kitty was determined to make the best of things; it

---

* Marie-Thérèse-Charlotte, Duchesse d'Angoulême, was the eldest child of the executed Louis XVI.

helped when people were kind to her. When Talleyrand, now the Foreign Minister, came to call, he was sent away by an abashed Duchess, too swollen-faced with toothache to receive visitors. When he insisted on coming up anyway, she enjoyed every minute of his charming company, forgot her pain, and admitted she was sad to see him go. Even Madame de Staël* – one of the greatest intellects of her age, and exceedingly critical of Wellington's army of occupation – found that Kitty's disarming honesty changed her view of her. Maria told her aunt the story.

> [Kitty] found that Madame de Stael was well received at the Bourbon Court, and consequently she must be received at the Duke of Wellington's. She arrived, and walking up in full assembly to the Duchess, with fire of indignation flashing in her eyes. 'Eh! Madame la Duchesse, vous ne vouliez pas donc faire ma connaissance en Angleterre.'
> 'Non, Madame, je ne le voulais pas.'
> 'Eh Comment, Madame! Eh Pourquoi donc?'
> 'C'est que je vous craignais, Madame!'
> 'Vous me craignez, Madame la Duchesse!'
> 'Non, Madame, je ne vous crains plus.'
> Madame de Stael threw her arms round her, 'Ah je vous adore!'[6]

Sir James Mackintosh, smitten by the brilliance of Madame de Staël, was among the throng visiting Paris in the autumn of 1814. He reported the numerous entertainments at the house in the rue St Honoré. 'A musical party . . . Grassini, Cini and a wonderful Spaniard who performed miracles on the guitar. Rather bored.'[7] On 9 December Mackintosh had queued up in the long line of carriages waiting to call at another Embassy reception; the line was so long that he didn't get in till eleven. Every European monarch wished to embrace the saviour of Europe in person. Such flattery would have turned most heads, the young and idolatrous Lady Shelley decided,

---

* In 1803 Madame de Staël had been exiled from Paris by Napoleon, whom she had initially admired. On her return to France she ran a famous salon where the terms were framed for France to achieve a strong constitutional monarchy.

but '[the Duke] retains that simplicity of character, and manner, which is still his distinguishing excellence. He remembers his old friends with the same interest as ever'. But Mackintosh was not entirely caught up in the gaiety of the post-war society. To him, at least, Napoleon's return was 'not so improbable an event'.

Napoleon fled from Elba on 26 February 1815, and made his entry into the French capital just three weeks later. It was almost exactly a year since Wellington had made his own triumphal entry. Kitty was in Paris when the news of Napoleon's escape arrived, whilst the Duke was at the Congress of the Allies in Vienna. She left in a 'violent hurry'[8] on 10 March with the 'shoals' of other English visitors and reached England just as the first reports of another disaster came to be known: the British loss at New Orleans. Meeting Longford in London, they crossed over to Ireland immediately to see their mother.

It had taken ten weeks for the news of Ned's death to reach Ireland. Kitty and Longford found the rest of the family already gathered at their mother's side: Hercules, Bess and Harry Stewart, Caroline and Henry Hamilton, and their brother Henry Pakenham, now ordained as a clergyman. It was the latter who read the daily prayers in the hall – Catherine's voice was no longer strong enough – whilst Henry Hamilton played the organ. It was a solemn gathering, all aware that the last time they had been together, Ned had been there too.

For Kitty, the sadness of the occasion was softened by the delight of reunion. She had not been in her old home for seven years. 'To find myself once more, my dear & valued friend, among my own people, has been to me the first of consolations', she wrote to Harry Stewart.[9] But for Catherine Longford, Ned's death was a blow from which she never recovered. It was the bitterness of failure that Ned had known at the very end that hurt her the most; even God was no comfort there. In her copy-book, Maria Edgeworth's 'mother of heroes' poured out an agonised prayer: 'Tho' thou Almighty Father thought it fit to embitter his last moments by want of success, yet I trust thou in mercy for the sake of our Lord & Saviour has received his Soul to happiness, thou wilt be mine & my dear childrens support that the storm overwhelm us not . . . Hear me O God . . . give me peace, still the anguish thou has thought to inflict.'

If the anguish was never stilled, it was well concealed. It was not in Catherine's nature to make others suffer by revealing her own anguish, and soon her remaining children were congratulating themselves on how well she was coping with this new trial. 'My Mother is wonderful!' Kitty exclaimed less than a month later, 'for there is now no unnatural exertion, she weeps for her poor noble child but she is resigned with meekness'.[10] In fact, Catherine had been in a weak state of health even before the news of Ned's death had arrived, having been dangerously ill with pneumonia for some weeks. Maria Edgeworth had written in February that '[Lady Longford] is getting well but requires quiet & Mrs Stewart & Caroline H. wisely prevent her from seeing people which she is eager to do'. Bess considered that this weakness of health made her mother better able to accept the loss of Ned.

When Maria met Lady Longford in Dublin, more than two months after she had received the news, she was full of admiration for this 'angel upon earth' – 'She gave me with eyes lifted to heaven & streaming with Tears a most touching account of her son Edward & of his sending her by his favourite servant his cap, the little bible which she had given him at parting & in which he desired his servant to tell her [he] had read every day a portion as she had counselled.' Two months later her admiration had not dimmed.[11] 'The resignation, the pious fortitude of this heroic mother are beyond all my powers of description – but not beyond my powers of feeling – I never *can* forget the impression Lady Longford has made on my mind.'[12]

For Hercules, now heir to Langford Lodge in place of Ned, it was a painful process to step into his brother's shoes. He had never been his mother's favourite. But by June, Longford was delighted to report to Bess that 'Every post brings some new proof that my good Mother is thoroughly taking to him – He is worthy of every confidence, & better able to give opinion than any one I know'.[13] Hercules was considered very clever, although he lacked the easy charm of either Ned or Longford, and was serious-minded and often critical. He was also partially crippled, and still suffering extreme pain from the injury he had received in 1812. Splinters of bone continued to emerge slowly from the open wound on his hip. Since then he had nursed a seat in Parliament, hard fought at the time against the pro-Catholic candidate in Westmeath, as Hercules followed his brother's anti-Emancipation line. (The 1812 election campaign supporting his brother had cost Longford £2,000, and he complained to the Edge-worths that he would not be able to buy the library table he had coveted.) But Hercules had entered into the field of politics with resigned commitment, admitting to Harry Stewart how much it saddened him to 'give up much of the Interest & Brilliancy of military life'.[14]

His mother, when her children had again dispersed, returned to the tranquillity and solace of Langford Lodge. Here, Letitia Balfour, her long-widowed friend at Castle Blayney, took her children's place as Catherine's dearest confidante. But it was another friend, Serena Holroyd, who had predicted six years before that Catherine could not survive the loss of her favourite son, should he be killed. 'Strong as her fine mind is, & great as I know her resignation to be, I do verily believe she would either lose her life or her senses if she loses him'.[15]

All thoughts turned on what was to be the fate of France. At Coolure, the Admiral made a bet with Edgeworth that the Emperor would be driven off the throne before the year was out. Longford, in the meantime, had returned to England and his seat in the House of Lords. He had now leased a small but comfortable house in New Burlington Street, only a stone's throw from his club. Writing to Bess on 12 June he predicted:

– In 3 or 4 days we expect to hear of the commencement of the desperate struggle in Flanders – Even now there are many who think that there will be no fighting – that Buonoparte will be *settled* by the Jacobins. I think there must be some sharp contest but I do not think it can last long perhaps not 3 months, possibly not 3 weeks.

He also reported with optimism on the state of their sister's health: 'Kitty is remarkably well & increasing in good looks & strength – as to her spirits you know how very variable they always were – I *refer* to long before her marriage but on the whole I do think in this point she is amending.'[16] Longford was eager to look on the positive, as ever. Whether Kitty was really 'amending' or not, was another question.

16

A Fragile Peace

❧

On 18 June 1815 the most decisive battle of the Napoleonic Wars was fought just south of Brussels, near the village of Waterloo. Outnumbered and outgunned by the French, Wellington fought a brilliant defensive action until Blücher's Prussians arrived to tip the balance. Bonaparte was forced to retreat and abdicate for the second time. The heads of the Allied powers convened to Brussels, to finish carving up the map of Europe which they had begun doing a hundred days before. France, for its sins, was to be an occupied territory. Naturally, Britain sent the Duke of Wellington, as the nation's hero, to be the Commander of the Occupying Army.

For most of the world, Wellington's position as a heroic figure was indelibly confirmed by his victory against Napoleon at the battle of Waterloo. In his own country, he was fêted almost beyond compare. More busts were made of Wellington than of any other figure in British public life, before or after.[1] Yet less than two months after the victory, Maria's friend Lady Romilly wrote to Maria in Ireland with some interesting news. 'But in Town at this present moment we are forgetting France, Bonaparte'. It was the behaviour of Napoleon's conqueror that was provoking excited gossip. Rumours were flying that Wellington was conducting a liaison with the charming Lady Frances Wedderburn-Webster, one of the coterie of pretty women who had surrounded the Duke since his arrival in Brussels. The lady's husband was now preparing to sue. 'Alas that so great a Man should tarnish his bright glory by his private misconduct.' Lady Romilly continued:

It is said that [the Duke] has offered any sum up to a hundred thousand pounds to make up the affair, but in vain. The injured husband remains quite inflexible, and the business is soon to come on in Doctors' Commons . . . but perhaps this scandal is not new to you, and you may have understood the hints of the papers long before this . . .*[2]

The hints of the paper were certainly clear enough. The society rag the *St James's Chronicle* conjured up a fine riddle:

> 5 Aug. Brussels 1815 – Fashionable Alliteration
> *In the letter W. there's a charm half divine*
> War – Wellington-Wedderburn-Webster – and Wine

and reported that 'a distinguished commander has surrendered himself captive to the beautiful wife of a military officer of high rank, in a manner to make serious investigation of this offence indispensable'.

Maria's reply to Lady Romilly was immediate and reflected her father's stern opinion of the Duke:

> As to Lord Wellington . . . we care for him only as a public character – But for the Duchess of Wellington we feel all the deep and tender interest which her sweet disposition must inspire in all who know her as well as we do – Her 12 years constancy, her refusal of that amiable hero General Cole who was desperately in love with her, her refusal of innumerable admirers who were at her feet during her reign as a beauty in Dublin has been ill rewarded by this Duke – She is not a woman who delights in titles or rank but she does enjoy her husband's glory and therefore I hope it will not like Lord Nelson's be tarnished.[3]

The scandal could not be kept from Lady Longford even in her retired life at Langford Lodge, and added to her increasing frailty.

---

* Lady Romilly was the beloved wife of the great legal reformer Sir Samuel Romilly, who was advising on Lady Byron's divorce case at the time. Doctor's Commons was the court reserved for such cases of 'Criminal Conversation', the legal ground for divorce before the 1857 Marriage Act.

Her daughters Caroline and Bess had grown particularly anxious for her health. When Longford suggested a visit to Paris that autumn, as the last opportunity to 'see what could never in all probability be seen again united', the great works of art that Napoleon had mustered,* and the 'assembly of the powers of Europe', Caroline did not want to leave her mother alone. But Catherine insisted that the Hamiltons should go.

When the time came for Catherine to travel to Pakenham Hall for her usual Christmas visit, she broke the journey at her niece Anna-Maria Ruxton's, Red House in Ardee. The Ruxton house had long been a convenient break in the journey, and usually Catherine enjoyed their company immensely. But this time Bess Stewart arrived there to find her ill and feeble: she had fallen downstairs, having suffered a minor stroke. By the time Catherine reached Dublin, she was unable to feed herself, and for a while could not even speak.

Caroline, Catherine's youngest daughter, wrote an account of her mother's last days. Hercules had just arrived from Langford Lodge; Henry was called to read prayers around her bed.

> My precious mother was the only person who was not agitated . . . 'God Almighty Bless you all, & may you have the same support & the same hope that I have, My Hope is Certainty, thro' the merits of our Saviour,' as she said these words her Countenance was quite beaming. To Kitty Hamilton she said, 'My Sweet Child do not think of me with regret, think of me as a Happy being', to John Hamilton – 'Always try to do your duty as you can, remember cleverness is not necessary to please God . . .'[4]

Her three younger sons lay beside her as she slipped into her last sleep, even with her final words of maternal advice on her lips.

Catherine Longford was buried, as she wished, 'in the most

---

* At the Second Peace of Paris on 20 November 1815 it was decided that all the treasures Napoleon had plundered from across Europe should be returned to their rightful owners. These works of art had largely been placed in the Louvre.

private manner'. Beside her in the family vault lay the remains of her husband the Captain and her son Ned. When Bess went through her mother's papers, she found a letter from Catherine addressed to her children, written soon after William Pakenham had drowned in 1811. It was a consolation. 'Accept my dearest children of my utmost heartfelt Gratitude for the kind consoling friendship you have each unremittingly had for me; which has given me a higher degree of happiness than I thought possible in this life after losing your dear Father'.

Out in the wider world, the wheels of the legal system had creaked forward. Mr Wedderburn-Webster's court case was settled in February, albeit in a rather different way than the public had expected. Instead of pursuing the Duke, the outraged husband sued the *St James's Chronicle* for libel, and won £2,000 in damages. Catherine's famous son-in-law was exonerated.

Bess wrote to Wellington to let him know he had not been forgotten in her mother's last prayers. The Duke wrote a polite letter from Paris in return – 'I assure you that I feel the value of Lady Longford's recollection of me in her last moments . . . She never ceased to favour me, and I hope I shall never forget her kindness to me.'[5] He had not, however, been treating Catherine's daughter with much kindness himself.

Maria Edgeworth wrote to her sister-in-law, Harriette Sneyd, in the summer of 1816, 'she has a hard card to play – and you who have with your husband no cards to play but the whole pack in your own hands will make allowance for her & pity her'.[6]

Kitty, the object of Maria's pity, had come on a restorative visit to Cheltenham. For once, the Duke and Duchess were together 'drinking water at the well arm in arm', and tactfully Maria had to explain to Harriette that it would not be a good moment for introductions. Caroline Hamilton had confessed to Maria that even she would not go and call on her sister if the Duke was about, in case it should 'embarrass' Kitty, the Duke was so 'excessively afraid of having her relations & friends come upon him'. Even the jovial Longford had become cautious of turning up too often. Maria herself thought at the time that Wellington was suffering from an excess of egotism. 'Poor Lady Longford', she wrote to a friend in London,

> was so deeply impressed with this part of the Duke's character that when the news of one of his victories was brought to her some years ago . . . thinking herself unobserved she vehemently ejaculated this prayer 'God keep him humble!' I wish you could have seen and heard the fervour of her expression – But it could not produce a miracle it seems, or work an impossibility.[7]

Maria's view of Kitty's position was not one Kitty would have liked to acknowledge. Kitty's letters often expressed an idolatrous worship of the Duke; she kept her unhappiness to herself. On this occasion in Cheltenham, it was understandable that Kitty wanted privacy for the Duke; she was concentrating on restoring him to health after the rigours of keeping the peace in Bourbon France. His brief visit to England that summer was a rare opportunity to reclaim the private man so often swept up by the huzzahs and halloos of his admirers.[8] And, for the time being, this plan was succeeding. On 18 July she reported to some old friends that her boys were 'as fond of, and as familiar with their noble and beloved Father as if they had never been separated from him . . . They accompany him in his walks, chat with him, play with him – in short they are the chosen companions of each other.'[9]

The Duke's pleasure in his young sons was genuine. His affection for children was frequently remarked upon, and one of the exceptions he made to a dislike of too many visitors was to allow Kitty to give homes to several needy young relations. But his time with his family was short. By 1 August he had left for London, and for Paris a few days later. The Duke and Duchess resumed their separate lives.

17

Marriage & True Happiness

25th August 1816.

> My dear Aunt, I lose not a moment in communicating to you a piece
> of intelligence which I am sure will give you pleasure – Ld Longford
> is going to be married . . .[1]

Maria Edgeworth was as usual the first to broadcast the news.
Although Longford's name had been connected with a number of
girls over the years, nothing had ever come to an engagement. Not
that the rumours of his love affairs weren't continually flying around.
As early as 1801, Ned Pakenham had written from St Croix that he
had heard Longford was engaged, and begged to know to whom.
In 1807 Maria herself had hinted that Longford was going to marry
Miss Emma Crewe, but that had come to nothing. In 1811 Ned was
advising his elder brother that, from his own experience, 'occupation
and not excess of novelty' was the only way to relieve heartache; in
1813 Lowry Cole was writing from the Peninsula that 'I am extremely
sorry to find you are still as great a vagabond as ever, and there is no
prospect whatever of reform'. 'Seriously speaking,' the bachelor Cole
continued, 'you are too much advanced in years to continue so long
on the town as you have done. I have often thought of writing to you
on the subject.'[2] By this time Longford was thirty-nine. It was all very
well for younger sons to play the field, but peers should hurry up and
produce their heirs.

Lowry Cole himself was married in 1815 – to Lady Frances Harris,
who at thirty years old was already long on the shelf. But he had

been in love with her for a decade. Longford may have been in the same position. There are frequent hints in Ned's letters to his brother that for years Longford had been pursuing an attachment that was doomed to fail. Unfortunately the name of the girl in question is never mentioned. In 1815, when the Marquess Wellesley's eldest daughter, Anne, was in the process of absconding from her dull husband William Abdy, Maria Edgeworth, ever-observant, commented with rather spiteful glee that she rejoiced that – 'Ld Longford did not marry Lady A's sister now Mrs Littleton whose bright eyes at one time made such an impression on him as to put good Lady Elizabeth in corporal fear & to bring from her ejaculations against the *drop of bad blood* of which she ever had a holy horror'. The respectable Mrs Littleton's only crime, in fact, was to be born the illegitimate daughter of the Marquess Wellesley.

Another possible attachment was Lady Sarah Lennox, the Duke of Richmond's beautiful second daughter, but the same holy horror had been felt for her – 'there was that drop too!'. The lovely Sarah had run off with Sir Peregrine Maitland – penniless hero of Waterloo – that year. But all these poor choices boded ill for Longford's future. 'I am afraid Lord L will be so frightened at the dangers he has escaped that he will never venture to think of any wife bad or good',[3] Maria had concluded at the time.

As he grew towards middle age, Longford had made no change to his lifestyle. It was easy enough to procure the favours of ladies in the streets of Pall Mall, just outside his club. Every expense – gaming, theatre, women – was still noted down in his leather account book. He did not attempt to hide his inclinations from Ned, who sent regular lectures on his behaviour. 'I suppose you are sporting the London Tactic, so keep within bounds of villainy for health sake.'[4] 'You are strong, but I dread these repeated trials of strength. To avoid the delights of abandonment, which you seem to understand, without total abstinence, which I do not pretend to recommend, there is danger of attachment to an unworthy individual'.[5]

It seems that Longford went ahead and proposed to the 'unworthy individual', but was turned down. His brother tried to cheer him up with a reminder that there were other ways to live, as

Ned himself knew only too well, after the bruising encounter with Miss Milbanke: 'give your ideas to the principles of *Retired* society. It is vastly singular, that in the difference of our lives, there should be such coincidence in the result of our objects, – but in making the comparison, I quite permit you the claim of an Elder brother, on the future attention of good providence.'[6]

But Ned's well-meaning advice was not heeded. Longford's 'restless desire' dominated his behaviour. He already had one illegitimate child, Miss Catherine Weekes, who lived a secluded life in Sussex. In London, at least two of his mistresses had children by him. One, Frances Chamberlain, gave birth to a daughter in 1814; the other, Margaret Forth, to a son in 1816. Perhaps he did become genuinely attached to them. For the rest of his life Longford paid these women and their children annuities, and left, with apologies, instructions in his will that the allowances should be continued after his death.[7]

The children themselves were taken away from their mothers and brought up by foster parents, with mixed results. The little girl was brought up by a 'respectable old lady, Miss Barland of London', who was paid a regular fee of £35 a quarter. Little Edward was lodged in the home of a Mrs Harding, in Bloomsbury. They were each christened with names that suggest a poor attempt at wordplay: Longford's daughter was called Catherine Chapman – which suggests Chamberlain and Pakenham, and his son Edward Frankford – which plays on Forth and Longford.

Perhaps it was not surprising that everyone had given up the thought of Longford becoming a respectable married man. 'Longford's going on the same way,' wrote Lady Enniskillen to her brother-in-law in India, '& I fancy will never marry.'[8]

Now, in the summer of 1816, Maria copied out Longford's letter to her father announcing his engagement. It had an unexpected touch of Mr Collins in *Pride and Prejudice*:

> You and yr most kind family have always taken the most lively & affectionate interest in all that concerns me & mine, I am sure you will be kind enough to extend that feeling to another whom I have

been fortunate enough to prevail upon to unite her fate with mine . . . Lady Georgiana Lygon is to be my partner & playmate & from what I know of her I flatter myself the choice will meet with approbation of my friends – possessing good sense & good temper – comely & companionable I deem myself more than fortunate in my fate – And I am sure that far from wishing me to desert my country & become an Absentee she would not permit it.

His bride's credentials were exemplary. The fifth daughter of Earl Beauchamp (not quite the tenth, as Maria described her), Georgiana had been brought up in the beautiful Queen Anne house of Madresfield in Worcestershire.* She was the first English bride to come into the family, but her elder brother was married into the Anglo-Irish set, his wife being Charlotte Scott, the sister of the Earl of Clonmell.[9] Georgiana herself was just eighteen, and a fashionable beauty. Perhaps with her dark hair and youthfulness there was something in her to remind Longford of his sister Kitty; certainly, Mr Edgeworth wrote to recall to Longford what he had vowed nearly twenty years before: 'Your bride has a pledge for happiness which I can answer for . . . if another such woman [as Kitty] has been found, England may claim some rivalship with Ireland.'[10] Whether Georgiana was physically like Kitty or not, in one respect she was quite different. When it came to money, Lord Beauchamp's daughter proved perfectly wise.

For the Beauchamps themselves, Longford must have seemed a nice catch. Even if his right to sit in the Lords as a representative Irish peer would end with his death,† his property appeared large and valuable. And it was something, after all, to marry the brother-in-law of the Duke of Wellington. Longford himself was elated: he wrote in hurried rhapsodies to Mr Swan, his London agent, 'I am the happiest man on Earth – the more I know of my future wife the more I

---

* Madresfield and the Lygon family later inspired Evelyn Waugh's *Brideshead Revisited*.

† In fact Lord Longford was made an English peer with the title Lord Silchester at the time of George IV's coronation peerages in 1821, so the family continued to sit in the Lords after Longford's death under that title.

admire her – Bred in a family of moderate & *careful* habits, she is no dasher & in every respect will make a prudent as well as a charming partner thro' life.'

This charming girl was worth 17,000 Irish pounds, far more, it turned out, than Longford had expected. In 1816 he was certainly in need of the money. Taxes were heavy to pay off the Government's war debts, and the post-war depression in agriculture meant that his estate income was down; the prices for oats, barley, beef and pork had fallen by half. Parts of Ireland were suffering a famine after the failure of the potato crop that August. Inevitably, the compulsory tithe rent paid to the clergy had become a renewed cause for resentment when times were hard – cattle were mutilated and houses burnt by members of new agrarian secret societies like the Ribbonmen in the south. The whole economy was affected; the elevated status the smaller landowners and middlemen had enjoyed during the boom years of the war came tumbling down again.

'Landlords who had set their lands at rack rents during the war are now all *racked* by the peace . . . the race of squireens who had sprung up, – and who kept gigs and had race horses have now suddenly sunk down again gigs and horses and altogether and are no more seen or heard of',[11] Maria explained to Lady Romilly. Moreover, Longford had just spent £4,000 improving the old Dublin house in Rutland Square, which he excused as all in a good cause to his agent, Mr Swan. 'I deemed [it] the best way of contributing my effort to relieve the severe pressure which lay upon all the trades people & workmen, in consequence of their not being able to find employment.'

He was also still paying out sums to several elderly annuitants, who refused to die. The annual interest on his debts alone was over £5,000. With these deductions, his total income was reduced to £10,634 a year – not much compared to his English peers. Georgiana's fortune was strictly meant to be held in trust for future children, but in practice it meant he could pay off some of his debts, particularly the one that irked him the most. This was the dowry money of £4,000 owed to the Duke of Wellington, which had been hanging over Longford's head since Kitty's marriage in 1806.

The business transactions for Longford's impending marriage went smoothly, perhaps because he felt no need to be completely honest about his own affairs. 'I shall only state that part which is legally obligatory', he warned Swan, 'I shall state all my debts & even ballance against me, all jointures and *positive* annuity – but not such as are voluntary . . . I do not think it either necessary or prudent *always* to put one's *worst* foot foremost.'[12] In other words, there was no need for Georgiana's father to know about the annuities paid to his natural children. He went on to give a very positive description of what he could offer his bride:

> I have a very comfortable & well appointed House & suitable offices & above 1200 acres of Ground in my own hands at Pakenham Hall – A large house in perfect repair £4000 having been lately laid out on it (Freehold) wants furnishing in Dublin . . . A small house in London for which I pay £200 per annum for 30 years . . . My farm also entirely supplies my house & family at Pakenham Hall with every necessary article.[13]

In fact, far from feeling depressed when he looked at his accounts, Longford decided to splash out in London. He ordered a curricle costing £100, and asked Swan to find him 'one pair of bright bay carriage horses – about 15 hands 3 inches high switch (not nicked) tails not younger than 4 nor more than 6 or 7 & good steppers – I think 35 or at most 40 guineas each ought to give me excellent ones'.[14] Nothing was too good for his lovely Georgiana. His main idea was to have the business settled as quickly as possible. 'When you see the person who creates this anxiety I flatter myself you will not be surprized at it', he wrote to Swan, on the last day of August, 'I am the happiest man alive.'

On the same day in September that he bought the wedding ring for his bride, he sent a cheque for £35 to Mrs Harding. She had written him a grateful report on his son a few days before. Little Edward, it seems, was teething.

Back at Edgeworthstown, Longford's neighbours were almost as happy as himself. Maria was delighted with him for writing so warmly to her father, who was far from well:

This letter is like his own kind hearted unaffected self – and how perfectly polite as well as kind – God grant that all those I love may marry well-bred people . . . My dear friends, I wish I could be with you at the moment when you read these letters & talk them over . . . Jabber! Jabber! Jabber! What fluency of joy! We all talked over and under each others heads as fast as we could for at least a quarter of an hour . . .

The only drawback to the match for Maria was that the bride's family name was the same as that of the 'reprobate young slasher' 'Beauchamp Courtington' in her latest, but as yet unpublished, novel. It would have to be erased 529 times from the manuscript.* 'Heaven help my poor Aunt Mary who must fall to *scratching* in the midst of the general rejoicings . . . Now there is . . . a *novel* distress he could never have forseen!'[15] Then the pale, anxious face of Kitty crept into Maria's thoughts.

I wonder whether [the Duke of Wellington] will rejoice, or whether he is too gloriously selfish to rejoice in his amiable brother-in-law's marriage & happiness. – Heaven help his haughty mistaken soul – he has mistaken his road to happiness I ween after all the noise he had made in the world – he must go back to his duchess to ask the way sooner or later.[16]

By mid-October all the deeds and trusts and declarations had been signed by both parties. Lord Beauchamp, his wife and children arrived in London on 20 October for the marriage planned for the following day. But in the night, Lord Beauchamp's heart stopped dead. This 'dreadful calamity, which has turned a house of joy & happiness into one of woe & mourning', meant all the proceedings ground to a halt. There was nothing poor Longford could do. Everything had to wait for the opening of Beauchamp's will, and a respectable period of mourning.

---

* In an earlier tale, *Manoeuvring* (1809), the character of Admiral Dashleigh had been removed by Maria on Sophy's advice, because of a close resemblance to Admiral Pakenham.

November slowly passed. In mid-December Longford went to Madresfield to spend Christmas in the grieving bosom of the Lygon family. On the 27th he returned to London for 'a dinner and play', paid a visit to the dentist, and bought himself a smart pair of new braces. Finally, on 22 January 1817, the waiting came to an end and Longford and Lady Georgiana were married at Madresfield Court. Elated, Longford took up his account book to make a last entry. 'The End of all Folly', he scribbled in thick black ink. 'The Commencement of true Happiness.'

True to his promise to the Edgeworths, Longford returned to Ireland immediately after his honeymoon, determined not to be labelled an 'absentee'. Back at home he wrote cheerfully to his cousins, urging them to visit. 'I certainly think when Lovell sees how comfortable & happy I am,' he joked to Edgeworth about his eldest son, 'he will feel much inclined to follow my example. I am now all surprise & astonishment at myself. How could I remain a Bachelor so long!!!!'[17]

Richard Lovell Edgeworth, who had known three generations of the Pakenham family, was dying in his seventy-third year. Until the very end of his life he was absorbed in improving the state of the countryside. He reminded Lord Longford of the need for a new bridge at Longford; the old one was in such imminent danger of collapse that the mail coach would have to be diverted. Longford had been happy to acquiesce; it was just the sort of project he believed worthwhile. Like his father the Captain he had been making improvements to his estates for nearly two decades. Unfortunately, as he confessed to Edgeworth, he had been so distracted that he kept forgetting to set the work in train. Georgiana, who had been feeling 'very delicate', was expecting a baby in October.

At her writing table Maria was hurrying to finish the last novel she would write in her father's lifetime – *Ormond*. It was the story of a young Anglo-Irishman who has been brought up – and corrupted – by a rascally pro-Union political jobber. The eccentric character of Sir Ulick O'Shane bore a strong resemblance to Admiral Pakenham, as well as another old neighbour, Sir John Blaquiere. As for Ormond himself, his love affairs with unsuitable women perhaps remind one of Longford.

And there were still visits to be made. Even an agonising stomach complaint could not prevent Edgeworth from going to meet Longford's new bride. On 16 February 1817, Maria and her father set off for Pakenham Hall, Maria reading aloud the first chapter of *Ormond* as their carriage jogged across the bog road. It was the last visit Edgeworth was to pay anywhere. On 13 June he died, and for months afterwards Maria languished in a state of profound grief, exacerbated by an eye affliction that meant she could not write without extreme pain. Then, true to her promise to her father, she buckled down to complete his *Memoirs*.

For the Longfords, the year ended on a jubilant note. Edward Michael Pakenham was born without difficulty on 30 October. And two months later, on Christmas Day 1817, Colonel Hercules Pakenham married Miss Emily Stapleton in Paris. She was the daughter of Lord le Despencer, and the match was 'much liked by the family'. Like her sister-in-law Georgiana, Emily was only a girl; just nineteen and extremely pretty. The only voice of dissent was Kitty's, who found Emily affected and saw her as a rival for the devotion of her brother Hercules. The latter's precarious health and loyalty to 'the Chief' had long ago made him her particular favourite.

18

Enemies and Friends

ᚱᚷ

Two weeks after Hercules' marriage, Kitty had begun a secret and urgent correspondence with her brother Longford on a rather different subject.

> Uncertain, dearest Longford, whether Lady Longford sees your letters or not, I enclose this note for *yourself* . . . knowing *His* liberality you will be astonished that money should be the subject but Longford it is not stinginess that I have ever to dread – Alas! Alas! – it is temper – and I hope you will believe it is from no extravagance of mine that I wish much I could get *now* the £1000 that must be mine at the death of our good old aunt Bess . . . do not be frightened there is no gaming in the case but much much distress of mind. Which would be instantly relieved by some arrangement which should put me in possession of the money . . . My dear Longford, I can enter into no further explanation will you answer me as quickly as you can for expedition is of consequence and give me your best assistance – God Bless you.[1]

Longford replied immediately. No questions, no remonstrating; in two days he had sent her half the money she asked for and promised to send the rest as soon as he could. Kitty's next letter was suffused with relief: 'Yes, dearest Longford, heaven blesses every act of brotherly kindness . . . You have saved me Longford, I can say nothing. For nothing that I could say would give you an idea of what I *have* suffered and *do* feel.' She felt the prying eyes of others all around her. Dining with Lady Liverpool was a trial, tempting as it was to confess and feel the sympathy of a friend. 'Heaven guard me from being softened to indiscretion. For great is her kindness . . . and also great is her curiosity.'

What was the cause of such a debt? Kitty only says that it was due to no 'fault of mine, but by a series of cruel misrepresentations . . . painful to explain in any way'. The most likely explanation is that Kitty was the subject of a fraud through one or more of her charitable causes – like the subscription funds for the poor of Portugal and Spain, or a needy relation. Such stories had always left her alarmingly short of housekeeping money. With the Duke in France, Kitty was once again in charge of all the household bills – and this time there were two houses to keep. She was now grandly installed in the Wellingtons' new home in London, Apsley House, which the Duke had bought from his debt-burdened brother Richard for £42,000. As well as Apsley House, there was the large estate of Stratfield Saye in Hampshire, which had been purchased by a grateful nation for the Duke in June 1817.* Kitty's book-keeping skills were severely put to the test. In a telling postscript to Longford, she promised to 'exactly follow [his] advice as to accounts'.

Meanwhile, in France, there had been an assassination attempt on the Duke. At about midnight on 10 February 1818, a man by the name of Cantillon† hid himself in the shadows at the entrance to Wellington's house in Paris. As the Duke's carriage approached, Cantillon fired a single shot – and ran off into the darkness. Luckily, the shot had done no damage. The Duke's men failed to catch the would-be assassin, but it was common knowledge that the plot to kill the Duke of Wellington had emanated from a group of disaffected exiles in Brussels.

The Duke himself was pestered by letters from his fellow Ministers to leave Paris for the safety of Cambrai, where the army had their headquarters. He stuck in his heels and refused to budge, still insisting as he had to his brother William two years before, 'I hope [the Cabinet] will allow me to do my own duty in the way I think best myself.'[2]

---

* From Lord Rivers, at a cost of £263,000.
† He was left a legacy by Napoleon, which Wellington considered the latter's only dishonourable act.

In England, Kitty was indignant but not hysterical. 'There is no doubt of it all being a plot of the Jacobins to whom the discontented halfpenny officers are become the ready agents', she reported to the family. She spoke crossly about the French police 'who are by no means as diligent or as active as if the attempt had been made upon the most insignificant French man'. Perhaps at a distance she could feel calm about this threat to his 'precious life'. Kind William Wellesley-Pole took the trouble to reassure her that Wellington really was quite safe. An avuncular figure, 'Old Pole' was always kind to Kitty, and had long ago earned her love and loyalty, just as Marquess Wellesley had. She had not forgotten their thoughtfulness in passing on messages from the neglectful General during the long years of the Peninsular War. 'I have often been accused of being in love with my Brothers in Law,' she once wrote to Marquess Wellesley, 'I should have been so were they not my Brothers in Law – a strict moralist would think this was coming too near the mark!'[3]

By degrees, the relationship between husband and wife themselves was worsening. Not only were they separated by international politics and domestic secrets, but also by the continuing allure of beautiful women. In 1818 Lady Charlotte Greville, the young, attractive daughter of the Duke of Portland, was rumoured to be the current focus of Wellington's attentions in Paris. And even Maria Edgeworth – now that her father was no longer there to defend his favourite – had become critical of poor Kitty.

In September 1818 Maria was staying with the Lansdowne family in England, and at Bowood had enjoyed a long, confidential gossip with a fellow guest. Lady Bathurst,[4] the niece of Lady Louisa Conolly ('very well bred, well drest, well rouged') had a good deal to say on the subject of all their Irish friends, and on Kitty in particular. 'I am very sorry . . . to be convinced that the duchess has been more hurt by her friends than her enemies and more by herself than both put together', Maria admitted in a letter. She added more cheerfully, 'but still if she does not quite wash out his affections with tears they will be hers during the long autumn of life – He lately said to Mrs Pole – "After all home you know is what we must look to at last" '.[5]

This revised appraisal of Kitty's position did not stop Maria

visiting her old friend again when she was in London the following
spring (1819). Maria arrived at Apsley House on St Patrick's Day, and
found a posy of shamrocks pressed into her hand by her smiling
hostess, with the words 'Vous en êtes digne'. Maria was captivated
once again. 'Nothing could be more like Kitty Pakenham, former
youth and beauty only excepted.'[6] They sat on two stools discussing
friends and relations, Kitty displaying all her old enthusiasm when
Maria showed her a copy of the newly published Edgeworth
Memoirs,[7] with an engraving of Kitty's father in the front.

Two weeks after the St Patrick's Day appointment, Maria found
herself in the company of the very man she had so often denounced
in her letters. To her embarrassment, she did not recognise him.

> I left off abruptly in my last to my aunt just as the folding doors at
> Lord Harrowbys were thrown open and the Duke of Wellington
> was announced in such an unintelligible manner that I did not know
> what Duke it was nor did I know till I got into the carriage who it
> was. He looks so old and wrinkled I never should have known him
> from likeness to bust or picture – His manner very agreeable
> perfectly simple and dignified. He said only a few words but listened
> to some literary conversation that was going on as if he felt amused
> laughing once heartily. It was lucky for me that I did not know who
> he was for the very fear of falling on dangerous subjects about
> husbands and wives in various novels we discussed would have
> inevitably brought me into some scrape . . . On the contrary I talked
> on quite at my ease.[8]

The Duke of Wellington had returned to London in December
1818, and was now in Lord Liverpool's Government as Master-
General of the Ordnance. Reunited, the couple's estrangement only
increased. They spent much of their time apart, Kitty chiefly in the
country at Stratfield Saye. The clever Princess Lieven* might have
thought it cold, ugly and uncomfortable, but Kitty loved it. Whereas
the Duke enjoyed hard work and social life combined, Kitty felt

---

* Dorothea Lieven was the wife of the Russian Ambassador to England, and a
great friend of Wellington's.

happiest away from the intrigues of court and Almack's. She disliked paying visits: 'I am much like a tree when planted in the country', Kitty explained to the Mackintoshes when they invited her to stay.[9] Kitty had been brought up by her mother to eschew all expensive vanities; her puritanical dress sense* was so ingrained that she saw no need to change things as she grew older. When a wig was suggested to cover her grey hair, Kitty shook her head firmly:

> my boys detest it, Papa sneers at it on others, I never had a pang for it, and *all the world of Fashion* is reconciled to my white *white* hair . . . I never conceal it *for the present* Poets of the day declare it gives me the appearance of the fairy in I forget what story who forgot to mention her hair when her youth was renewed, I supposed she put on a farthing cap when she plunged in the fountain . . .'[10]

Kitty's short-sightedness and shyness dictated her behaviour: she was as conscious as ever that she did not wish to be part of a 'spectacle'. She felt no desire for a more intimate relationship with the royal family, whatever courtesies they showered on the Duke and his little boys. When Eton held their medieval procession, the 'Montem', in July 1820, Kitty stayed at home, because 'finding there was a Royal Party, and that Lady Conyngham [the King's mistress] & her son . . . were to be of it, I feared the Dchss of Wellington and her sons might be pressed into the service, so thought I should just wait for the next Montem which will be in three years hence was not that wise?'.[11] Mistakenly, Kitty's instinct was to focus all eyes on her husband. As an early biographer of Wellington put it: 'If there was one thing for which the Duke had more aversion than another it was being "shown of"; yet the Duchess never learnt to avoid it, and delighted in drawing attention to his great qualities and achievements.'[12]

The unhappy relations between the Wellingtons were common knowledge. Indeed, a group of would-be revolutionaries apparently claimed that the Duke's 'cruelty' to his Duchess – and to the masses – was a valid excuse for his assassination. The Cato Street gang, as they

---

* Lady Shelley called it 'Calvinistic'.

became known, conceived an idea that they would destroy the whole Cabinet. On 23 February 1820, constables and soldiers raided their hideout in an alley off the Edgware Road. The five ringleaders were later executed, and the Cabinet continued as before. But the incident caused Wellington to explode. In one of his most terrible letters to his wife, he accused her of spreading lies and complaints about his behaviour:

> . . . you and your family have complained of my conduct towards you without Reason . . . your whole conduct is one of watching and spying [on] me, and . . . you have employed my own Servants in doing so . . . I really don't believe you have any bad Intention. But every day's experience convinces me that you do more foolish things . . . which you must regret . . . upon the first moment of Reflection than any woman in the world.[13]

The Duke was perhaps right to be aggrieved. Using his servants to 'spy' on him, as he had determined she had been, was akin to the washing of their dirty linen in public. Their relationship reached a new low a year later when the Duke thought – mistakenly – that Kitty was accusing him of being uncharitable – and worse. For the first time he threatened her with the ultimate humiliation:

> I have given all that I chuse to give. Upon this point I cannot help observing upon your mode of enquiry into my Transactions from Servants and other Underlings. It really makes my life a Burthen to me. If it goes on I must live somewhere else. It is the meanest dirtiest trick of which any body can be guilty.[14]

Kitty at times believed his harsh words would kill her. 'I hope that I forgive you. I would and I am sure I could have made you happy had you suffered me to try, but thrust from you I was not allowed, for God's sake for your own dear sake for Christ sake do not use another woman as you have treated me'.[15]

Although this nadir in their relationship passed, it was many years before the two households of the Duke and Duchess trusted each other. 'When you are so kind as to call here again', Kitty wrote once in paranoid strains to an old family friend, Lord Bristol, 'do not let the Porter turn you away. He has a trick of sending *away* my friends saying "I thought you would like *not* to see them" and of sending *in* Enemies saying "I thought you would just like to see them".'[16] Yet through all this her sons remained sweetly adoring of their mother, and gave her hope for the future:

Jan 1ˢᵗ Stratfield Saye 1821

My Bess I was awoke this morning by two young and beloved voices singing Mama Mama happy new year! One at each side of me on my bed. May it indeed be a happy new year! Nothing is impossible to the merciful God who sees us.[17]

The white-haired fairy had her consolations.

19

Room for Improvement

❧

With the death of George III on 29 January 1820, the Prince Regent was now officially in the position of power he had long held in trust. To the surprise of his former Whig allies, however, the new King kept Lord Liverpool's Government in office. Another person, too, was keen to retain her office – or rather claim it for the first time – and that was his estranged wife, Queen Caroline of Brunswick.

The Queen's return to England in early June 1820 and her troublesome campaign to rejoin her husband came to a public climax three months later. An extraordinary 'Bill of Pains & Penalties' was drawn up by the King's Ministers, proposing that Caroline's adulterous habits whilst abroad disqualified her from sharing the throne. In fact, it said, the King should be allowed to divorce her. Every member of the Lords was summoned to Westminster whilst the 'trial' went on, including the thirty-two Irish representative peers. Longford took his seat with weary submission. It all appeared a pointless exercise.

'Here we are again wasting our time in frivolous disputes about forms of questions', he complained to Bess on 6 September, and continued in the same vein to his cousin, Edward [né Pakenham] Conolly of Castletown,* a month later. 'I can form no idea as to the result of the Queen's trial . . . we are shut up 6 hours each day it is very tiresome indeed. Whether the bill drops or not, all are fully

---

* The son of Admiral Pakenham who had inherited Castletown from Tom Conolly, and changed his name to 'Conolly' under the terms of the latter's will.

convinced of the vice guilt & depravity of our most Gracious Queen.'
The Defence had just begun.

Longford's own lifestyle since his marriage continued whiter
than white. His good habits now would have astonished his brother
Ned:

> Since I came to London I have *not once* lain in bed at 7 O'clock. I
> lodge close to the House in Parliament street – I then go up to
> Harley Street near Portland Place to the cold bath, walk home to
> Breakfast at 9 – then go to the House about 9 1/2 stay till past 5 – I
> very seldom dine out, & *never* at a club dinner as full living does not
> answer either in comfort or in health . . . I am always in bed at 11
> and up again at 7 – I generally get a good walk after 5 oclock before
> dinner –[1]

The Bill was indefinitely postponed in November, by an exhausted Lord Liverpool who could not persuade his Cabinet col-
leagues to vote for the King's divorce, even if they believed the
Queen was guilty. Everybody involved was heartily sick of the whole
affair, Longford as much as any. Delighted to get away, he installed
the family in Brighton for the winter, like the rest of the fashionable
world who followed the King to his seaside pavilion. From there
Longford only made the odd flying visit to Dublin and Westmeath.
This was to check on the building works in progress.

Since the arrival of Georgiana as mistress of Pakenham Hall, Longford's appetite for building had returned more strongly than ever. He
decided on some fashionable improvements along the same lines he
had begun two decades before. Francis Johnston's alterations had left
certain structural defects: at least that was the excuse Longford made
to himself and anyone who asked him. 'I am in a sad heavy job now
at P Hall – all that was done in 1801 when I first altered the House, is
now obliged to be taken down, as it was done so very negligently and
ignorantly', he explained to Kitty, '& since I am obliged to do so
much I am decided to do a little more and make my house complete
and secure. Among other things I am putting a large area round the
house, underpinning the old thick walls – it is troublesome, but I

expect during my life that an area will be a pleasant thing round every House in Ireland.'[2]

This time James Shiel was employed to extend the gothicisation of the house. This meant building out a bay window from the dining room and adding half a dozen battlemented turrets. Inside the ceilings were plastered with rib vaulting, which gave the rooms a grandeur they had never had before.[3] Further down the great drive that Longford had planted with beeches and oaks, Shiel replaced the classical entranceway – now so out of fashion – with a cut-stone castellated gatehouse. His father's Coade stone sphinxes were consigned to the flower garden.

In truth, Longford was finding domestic happiness a little dull. Now that Georgiana had successfully produced a quiver of heirs – three boys by the autumn of 1820[4] – the peer needed a project. As his household grew, Longford enlarged his home. After all, it was what he liked doing best; he had his father's building genes in his blood. Hercules was doubtful about the whole thing:

> Longford who has been some time very figgity from want of something to do, has now made himself work enough . . . he has after all his expenses on Pakenham Hall, nearly gutted the house from top to bottom, the entire side next Castle Pollard has been taken down to the ground, the Roof being supported on scaffolding.[5]

By September he was trying to raise money from Edward Conolly at Castletown, who had owed him £15,000 since 1810. It was hardly Edward's fault. He had inherited this old debt of Tom Conolly's with the Castletown estate, and Longford had taken on the payment himself because, if it had been paid at the time, it would have meant the 'utter ruin' of Lady Louisa. Longford admitted that his costs for improving both Pakenham Hall and No. 10 Rutland Square were twice what he had estimated they would be. He had 'not a prospect' of receiving his rents, the state of the country was so low – and, most annoying of all, the oldest of his clutch of annuitants, eighty-three-year-old Mrs Iremonger, was still heartily alive when she was 'really supposed to be in *articulo mortis*'.[6] But Edward Conolly was in no better state than his cousin to pay out such a large sum, and could not help to refund him.

Pakenham Hall was not the only family home undergoing changes. At Coolure, Admiral Pakenham was extending the old house for reasons his daughter Bess could not fathom. 'They are building away here at a great rate, a great deal larger addition to the House than they will ever want', she wrote crossly to her brother Richard in late July of 1821. 'I believe it will cost lots of money, about £1000 . . . before they leave it finished, and there is now no peace within the demesne of Coolure, for between the carpenters hammering and the masons chipping the stones, your brains are so bothered with it and so full of it, that positively it goes on in my ears all night, so that even our pillows are no refuge to us.'

It may have been that Louisa and Thomas were looking for a distraction, for in the early months of that summer they had lost two of their daughters, twenty-year-old Kitty in May and then the youngest one of all, little eight-year-old Emily a few weeks later. The old Admiral had always been an affectionate father, and according to Lady Louisa Conolly had particularly loved his daughters. Now she saw him 'quite broke down'; whilst Bess wrote to her brother that 'it goes to my heart to see Papa . . . [he] struggles so to conceal his feelings'.[7] Yet it is incredible that in an age of high child mortality, these were the first two of fifteen Coolure children to die.

At Castletown, an era was coming to an end. For two months Lady Louisa had been suffering greatly from an abscess on her hip, which had become a mortal infection. She had accepted her approaching death with the calm serenity that characterised her life. She had a tent erected on the lawn at Castletown so that her last days might be passed surveying the creation she had so loved.

After Lady Louisa's death, Edward Conolly began work on restoring the estate. Ever since Tom Conolly's death in 1803, much of Castletown had been in a state of dilapidation, due to the massive debts left by its former owner. But his programme of improvements was not universally admired. As ever, Louisa Pakenham found herself trying to mediate between her family and the Napiers, who still resented the Pakenham takeover. 'I cannot say how much it gratified me to learn that you approved of Dear Edward's proceedings here', she wrote to her sister Harriet Clancarty,

> I know how much it is his wish & study to do everything that was intended & to fulfill every wish as far as he can & if he has failed in some, it may be from error of judgement & unforeseen difficulties, but in no way want of respect & veneration for the opinions & affection for the memories of those dear Parents to whom he owes so much, & nothing vexed & dissatisfied me so much as finding how much he has been misunderstood by dear Emily Napier . . .[8]

It may have been Edward's 'proceedings' that decided Emily Napier on leaving Castletown for good, and returning permanently to England. The Pakenham-Napier relationship at Castletown had never been an easy one. When Emily's mother, old Lady Sarah, came out for a final visit to her sister Lady Louisa just before she died, Bess Pakenham, Edward's sister, showed no enthusiasm. 'I intend to go home,' Bess wrote, 'as I hear Lady Sarah is steering her weary course this way, the tiresome old hag, she will be such a bore here to Aunt and Emily.'[9]

That August, another interesting person was approaching Dublin. The newly crowned King George IV – whose delayed coronation had been held the month before – was coming on an inaugural visit to Dublin. For the first time in 130 years, the reigning monarch was to greet his Irish subjects. Dublin was 'in ferment'. Bess Pakenham reported in her father's dry tone, 'Everybody is quite taken up by his Majesty's visit to Ireland. All the Castle people are turned out to get the Castle ready for him. I hope he will spend some money if he does come, for certainly, as I hear, his representative spends none'. The Lord Lieutenant, Talbot, was indeed notoriously careful – which made him unpopular in such hard times.

Whether the King spent generously during his three-week visit or not, the Irish took him to their hearts. Crowds flocked in from the country to see their monarch, every lodging house was packed with the curious. He landed on his birthday, 12 August. Whilst the official greeting party waited at Dunleary pier for the royal yacht, a steam packet carrying the King sailed discreetly into the opposite port of Howth. Crowds lined the quayside, cheering the steam packet as it sailed towards the harbour. The day before, when already at sea, George had been told that his wife Queen Caroline had died,* so a more subdued entrance to Ireland seemed appropriate. Yet his itinerary was hardly affected. He spent five days in retirement at the Viceregal Lodge in the Park, but this was the slightest possible mark of respect to an unloved spouse. Then the celebrations began in true Irish style, with the grand arrival into Dublin on 17 August. In that city, at least, nobody cared for the poor dead queen.

As the appointed hour dawned for the King's entrance into the capital, Mr Richard Morrison, the fashionable architect, was hurriedly putting the finishing touches to his newly built triumphal arch. It stood at the entrance to Sackville Street, just below Rutland Square, with 'One Hundred Thousand Welcomes' inscribed across the top in Irish. The scaffolding had just been removed when the civil procession came into view on Carlisle Bridge. According to *The Times*, Morrison had to pluck out all the decorative orange paper flowers at the very last moment, in case they should be mistaken for party symbols.

In fact, the King went down remarkably well in Dublin. He appeared in his uniform with a huge rosette of shamrocks pinned on his hat. Everyone could see he was in the best of spirits, certainly not marred by the small band of black crêpe on his left arm. As his appearance was greeted with affectionate cheers, the King did his best to reciprocate, and 'repeatedly held up his hat, and pointed with his right hand to the large shamrock which decorated the front, and then with his finger touched his heart'.[10] A great train of carriages followed the King's, including Longford's. Other Pakenhams and their friends watched from the tall windows of the house in Rutland Square – where they had a 'grand view'. Then the gentlemen set off to the King's levée at the Castle. 'You and Tommy', one Pakenham relation wrote to her daughter, 'would have been amused to see them practising their bows'.[11]

* She died on 7 August 1821.

Three days later the King held another crowded levée that even included the Catholic bishops. Twenty-year-old John Hamilton, Longford's nephew, found himself dancing a quadrille just as the King arrived and was charmingly obliged to continue under his gaze. Longford too was once again in the throng, and on his arm was a proud old man who wore a magnificent silver star on his breast. Admiral Pakenham, at sixty-two, had recently been rewarded for his long service to the Crown and made a Knight of the Bath. In dutiful style Lady Longford, with several others, hosted a patriotic ball at the Rotunda, although she was only a month from giving birth.

When the King finally embarked from Dunleary on 7 September it was with a 'heart filled with sorrow', and a last blessing on his people.[12] Dunleary itself was rechristened 'Kingstown' in honour of the royal visit.

At the close of 1821, Wellington's eldest brother, the Marquess Wellesley, was made Lord Lieutenant of Ireland. The new Viceroy was popular with many because of his known sympathy to the cause of Catholic Emancipation.[*] These hopes were strengthened further when he dismissed William Saurin,[13] the long-serving Attorney General whom many saw as being at the centre of anti-Catholic opposition, and ejected the incumbent Castle staff ('*impetuous*', declared the Whig hostess Lady Cowper when she heard the news). The renowned Catholic barrister and campaigner, Daniel O'Connell, made a public welcome address to Wellesley, and was invited to attend the first levée of the new viceroyalty.

In the next few months Wellesley had at least achieved some reforms. He had steered the Composition of Tithes Act through Parliament to allow cash to be paid to the tithe collectors, where before payment was in kind. But the economic situation in Ireland remained dire. The post-war depression in agriculture continued to have a dramatic impact on a country where there was so little industry to provide employment. The continuing subdivision of

---

[*] He was to marry the Catholic widow Mrs Marianne Patterson in 1826, much to Wellington's disgust, as she had been a favourite of his own.

land as the population boomed only made things worse. For land-lords, rents were hard to get, and many evicted their smaller tenants or cottiers.

Tom Longford, with numerous debts crowding in on him, began negotiating to sell the Hampshire estate in England he had inherited with his distant cousin Viscount de Vesci. This made up part of the unexpected inheritance his father had received in 1778. By chance, the Hampshire estate of Silchester* adjoined the Duke of Wellington's property at Stratfield Saye, and the Duke was willing to buy it for a very fair price. Unfortunately Lord de Vesci, the joint owner, was in no hurry to sell. The negotiations rumbled on for three years, and were a further cause of friction between the Longford and Well-ington families. In the meantime his domestic costs continued to rise, as his tribe of children grew ever larger. It was fortunate, indeed, that Lady Georgiana had no expensive tastes.

The 'heavy job' of improving Pakenham Hall had finally come to an end after three years' work. Maria Edgeworth, who had not stayed there since 1817, scribbled a breathless report as she sat in the library.

Jan 21st 1824.

We – Mrs E – Fanny Lovell and I, are very glad to find ourselves once more at Pakenham Hall – and to see Lord Longford sur-rounded as formerly by his friends in the old Pakenham Hall hospit-able style – himself always as cordial, unaffected and agreeable as ever . . . the house has been completely new-modelled, chimneys taken down from top to bottom – rooms turned about from length-ways to breadthways – thrown into one another, and thrown out of one another, & feet & inches added to the height of those below by taking from the floors of those above & the result of the whole is that there is a comfortable excellent drawing-room, dining-room, & library – all rather too low for their size but this cannot be helped, & in my opinion is of little consequence. The bed-chambers are admirable and most comfortably furnished with all that the most

---

* The English peerage given to Longford in 1821 was named after this land.

luxurious sleeper or waker or sleep awakened can desire – No frippery – no tables covered with china toys to be knocked down . . .[14]

The Edgeworth visits to Pakenham Hall were not as frequent now as they had been before Longford's marriage. It seems Georgiana did not appeal to Maria, although she admitted she had been 'very attentive to us – her beauty is not what it was'. But when the novelist did visit she was struck by the cheerful domestic scene. '[Lady Longford] has the finest & most happy open-faced children I ever saw – Not the least troublesome, yet perfectly free & at their ease with the company & with their parents.'

20

True History

⌇

In England, Kitty still had hopes of repairing her marriage. A year after her worst moments with the Duke in 1821, she wrote to her niece Kate Foster describing an almost tender exchange with her husband. She had just been on a jolly river outing with her boys at Eton.

> I arrived in Town about 7 o'clock and saw the Duke for a few minutes. My Hair was in the beautiful state in which Eolus, Borios and other gentle breezes on the Thames had left it, and certainly struck the Duke with wonder! for he took hold of it and very gently said 'Had not you better do something with them, had not you better?' to which I answered 'I feared you hated anything approaching to a wig,' to which he answered 'Oh, no. I am sure you would look better,' and so dearest Kate, to your triumph, one word or two from one man has done what boys and girls and men and women failed in accomplishing and now, as far as belle chevelure goes I am within a trifle as young as you. He has not yet seen the change but we shall meet tonight at Devonshire House where I hope he will observe that I have lost no time in complying . . .[1]

She still wished so hard to please Arthur. But even a change in her appearance would have made no difference now to Kitty's failings in the Duke's eyes. He had found the pattern of a truly 'sensible woman' in Mrs Harriet Arbuthnot.

The Duke had known Harriet since his time as Ambassador in Paris, when she had been brought out as the new bride of a hard-working Treasury Secretary, Charles Arbuthnot. She numbered one

Ned Pakenham's moment of glory came at the Battle of Salamanca, 22 July 1812.

The newly created Duke of Wellington, victor of the Peninsular War,
painted by Sir Thomas Lawrence, 1814.

Above: A contemporary print of the Battle of New Orleans, which shows General Sir Edward Pakenham lying in the arms of Major MacDougall. His body was sent home to Ireland in a barrel of rum to be buried in the Pakenham family vault at Killucan, Co. Westmeath. *Below left*: General Sir Edward Pakenham by Martin Cregan, painted posthumously with his Peninsular medals and the Star of the Bath. He is holding the Treaty of Toulouse, which brought the Peninsular War to an end. *Below right*: The commemorative word given by the grateful inhabitants of St Croix to their 'conqueror' Colonel Edward Pakenham in 1802.

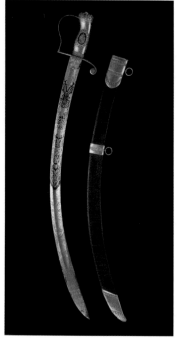

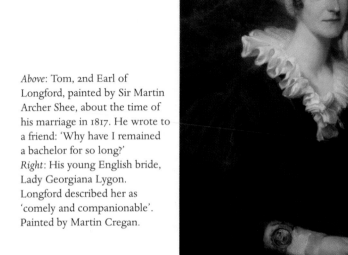

Above: Tom, 2nd Earl of
Longford, painted by Sir Martin
Archer Shee, about the time of
his marriage in 1817. He wrote to
a friend: 'Why have I remained
a bachelor for so long?'
Right: His young English bride,
Lady Georgiana Lygon.
Longford described her as
'comely and companionable'.
Painted by Martin Cregan.

Above: 'A Sketch in the Park'. The Duke of Wellington arm in arm with his constant companion, Mrs Arbuthnot, in Hyde Park. They were rumoured (incorrectly) to be lovers.

Left: The painfully short-sighted Kitty, dressed in her habitual white muslin, leans over her easel.

Facing page above: Kitty's two sons in Eton dress, with Gerald Wellesley. Stratfield Saye, the Duke of Wellington's country house, appears in the background. *Facing page below*: Georgiana with her three daughters in 1833, painted by Miss E. Scott, who charged £28. Georgiana was to be widowed two years later, but lived on until 1880. *Above*: Georgiana's four eldest sons, the youngest still in petticoats astride the family dog.

Pakenham Hall – now Tullynally – as it is today. Tom Longford's creation photographed from the same viewpoint adopted by George Edward Pakenham for his sketch of 1737–8. (See pages 2–3 of plate section 1.)

of his close circle of female friends and admirers, although her particular hero was Lord Castlereagh. In August 1822, Castlereagh – suffering a nervous collapse brought on by overwork and the threat of blackmail* – cut his throat. In the aftermath, Mrs Arbuthnot and the Duke grew closer still. 'He has promised', Harriet wrote in her confidential journal, 'to fill the place of the friend I have lost.'[2] The Duke made confidences to Harriet that he rarely made elsewhere. Their common interest in politics, their energy and deeply practical natures made them kindred spirits. It was to her he poured out the sad tale of his unhappy marriage:

> He assured me he had repeatedly tried to live in a friendly manner with her, had determined that he wd. communicate all his projects to her and endeavoured to make his pursuits & interests the same as hers; but he assured me that it was impossible, that she did not understand him . . . and that he found he might as well talk to a child.[3]

The complaints went on and on. Kitty was trivial-minded, obstinate and quite stupid when it came to politics. Her presence had even left his home friendless, when he was a domestic animal who loved having people about him. When Harriet asked Wellington why on earth he had married Kitty, he could hardly contain himself:

> Is it not the most extraordinary thing you ever heard of! Would you have believed that anybody could have been such a d . . . d fool? I was not the least in love with her. I married her because they asked me to do it & I did not know myself. I thought I should never care for anybody again, & that I shd be with the army, &, in short I was a fool.

He had conveniently forgotten the appealing letters he had written

---

* Castlereagh, who had recently inherited the title Lord Londonderry, was anonymously accused of homosexuality. When Wellington had found him in a state of terror the day before he killed himself, he initially said: 'Depend upon it, this is all an illusion. Your stomach is out of order.' Quoted in Elizabeth Longford, *Wellington: Pillar of State*, p. 93.

to Lady Olivia Sparrow at the time. As the Duke commented to Mrs Arbuthnot on another occasion, 'who ever heard of a true history?'.[4]

That September, 1822, George Canning was appointed Foreign Secretary in place of Castlereagh. Almost immediately Wellington was ordered abroad on a diplomatic mission to Verona, where the great powers of Europe were assembling.

Lady Cowper, a devoted fan of Wellington, thought the new Foreign Secretary should have been Wellington himself. In fact the Duke had been extremely ill because a celebrated doctor had poured caustic soda into his ear in an attempt to cure an infection. Lady Cowper fretted for him: 'I quite doat upon that dear Duke; he is so open hearted and kind and unostentatious & after one misfortune one always fears another . . . & he is so very good natured to me.'[5] But the Duke's high sense of duty prevailed, and he set off to join the Congress. He wrote Mrs Arbuthnot a last note, saying that he hoped she would think of him sometimes, since all his 'thoughts and wishes are centred on you'.[6] He would not return to England until December.

In the meantime Kitty was full of good intentions. She had formed a friendship with Elizabeth Fry, the prison reformer and Quaker, and was busy buying baby clothes from the female prisoners at Newgate. She made the best use of her good relationship with Wellington's brother, Marquess Wellesley, the new Lord Lieutenant of Ireland. She wrote begging him to help her brother Henry up the clerical ladder; Henry was the rector at Ardbraccan in Meath. Her appeal was successful, for by the following March Henry was installed as Archdeacon of Emly in Limerick. Kitty glowed with thanks: 'In gratifying my brother you have obliged me more than I can express & your kind message to me has gone to his heart. I will only add that, next to my Husband, you my dear Lord Wellesley are the man on earth to whom it gives me most pleasure to be obliged.'[7]

She was also planning a surprise for Wellington's return to Stratfield Saye, writing a charming letter to Sir Thomas Lawrence about the portrait he was finishing of the Duke:

Our library is now complete . . . the room is a handsome one, the Duke has done everything to it he could to make it beautiful and comfortable, and my own ardent and earnest wish is to place in that room the portrait . . . The Duke is now abroad and I should be everlastingly grateful to you if you could let me have this portrait that I might have it placed in this, his favourite room, before he returns to this country.[8]

Whether the portrait was finished in time, and whether the Duke was pleased by it, history does not relate. But Wellington was, as usual, being endlessly discussed behind his back. In Verona Frances Stewart, the wife of the new Lord Londonderry, carefully noted his nightly trips to the theatre. Wellington appeared quite broken down, she remarked with satisfaction, having always felt that he had not given her husband the patronage he deserved: 'He looks very old, stoops and is deaf as a door. He is treated here with great respect and égard from his name and station, but his excessive brusque manner is very much disliked.'[9] Even Lord Liverpool was quite cross that the Duke was not looking after himself. 'The Duke must be made to recollect that he is passed fifty, and cannot play the same tricks with himself as he could formerly', he complained to Charles Arbuthnot. A month later Liverpool took a hit at poor Kitty: 'It is most unlucky that [the Duke] should not find in domestick comforts a proportion at least of that repose he so much wants.'[10]

After his return, the Duke found both comfort and repose in Brighton rather than at home. Here the Duke enjoyed the adoration of several grandes dames, actively competing for pole position. Lady Cowper* was quite disgusted by Lady Jersey's† fawning over the great man. Lady Cowper had wanted the Duke to meet the Princess Lieven at her house, but he had refused, saying he was obliged to

---

* Afterwards Lady Palmerston and wife of the Prime Minister. Her other brother, William Lamb, afterwards Lord Melbourne, was married to the theatrical Caroline, another admirer of Wellington's.
† Lady Sarah Sophia Jersey was the daughter of Earl Westmorland, to whom Wellington had been ADC when the latter was Lord Lieutenant of Ireland. She and Mrs Arbuthnot were cousins.

stay in town that week; 'perhaps it is to be near *sa belle* . . . He sent an excuse here for this time, but people say he is more in love than ever with Mrs Arbuthnot. I wish L[ad]y Jersey would make a diversion, for she is an odious little woman.' She must have truly disliked Mrs Arbuthnot, to have preferred even Lady Jersey. Some days Lady Cowper dug the knife in there too: 'Lady Jersey thinks no more of politics; all her thoughts are how to catch the Duke of W. – all ambition & yet as eager as if it was love.' The Duke had even given Lady Jersey a fine diamond ring, which she insisted on wearing 'constantly' a move which naturally delighted the Duke, who 'laughs at it & at her always saying "not at home" to others when he calls – pardi, cette femme elle m'affiche', wound up Lady Cowper to her brother Frederick Lamb.[11]

To do Lady Cowper justice, her interest in Wellington was not entirely selfish. She cultivated the Duke as much out of anxiety to promote her brother William's Foreign Office career as for her own vanity. But in the circle of fans that surrounded him, only Mrs Arbuthnot really provided the fireside friendship[12] that the Duke had not found at home.

Kitty, as everyone could see, was now actually frightened of him. His famously abrupt manner of speaking was rarely softened for his wife's ears. By 1825 she had been reduced to such a state of nervous tension that she no longer dared to ask her own friends or relations to stay. When her niece, Kate Foster (née Hamilton) wrote inviting herself for a long visit, Kitty begged Lord Oriel – Kate's uncle by marriage – to prevent the plan. 'There can hardly exist a case in which it is wise in any Woman to fill her husband's house . . . with her own Relations however dear they may be,' she appealed,

> but my dear Lord Oriel there exist circumstances in my situation which would make any length of visit from any of my own family . . . to me totally destructive of every hope of happiness. Even my own sister my precious Caroline whom I had the happiness of seeing after an absence of years, stayed with me but three days . . . It is of the most vital consequence both to my present peace, and to my future hopes that I should be at perfect liberty to go any where, at any moment.[13]

She did not explain any further to Lord Oriel what she meant by 'go any where', but it signified that she could not bear to be trapped in the house if Mrs Arbuthnot should arrive. The kindly old man did as Kitty begged, and put off the Foster visit.[14]

Was the Duke's relationship with Harriet Arbuthnot more than friendship? Robert Peel, the Home Secretary and a great admirer of the Duke's, certainly believed so. Deeply uxorious himself, Peel was sickened by the Duke's treatment of his poor little Duchess. Staying at Stratfield Saye just after the icy funeral of the Duke of York in February 1827[15] had reduced the Duke to an invalid, Peel could hardly bear the pitiful scene; as he told his wife:

> I came down . . . earlier than the rest, and found the Duchess of Wellington alone in a small room near the breakfast room. Poor thing, she was as affected and uneasy about the Duke as if he had treated her with the kindness which is her due. I told her not to be alarmed, for that I thought the Duke before his attack was better than I had seen him for years . . . She replied 'I am so short-sighted I cannot remark his features, I can only judge of the colour, and when I look at that precious face, it seems to be very pale.'
>
> She burst out a-crying, and such things make me still more hate the sight of those who can find it in their heart, even if they have no sense of virtue, to usurp her place . . . What wickedness and what folly to undervalue and to be insensible to the affection of a wife! God bless you, my dearest love, and may He ever preserve us in the happiness we have enjoyed.[16]

On another visit in 1828, Peel complained: 'I see no signs of the influence of Mrs A. having abated. She takes her place next to him [Wellington] at dinner as if it were a matter of course'.[17] And yet Lady Shelley – who saw them all frequently throughout the decade – was convinced there was no impropriety. Mrs Arbuthnot was simply his 'fireside' friend. 'He admired her very much – for she had a manlike sense – but Mrs Arbuthnot was devoid of womanly passions, and was, above all, a loyal and truthful woman.'[18]

What did Mrs Arbuthnot think of Kitty? At times she showed

actual dislike, calling her 'odious' to Mr Arbuthnot, when advising him that they must make up some quarrel with her. She found Kitty's company dull too, and was delighted when the 'foolish' Duchess had decamped to whichever house the Duke was not then staying in. In Mrs Arbuthnot's eyes, Kitty's failure was twofold: she had failed Wellington intellectually and domestically:

> . . . if she had good sense all wd now be right, for what he now wants is a comfortable home, but she is totally unfit for her situation. She is like the housekeeper & dresses herself exactly like a shepherdess, with an old hat made by herself stuck at the back of her head, and a dirty basket under her arm. The Duke says he is sure she is mad.[19]

Yet occasionally she even admonished Wellington for his lack of civility to his wife: 'he is not aware that his manner is abrupt to the greatest degree to every body, particularly to her; and, as she is frightened to death at him (a thing he detests) she always seems *consternée* when he comes near her'.[20] But chiefly she felt that the Duchess was to be pitied, for naturally she could not 'help' being a fool.

Poor Kitty was not a fool, but short-sighted and stubborn. By trying to leave the Duke discreetly alone, she only provoked him. Lady Shelley, who had a diplomatic touch, traced Kitty's shy habits to the quiet years she had spent in Ireland, caring for an 'invalid relative'.* When she stayed with the Wellingtons in 1825, Lady Shelley reported that Kitty 'always sat apart from her guests, dressed, even in winter, in white muslin, without any ornaments, when every one else was in full dress! [She] . . . seemed to be uneasy at being taken to dinner by a Royal person or an Ambassador. She seldom spoke'.[21] That Kitty should prefer talking to the parson and the tutor at grand Stratfield Saye dinners the Duke found insulting. In his mind, she refused to show the respect to those political ladies and gentlemen that her position demanded. He made this the perfect excuse for leaving her alone.

* Probably the crippled Robert Pakenham, who had died in 1808.

Yet Kitty still believed she had insight into her husband's inner-most feelings, and was even prepared to enlist Mrs Arbuthnot's help in watching over him. 'Do you recollect what day this is?' she wrote to her one sad May Day, in 1827:

It is the Duke's birthday! On this day last year we dined with you, we were together! He was lately returned from Russia,* and in high spirits and in high favour! And now I am here alone, and most anxious, while [he] is probably with you! Pray for me, Mrs Arbuth-not, it will be praying for me to wish everything good to him. He feels far more deeply & more often painfully than he allows himself to express, and I cannot but apprehend that he often suffers that which none suspect.[22]

---

* Wellington had been sent on a special mission of condolence and congratulations on the accession of Tsar Nicholas I.

21

The Great Question

The movement for Catholic Emancipation – most essentially, the right of Catholics to sit in Parliament – had been growing with renewed vigour in Ireland ever since 1823. That year Daniel O'Connell had formed the New Catholic Association and found a method of raising funds. He had initiated a Catholic 'rent' – monthly contributions of a penny upwards – which could compensate those tenants evicted for not voting with their landlords. Since there was no secret ballot, this meant that the forty-shilling freeholders – encouraged by their priests – could now openly vote for Emancipation candidates.

Although numerous Bills on the subject of Catholic 'relief' had been introduced into Parliament over the last two decades, an increasing number of MPs now believed the moment had come. In Ireland the subject haunted all political conversation, as great public meetings were held across the country inspired by O'Connell's unrivalled oratory.

In March 1825, the famous Whig reformer, Sir Francis Burdett, introduced a new Bill for Catholic Relief. Colonel Hercules Pakenham, MP since 1812, found himself for the measure for the first time in thirteen years. Up until then he had always followed the family and the Government line on the matter: Longford was a determined 'Anti' when it came to the Catholic question. Only their brother Ned, back in 1811, had felt that some legal change was the only solution to Ireland's troubles.

Although he held one of the two seats for County Westmeath, Hercules' own estate was in Antrim and he had seen the contrast between Protestant and Catholic tenants. He believed the country

would only suffer if landowners like himself did not take action. Even
two years before, his agent had written to him that a 'crisis' was
approaching, that would 'end in nothing short of our being obliged
to fight the battle of the Boyne over again'.[1]

In the Commons, he spoke with appealing honesty about his
change of heart. Ireland, he said, had undergone great 'physical'
prosperity in the last twenty years, yet 'when he turned to its political
state, what a dreadful contrast appeared: with the exception of the
happy Province of Ulster, the country was staggering from one
convulsion to another'. It had become patently clear, even to him,
forced as he was 'to separate in opinion from many of his oldest,
dearest, best friends' that the 'baneful influence of the penal laws' was
the 'paramount cause'. Catholics had been given power, but these
laws prevented that power from being useful to the state. A Catholic

> could scarce begin his career when he was checked, not by difficul-
> ties that might be overcome by daring spirit or patient resolution,
> but by a statute, that impenetrably barred his advance, and that for
> ever. Could any man with common feeling and sympathies bear this
> state of things with content? He could put his hand to his heart and
> confess that he did not feel that he could bear it.[2]

Burdett's Bill was narrowly carried in the Commons, but lost in
the Lords by 130 to 178 votes. The King's heir, the Duke of York,
voted against it with a rousing speech. 'London is quite mad, with
parties & with Politics', Lady Cowper reported to her brother
Frederick, 'the Duke of York is very proud of himself. "The constitution saved" is placarded in the streets & the Catholics are all
furious.'[3]

After this failure, Hercules did not stand at the next general
election a year later, but resigned. It was impossible for him to
stand for a seat where he had been supported by Longford's interest.
The Irish papers reported that there had been a family rift:

The Freeman's Journal Dublin, Friday June 2nd 1826.
COUNTY WESTMEATH. – It is with regret, and indeed almost
with a feeling of shame, that we have to announce the retirement of

Colonel Pakenham from the representation of this County. Colonel Pakenham is the victim of the vote he gave and of the speech he made in favour of Emancipation, during the last Session. His brother, Lord Longford, has withdrawn his interest, and though we have reason to believe that if he stood upon liberal and Catholic grounds, he would head down the influence of the Noble Lord; yet he is a man of too much private good feeling to put himself . . . in active hostility against his own family. The motives which have influenced him, cannot however be appreciated by such a man as Lord Longford himself. As to the feelings which Colonel Pakenham will carry with him into his retirement, they are such as Lord Longford can never hope to enjoy.

Meanwhile, O'Connell's Catholic rent system was such a success that in the ensuing general election four counties – including Westmeath* – threw out and replaced the sitting anti-Catholic MPs.

Whatever the papers said, there was no serious quarrel between Longford and Hercules. The casual friendly tone of all their later correspondence remains. But like the Duke of York, Longford would not be moved on the great question. For him, Catholic Emancipation was a constitutional impossibility. How could Catholics swear fealty to the Protestant King, since the Pope was at their head? The very oath required abjuring the Catholic creed. How could a legislator have any form of free will if he was bound to follow the rule of his priest? How could an Irishman disentangle politics from religion – certainly Longford could not.

In his own town of Castlepollard, Longford blamed the increasing unrest of the last few years principally on the Catholic Association. As a county magistrate for Westmeath, he had taken part in numerous trials of men convicted of concealing arms and destroying property; and his tenants were now being threatened by gangs of Ribbonmen, in the same tradition as the 'Defenders' of the eighteenth century. He saw the situation as inflamed, and a strict

---

* The Emancipationist candidate, Hugh Morgan Tuite, ousted the landlords' choice by a narrow majority of twenty-four.

adherence to the status quo as the only way to keep the country from falling apart.

In England, Lord Liverpool's long ministry came to an end in the autumn of 1827. There was no general election and the Whigs remained out of office. Liverpool was succeeded by George Canning, who died a mere four months after accepting office. There then followed the feeble ministry of Lord Goderich, but that too came to a swift end. On 9 January 1828, the King made Wellington the offer of the premiership. With the Duke in charge, the King assumed, the Government would remain safely anti-Emancipationist.

Kitty's response was enthusiastic. To her sister Bess in Ireland she wrote:

> Thank God the Dukes strength seems to encrease, his powers to rise as they are called for, and his popularity with those who were of the party adverse to him in politics is positively wonderful! The respectable Whigs say decidedly that if he goes on as he has begun he will be the most popular minister England ever knew, and that beyond a doubt he shall, even now, have their support.[4]

With the change of ministry, a new Lord Lieutenant had arrived in Dublin. The Marquess of Anglesey, formerly Lord Uxbridge and a veteran of Wellington's campaigns, replaced Marquess Wellesley. Anglesey was popular in Ireland for his well-known liberal views and his anxiety to please all religious parties. Although the official line of the Government remained against Emancipation, factions within the Tories were breaking out. It seemed that the 'great question' was finally going to be answered.

In late June 1828, Daniel O'Connell declared that he would stand in the County Clare by-election, even though, as a Catholic, he would not be able to hold a seat. A group of Irish 'Ultras' – those most opposed to Emancipation – decided that something must be done. The immense power the Catholic Association had achieved was proved by O'Connell's temerity in making such a move. Some opposing force must be set up to contest it.

Accordingly, on 4 July, the day before O'Connell's election

victory was confirmed,* a group of anti-Catholic peers and com-
moners met in London. The venue was Lord Longford's house in
New Burlington Street. In the chair was Lord Chandos – in direct
opposition to his father, the Duke of Buckingham – and the speakers
were the Duke of Cumberland, Lords Farnham, Hotham and the
Duke of Newcastle. They decided to form a 'Protestant Club'. On
the former Lord Chancellor Eldon's advice, they changed its name to
the Brunswick Constitutional Club, and planned a mass petitioning
of Parliament.

On 14 August the Brunswickers held an inaugural banquet in
Dublin. Longford was elected President, and was soon busy sum-
moning support from all corners of the country, with some success.
By early November, 108 clubs had been formed in Ireland, with many
more in an embryo state. But in England the majority of MPs did not
take the Brunswickers too seriously. These Ultra Protestant factions
were nothing new; the diarist Charles Greville dismissed them as
'that old worn-out set'.[5] Yet the most prominent supporter of the
new club was far from worn-out. The King's brother, Ernest, Duke
of Cumberland – whom Mrs Arbuthnot called 'the most mischievous
person in the world' – was brimming with outraged zeal. Princess
Lieven was astonished: 'What idiots your high tories are!' she
exclaimed to Countess Cowper in September, '[Cumberland]
boasted to me the other day that he had an organisation which
would defeat the Catholic Association. A fine state of affairs when a
country is governed by clubs!' Then she put her finger on it. 'What
will the Duke of Wellington have to say . . . ?'[6]

Just as Princess Lieven had suggested, Wellington was furious
about the Brunswick Clubs. In fact, by October the whole subject of
Ireland had put the Duke 'in a fury'.[7] Only his most intimate circle
knew that he had privately concluded that the Catholic claims must
be met one way or another as soon as O'Connell had been elected in
Clare. A new situation called for a new political solution. Wellington
began by quietly pressing the King with the urgent need to discuss
the Irish question in early August. In a lengthy memorandum,[8] he

---

* 2,057 votes against Vesey Fitzgerald's 982.

insisted that rebellion in Ireland and the collapse of the Government at home would result if this advice was not followed.

And now, in the midst of his difficulties with both a truculent King and the real threat of civil insurrection in Ireland, he found the King's brother and his own brother-in-law plotting extremist demonstrations. He dismissed them with a stroke in a letter to Mrs Arbuthnot:

> Will Lord Aldborough, Lord Longford, Lord Farnham and a long &c remain in Ireland if there is a cutting of throats in consequence of their Brunswick clubs? Will they each of them spend a few pounds to perfect a real system of Association amongst the Protestants for general security? No! Their object is Faction and nothing else; and there I leave them . . .[9]

Far more worrying was the behaviour of the Lord Lieutenant. Over the preceding months, Anglesey had given the popular impression that he was working to get Emancipation carried. Far from leaving policy-making to Westminster, he appeared to have stolen a march on the Government. He had invited leading Catholics to his levées, and had had a personal meeting with O'Connell. Mrs Arbuthnot blamed the choice of Anglesey for factional behaviour in Ireland, complaining that if the Duke had only sent 'a sensible man & not a partizan, the Protestants wd not have set up Brunswick Clubs, & that irritation & fury wd not have been excited which has tended, I think, to complicate the question'.[10]

In fact, Anglesey had become such a thorn in the Duke's side by the end of November that the Duke complained to Lord Bathurst, 'Lord Anglesey is gone mad. He is bit by a mad Papist: or instigated by the love of popularity.'[11]

In Westmeath, Longford's rallying cry provoked differing reactions. Several of his Protestant neighbours, like Mr Wood of Rosmead, and Sir Thomas Chapman of Killua Castle, refused to join the new club. They took the view that any involvement in political subjects was dangerous, when Ireland was in such a state of agitation. Chapman went further and said he did not approve because he saw nothing serious in Brunswickers' actions: 'They want to put down the [Catholic] Association by Eating & drinking their annihilation. This never will do'. His wife, Lady Chapman, wrote an appealing letter to Longford begging him not to continue petitioning her husband to join a cause which could not be won, and of which she did not approve:

> I think the state of our unhappy country is owing to our Government, the Duke of Wellington I consider nearly despotic and am sure if he has decided that Emancipation should be given the petition of all the Protestants in Ireland will not influence him. And if he is of the contrary opinion Martial Law must very soon be declared in which case I think the unfortunate resident Gentlemen in Ireland should be quiet and leave the English military to execute the Government orders . . . I have every expectation that if Emancipation is Given, it will tranquillize our country . . .[12]

Even Mr Smyth of Drumcree, who had stood and lost against the Emancipationist candidates in the 1826 election, declined to join. 'Clubs sometimes commence like Lambs & make their finale like Tigers', he warned, enclosing a £20 note for the cause. Instead, he decided to take a year's travel abroad.

Nevertheless, when the first annual meeting of the Irish Brunswickers was held at the Rotunda on 4 November 1828, about 600 members were present to cheer Lord Longford's speech. He was at pains to remind them all of how they should proceed: 'We are called upon to act – but, in doing so, we are not to oppose clamour by clamour, but to oppose clamour with temper and moderation – let us oppose fiction by facts, for we should not, in the furtherance of our objects, adopt that well known figure of speech, "rhetorical artifice" '. A long series of extremely rhetorical speeches then followed, and Alexander Saunderson, MP for County Cavan, raised cheers by urging that unless 'the Protestants of the empire combine for their personal safety, their liberties, their properties, and their lives, [they] will fall a sacrifice to the disaffection and the treason of all enemies'.[13] For most of those in the room there was no doubt, as Newcastle put it, that 'the enemy was at the gate'.[14]

Longford himself, with memories of 1798 alive in his mind, saw conspiracies everywhere. He took it upon himself to pay informers to report on the 'seditious' Catholic meetings taking place in the disturbed southern counties. He wrote to Wellington about the 'dangerous plans which [they] are quietly and nightly discussing and arranging at Limerick', far from the Government's watchful eyes, and had compromising cipher messages decoded for his brother-in-law to read. By November Longford believed that the mass agitation had increased to such a degree that no such secrecy was seen as necessary: 'business is carried now on, in too open & avowed a manner to require the protection of mystery or cipher'.[15] What he had failed to realise was that he was only fuelling Wellington's determination to conciliate the Catholics. Writing to Leveson Gower, the Irish Chief Secretary, the Duke shrugged the Brunswickers off as a nasty irritant: 'I don't think that the Irish landed Gentleman has yet discover'd that He is the least influential of all His Majestys subjects and these Clubs may tease the Govt by their Interference in Politics'.[16]

A radical wing of the Catholic Association was developing which had begun to look for more than mere Emancipation: a repeal of the Union. Concurrently, in Armagh in the north, the Orange yeomanry appeared to be gearing up towards a conflict that could spark a civil war. From there, the pro-Emancipation Pamela Campbell – the daughter of Lord Edward Fitzgerald – wrote anxiously to her friend in London that the factionism was infectious, and even she felt no safety from either side. 'I am constantly told *indirectly* that the friends of the Catholics should fear their ascendancy, for if they begin a *masssacre* they will cut down friend and foe. Pleasant little images!' In the south, even a moderate like Maurice Fitzgerald, Knight of Kerry, had written to the Duke that 'the danger is appalling and it is rapidly progressive . . . The line is strictly drawn between the religions . . . the array of the people is complete. Every parish is a regiment'.[17]

Wellington, realising that no further delay was possible, persuaded the King that he should be allowed to consult the bishops of the Church of England on the subject. The King agreed, adding however that 'on the point in question I need not tell you what my feelings are'.[18] Nevertheless, Wellington believed that he could be persuaded on the matter, if only Ireland could present itself in a more peaceful light. In this he was hampered by Anglesey, whose friendly approach to the Catholic Association members he felt was encouraging agitation. By Christmas Eve 1828, he had got the Cabinet's and the King's agreement to recall Anglesey.

Amongst the Ultra Protestants in Ireland, Anglesey's recall was seen as a sign that Wellington would not conciliate the Catholics. Wellington had kept his real view so obscure that when the King's speech at the opening of the new session of Parliament on 5 February 1829 announced that the matter was to be debated, it came as a nasty surprise to the Ultra Tories. The King continued to dither on the issue, in an agony of doubt whether it went against his coronation oath to allow Catholics into Parliament. But Wellington pressed on with his scheme.

When the furious Duke of Cumberland hurried back from Hanover to try and sway the King against him, Wellington threatened the King with resignation, which finally did the trick. 'He treats with him [the King] as an equal, and the King stands completely in awe of him'[19] wrote Charles Greville. Whether it went against his conscience or not, the King could not allow his Government to fall.*

Five weeks after the King's emotional capitulation to his Prime Minister, Longford wrote his sister Bess a weary letter from London: 'This morning at 11 1/2 O'clock the Popish bill passed by a very great majority . . . None hope more nor expect less from this measure but in every way I shall do my best to make it succeed according to the anticipations of its promoters – & shall be truly happy to find I have been mistaken in my views –.' The 'Bill for the Relief of His Majesty's Roman Catholic Subjects' received the royal assent on 13 April 1829. But in the end the 'relief' was spread very thin indeed. An Act disenfranchising the forty-shilling freeholders in Ireland immediately followed the passing of the Emancipation Bill.

---

* The King actually dismissed Wellington and his Ministers but was persuaded by Lady Conyngham to reinstate them. Wellington then pressed for written confirmation that the King approved Catholic legislation.

The threshold of the county electorate was thus raised to a property qualification of £10 a year; the electorate, which had numbered a little over 100,000, fell to about 16,000.[20] (The boroughs were not affected.) This was the *quid pro quo* that Wellington had used to win support in the Lords.

The Duke, meanwhile, had fought a duel with an Ultra Tory, Lord Winchilsea, on 21 March in Battersea Fields. The furious Winchilsea had accused him of deceiving the public about his intentions, and planning 'the introduction of popery into every department of our lives'. In the event, Wellington fired wide, and Winchilsea did not fire at all. After the encounter the Duke went to have breakfast with Mrs Arbuthnot, and said: 'Well, what do you think of a gentleman who has been fighting in a duel?'[21] Kitty was unaware that anything had taken place.

Maria Edgeworth rejoiced at Wellington's victory. Her father and mentor had long been in favour of Emancipation. The Duke, she wrote,

> must now indeed feel that he is a happy as well as a Great man – He has certainly prevented a civil war and has by his civil courage saved both England & Ireland – The Catholics in this moment of triumph behave wonderfully well – with a noble spirit that strikes (as Mrs Henry Hamilton wrote me word) even those who were formerly least favourable to their cause.[22]

She saw with approval that Longford meant to go quietly:

> He opposed the measure as long as he could but now opposition can do no good & demonstrations of difference of opinion could only do harm therefore tho' his opinion remains unchanged he submits & wishes all who can be influenced by him to submit with a good grace to the law of the land. Very wise & good.[23]

Hercules wrote to Kitty that now their brother's intention to 'do away with all party feeling' had been made known publicly, it had 'caused the greatest satisfaction. The Deases' – an ancient Catholic family and neighbours of the Pakenhams – 'invited all the Pakenham children over from Pakenham Hall and gave a little fête to show how sensible they were of the value of the declaration.'²⁴ Archdeacon Henry Pakenham issued a word of warning. Longford was storing up trouble, he told Kitty, since he still followed a policy of discrimination. By opposing the 'education of the Catholics', Longford had 'acted with the Priests'. Those priests were naturally the Reverend Pakenham's greatest rivals. Education should have been the chief weapon of the landlord, the

> only thing ultimately to break the power of the Priests – by their opposition to all instruction the priests show they are quite aware of this danger, thank God they do not succeed . . . Hercules, who voted for Emancipation, does all he can to circulate the Scriptures and promote instruction . . . Thus their line of Politics and line of conduct seem to interchange oddly.²⁵

Kitty's belief in the Duke's power had never wavered. To a friend she admitted proudly that

> the agony of anxiety which I have felt on this most awful subject, has been unmixed with fear of the success of a measure brought forward by *Him*! And such a measure! I know what his opinion *was* upon this subject; he has explained what it *now is*, and the grounds on which his present opinion is formed. The firmest of them would not have adopted the present mode of acting had he not known it was necessary so to act! The most upright of them would not have proposed the measure had he not felt that it was *right in the sight* of his *God*!²⁶

Miraculously, things had improved in her relations with Wellington. She now felt confident enough to offer a room at Downing Street to her nephew Thomas Stewart, writing to his mother, 'This house is enormous, there are on the same floor 2 Dining Rooms, 3 Drawing Rooms, a Bed room for me, a dressing Room and 3 smaller bedrooms so you see it can possibly be no inconvenience . . . I will answer for the Duke's kindly feelings towards your child.'²⁷

The new understanding between husband and wife partly stemmed from a testament of trust the Duke had made to her.

When he had become Prime Minister, Arthur had asked Kitty to be a joint guardian of the Long-Wellesley children, the motherless sons and daughter of his nephew William. 'Wicked William', who had abandoned his wife long before she died, was attempting to spend all his children's inheritance,[28] and the Duke had stepped in to protect them. Kitty accepted with alacrity. The task of looking after the emotional welfare of three waifs could only appeal to her, as a 'most serious & sacred one'. She succeeded admirably. The three children blossomed under the care of their quiet, affectionate aunt and for once the Duke recognised Kitty's maternal talents.

In Ulster, sectarian unrest was still evident as members of the Orange Order continued to protest against Emancipation. From Langford Lodge, Hercules blamed the club his brother had so keenly promoted. 'I apprehend our infatuated Orange-Men . . . mean to make a great Parade on Sunday next, the Mischievous exertion of the Brunswick Club, blew up last year a spark that had nearly extinguished itself.'[29] This was to be the 12 July march to celebrate King William's victory at the Battle of the Boyne, which had been made illegal. Just as in the previous year, riots and disturbances followed. Moreover, the most extreme Brunswickers in Westminster were still intent on upsetting the Government. The Duke was well aware of this, but dismissed them: 'The Brunswickers are very foolish', he wrote to old Admiral Pakenham on 12 June, stating his conviction that the Protestants of Ireland were better-off than they had ever been. 'If men of property continue to quarrel about a religious question which is decided they must become the victims of the more numerous class who have everything to gain and nothing to lose.' Their best option for continuing security was to 'hang together' and 'adhere to Government'.[30] Government, after all, had now raised the franchise to a higher level.

In Westmeath, however, Longford was still not eager to 'hang together' with anyone. Perhaps the unhappy Brunswicker experience had put him off. He might have resigned himself to Catholic Emancipation, but that did not mean he would embrace ecumenism. When asked to join a non-denominational agricultural improvement society* by Lord Downshire, Longford demurred with the comment, 'certainly till the state of feeling is very greatly altered I shall decline belonging to mixed clubs – and very probably to any club – I do the best I can individually . . . You and I have very different ways of aiming at the same object . . . We are all quiet here as can be – a fair Harvest but prices seriously low'.[31] His instinctive aversion to any hint of increasing the Catholic vote remained strong, and a year later he was speaking out again against further electoral reform. Even his friend Maria now despaired of his political judgement: 'Lord L has been so violent & foolish on this subject and has so *advertised* his folly in the house of Lords that I really could not conceive you who knew everything did not know *that*', she wrote to Sir Philip Crampton, the liberal-thinking Surgeon General:

> It is most odd & unnatural that I should be here writing to you *against* my own neighbour & *relation*, and a man I really think a very good natured good hearted man – and whom I know to be an excellent prudent landlord [whom the] Knoxes and Hamiltons praise . . . But still not one of them would honestly tell you they think him judicious or a man of judgement . . .[32]

Wellington would certainly have concurred.

As for Hercules, who had resigned his seat in order not to cross his brother, he had given up thoughts of politics entirely. Two years later Wellington urged him to return to the political fray, when the Tory Party were in desperate need of support:

> I am the last man who would recommend to any man to ruin or even distress himself, by standing for an election. A seat in Parliament is nothing but gratuitous trouble and vexation. But I am afraid that the times are come when the gentlemen of property and consideration and good principles must come forward in order that we may, if possible, keep a country in which any of us can live or can preserve anything.[33]

* The Leinster Society.

But even such an appeal from the 'Chief' did not tempt him.

That autumn, 1829, Hercules took his large family to stay with Longford at Pakenham Hall. After his return, he wrote to Kitty describing the changes that had occurred. 'The place has been much improved . . . Lady L. appears to really enjoy it.' If a small rumble of difference remained between the two Pakenham brothers, it was not mentioned. Only Georgiana made a public show of feeling on the matter: 'she still is much excited both on General & County politics but when those subjects can be avoided, is really animated & cheerful'.[34] No doubt Hercules found it safer to stick to talk of gardening.

22

Happy at Last

Kitty was dying. During the long, unusually cold winter of 1829–30 she had become an almost permanent invalid. Stranded at Stratfield Saye for months at a time, she dined alone and went to bed early. She suffered cold after cold, whose 'incessant coughing so weakened me', she explained to Bess, 'as to occasion an internal strain'. But she was still thinking keenly of her duty to her wards who were spending their school holidays at Stratfield Saye. Her patience was paying off. The elder one, William's 'poor hard eyes over flowed' when she asked him to stay with her until she was better. 'The unfortunate boy had often said that he did not know what it was to care for anybody, and that he knew nobody cared for him but for his money. These miserable opinions are now shaken . . . this "Brand will be saved from the burning".'[1] Douro and Charley too were affectionate, devoted sons, riding down to Hampshire to see their housebound mother whenever chance afforded. But both were busy with their careers: by now, Douro was in Parliament and Charley in the Army. The Duke, 'entirely occupied & engrossed with public matters',[2] she hardly saw. When she did see him she worried and fussed – and drove him away again with her concern. The Duke, as usual, had far more serious worries than his wife's fretting.

Since the passing of the Catholic Bill, the Government's support in the Lords was at a dangerously low ebb, in spite of the Tory majority. Many had not forgiven the Duke for what they saw as a betrayal. 'Everything in this country is in the most extraordinary state possible', the loyal Charles Arbuthnot wrote to one of

Wellington's brothers. 'We met Parliament with the King notoriously & almost avowedly against us, the Duke of Cumberland & the Brunswickers resolved to go all lengths, even unto Radicalism, rather than not do their utmost to destroy us.'[3] Mrs Arbuthnot was convinced that Anglesey and Londonderry were busy 'laying their heads together how to form a Government without the Duke'.[4] At the same time, the Whigs under Lords Grey and Holland were pressing for parliamentary reform, and exploiting the Duke's weak position.

That spring, Kitty thought herself well enough to travel to London. When she arrived at Apsley House she was greeted by an exultant Charley, who carried her upstairs in a swinging chair on his back. When he heard she had arrived, Douro came 'flying' to her side. Old friends like Florence Balfour came to call, and Kitty wrote cheerful bulletins to Bess about her progress.

On 26 June 1830 King George IV died, his gouty frame swollen by dropsy. At Apsley House, Kitty's own health had not improved. By July she was unable to go up or downstairs without pain 'in every muscle' and meekly accepted the help of her sister-in-law to perform all the duties of giving a breakfast to the new King and Queen. William IV, a naval veteran, endeared himself to her immediately. 'He knew my Father's picture instantly & spoke of him most kindly. Douro says that now he has established himself in my heart as the first and wisest King that ever reigned and perhaps, so he has.'[5]

At this time, the pressure on the Government to introduce electoral reform was becoming extreme. Public feeling was volatile and expectant. November 9 had been planned as the Lord Mayor of London's day of state, when he would receive the new King and his Ministers. At the last minute Wellington cancelled it, fearing there would be a city riot. From her bed, Kitty pencilled her feelings to Bess:

> . . . all is perfectly quiet except the talkers in the 2 Houses of
> Parliament, and the disappointed Pickpockets Thieves & Radicals
> of London. In my heart I think that in the Duke's Warlike life, he
> never did any thing so valiant, and that no Government ever did a
> wiser thing than preventing the Lord Mayor dinner . . . but for the

advice of our ministers, so judiciously complied with by our King, London might have been flowing with blood that night, and all England drowned in tears now![6]

She wrote jokingly to Bess that the hardest part of being an invalid had been to break the habit of doing everything for herself: 'I have been compared to the cat turned into a Lady, who bounced out of bed to catch a mouse that crossed the floor.' If she tried to move, she was 'hunted back to my nest, by all my friends, with threats of being strapped down, and scoldings'.[7]

The day after Kitty had written, 16 November, Wellington re-signed. The Government had lost the vote on a minor Bill; as ever, the General knew when it was prudent to retreat. The Whig leader, Lord Grey, became the first Whig Prime Minister since the coalition 'Ministry of all the Talents' in 1806. Kitty was as positive as ever, describing the event as 'the direct Hand of that God who has ever protected him . . . Every body saw that the Duke's health was altering, that his countenance was acquiring a drawn and fallen look, his figure to shrink and many other appearances that preceed the breaking up of a constitution from over work. Thank God he has resigned in time'.[8] She was perfectly convinced that her own recovery was imminent too. Although she could now no longer sit up, she hoped cheerfully 'that that which has been injured will recover & in the meantime I am most comfortably established on the ground floor, and certainly see as many people as I ought'.[9]

Two months later Maria Edgeworth made the journey to Apsley House. There she found Kitty still installed in a long, low room on the ground floor, surrounded by the trophies the Duke had received from all the sovereigns of Europe:

> In the midst, on a narrow, high mattressed sofa like Lucy's – all white and paler than ever Lucy was paler than marble – more delicate than life lay as if laid out a corpse the Duchess of Well-ington. Always little and delicate-looking she now looked a mini-ature figure of herself in wax-work. As I entered I heard her voice before I saw her; before I could distinguish her features among the borders of her cap – only saw the place where her head lay on the

huge raised pillow. The head moved the head only, and the sweet voice of Kitty Pakenham exclaimed 'Oh Miss E you are the truest of the true – the kindest of the kind' – and a delicate little death-like white hand stretched itself out to me before I could reach the couch and when I got there I could not speak – not a syllable. I dared not trust my voice but she with most perfect composure – more than composure, cheerfulness of tone and look, went on speaking; as she spoke, all the Kitty Pakenham expression appeared in that little shrunk face . . . And she raised herself more and more on her elbow as she spoke and spoke with more and more animation – in charming language and with that peculiar grace, and elegance of kindness – recollected so much of past times of my father most particularly whose affection she convinced me had touched her deeply and whose admiration I more than ever felt had been deserved . . .

While I looked at these [trophies] the Duchess . . . exclaimed with weak voiced, strong souled enthusiasm 'All tributes to merit! – there is the value! And pure! Pure! – no corruption – ever suspected even. Even of the Duke of Marlborough that could not be said so truly.' The fresh untired enthusiasm she feels for his character – for her own still youthful imagination of her hero – after all she has gone through is quite wonderful! most touching. There she is fading away – living to the last still feeding, when she can feed on nothing else, on his glories . . .

Even Maria, whose own family tragedies might have inured her to the sight, was overcome. Although her friends told her that the prognosis was not hopeless for the Duchess, she was not convinced. She concluded her letter with a grim wish. 'I hope she will not outlive the pleasure she now feels, I am assured, in the Duke's returning kindness. I hope she will not last too long and tire out that easily tired pity of his.'[10]

Maria's wish was fulfilled. It seems from the description of her symptoms most likely that Kitty was suffering from stomach cancer, and the doctors could do nothing but wait for nature to take its course. Kitty herself had never shown a sign that she knew her illness was life-threatening. She continued to be preoccupied with the Duke's happiness, writing in letters to Bess her fear that without office he was 'uncomfortable . . . Inactivity does not suit him . . . I look forward to some change which will place him in some situation of useful activity. Not Prime Minister. On being employed both his health & his happiness depend! We are all such creatures of Habit'.[11] The Duke, however, expected no recovery. On 16 April 1831 he wrote to the organisers of the Irish ball to say he was unlikely to attend, because his wife's health prevented him leaving Apsley House. By then he was sitting with Kitty daily, feeling her pulse and giving her all the quiet attention she had never known before. For once she was 'quite composed not in the least agitated & quite at ease'[12] when she saw her husband. As Maria sadly reported, 'They say he is very kind now and that she says she is happier now than ever she was'.[13]

In the end, Kitty died quite suddenly. Her brother Longford had just been to see her the day before, and wrote to Bess that Kitty had been in cheerful spirits, happily receiving visitors in her wheeled bed. 'How little did I expect', he wrote on 24 April, 'that I should so soon have to state that all was to end in this world with our dear Kitty.' She had fallen into unconsciousness soon after his visit, and could not be aroused. Apart from a brief period of pain in the early hours of the morning, she remained in 'a quiet torpid state . . . till it pleased God to call her to a better world – Douro was with her to the last & felt most acutely – Charles was at Dover'.[14] The news flew over to Ireland. Poor Hercules had missed Longford's letter, and only heard when, coming in from his daily ride, he picked up the newspaper. He had been exceptionally fond of her, since the time he had been invalided out of Spain and stayed with her in Cheltenham. But he summed up what was probably the family feeling in his reply: 'She could no longer be of Essential Service to her Sons, & had the Sufferings of protracted Disease been added to her Already Bitter Cup, how sad would have been her Lot; as it was her Christian Spirit & Gentle Heart retained & enjoyed all their Fine Feeling to the last.'[15]

The Duke wrote a brief note to Mrs Arbuthnot: 'The Poor Duchess died at about half past ten this morning. She suffered some pain in the Night. But none this Morning. This End was quite unexpected so soon'.[16] To Mrs Arbuthnot he even betrayed some sentiment:

'It is a strange thing,' he remarked, 'that two people can live together for half a lifetime and only understand one another at the very end.' After a pause, his friend remaining silent, he related that the Duchess had run her thin fingers up beneath his sleeve to assure herself that he still wore an armlet she had once given him, and which she believed he had long ago discarded. 'She found it,' he said, 'as she would have found it any time these twenty years, had she cared to look for it.'[17]

One last visitor came to see the Duchess. Unconscious of what had occurred, Maria Edgeworth returned to Apsley House two days after Kitty's death. The Duke and his sons had already left for Stratfield Saye, whilst the corpse remained in the darkened house. Maria gave her card to the porter only to be told the news. Shocked, the ever-inquisitive Maria did not forget to question the maid about the last details:

'Was the Duke in Town?' 'Yes, Ma'am – beside her.' Not a word more on that subject but I was glad to know that certain . . . The poor maid could hardly speak. She went in and brought me a lock of her mistress's hair – silver grey – all but a few light brown that just recalled the beautiful Kitty Pakenham's formerly! So ended that sweet innocent – shall we say happy or unhappy life of hers? Happy I think – through all – in her good feelings and good conscience and warm affections, still loving on! Happy in her faith – her hope and her charity – Yes happier I am sure than those who injured her can ever have been or ever be.[18]

In the outside world, Lord John Russell's Parliamentary Reform Bill had just been passed in the Commons, but only by a single vote. Under pressure from his Prime Minister, William IV had dissolved Parliament. On the day after Maria's visit, 27 April, the Lord Mayor ordered general illuminations in honour of the dissolution. Outside the darkened windows of Apsley House, the jeering crowd lobbed bricks at the Duke's home, smashing the glass.

From the country the Duke wrote to Mrs Arbuthnot: 'They certainly intended to destroy the House, and did not care one Pin for the poor Duchess being dead in the House'.[19]

23

A Fairy Land

$\sim$

At home in Westmeath, Tom Longford was busy with his garden. Like many of his peers, Longford was caught up in the rage for new exotic plants. Clubs for gardeners were the only ones he was prepared to join. By 1830 he was a subscriber to both the Irish and English Horticultural Societies, and by 1832 a Vice-President of the Irish one. He ordered shrubs and young plants by the hundreds from Simpson's in Dublin, Miller's of Bristol, and Lees' famous Hammersmith Nursery in London. And he had always loved trees. For over twenty years, Longford had been planting oaks, beeches, larch and pine in ornamental clumps in the pleasure ground and demesne, and on the newly drained bogland. Oaks were his particular favourite. One visitor, walking around the garden in 1835, described a new 'quercetum . . . containing all the species of hardy oak which may be procured'.[1] There seemed no limits on what he might do; when Maria Edgeworth asked if he planned any more improvements, he joked 'Oh yes, I never was intended for a finished gentleman!'.[2]

His wife Georgiana had also found her *métier* in gardening. Maria Edgeworth, who had never taken to the new Lady Longford, initially turned her heart against Georgiana when she came for a visit in the autumn of 1832. Although Longford was 'quite well & Lord Longford forever! . . . the children beautiful – the place much beautified', it was not the old hospitable Pakenham Hall she had known for so long '– there's an end of that'.[3] Without doubt the change was due to the mistress of the house. 'Lady L is very civil – But there is a sharpness *& hardness* even in the beauty of her face & in her manner and voice that prevent the *probability* of my loving her'. Several hours later,

Maria rushed back to her writing table to finish her letter to Sophy with a fresh glow of enthusiasm.

> 5 o'clock. I have been out all morning – walking and driving and have much improved my opinion of Lady L by seeing all she has done – both in beautifying this place and employing the people – One should see & hear both sides of character before one pronounces judgement – Her manners do not *shew* good taste or good judgement – But all she has done prove that she has both in no common degree – I never saw in England or Ireland such beautiful gardens & shrubbery walks as she has made – In a place where there was formerly only a swamp and an osiery[*] she has made the most beautiful American garden[†] my eyes ever beheld – took advantage of a group of superb old chestnut trees, oak and ash for a background – trees which had never been noticed in that terra incognita before & now it is a fairy land – Embowered round with evergreens & even now when the rhododendron bank was not en blow & all summer plants out of bloom it was scarlet-gay with Lobelia Fulgens[‡] and double dahlias of all colours in the green grass their flower knots looking most beautiful – Pray make Mr Hamilton and Caroline describe the Italian garden & the pheasantry etc to you – all new creations since I was here – Considering the ill health Lady L has had it is quite wonderful how much she has got done.[4]

By now, Georgiana had given birth to ten healthy babies. The youngest was little Frank, born in February 1832. Longford, now approaching his fifties, had become quite the family man, doting on this tribe of children. He was a loyal and protective husband to the nervous Georgiana, refusing all invitations to travel when she was due to give birth. In fact he shone as a husband and father, proudly bringing them about with him whenever he was at home. He even saw himself as an expert on post-partum women. 'You will be glad to

---

[*] An area where willows are grown for basket-making.
[†] An 'American garden' used plants from America, primarily of the ericaceous variety.
[‡] A synonym for *Lobelia cardinalis*, a scarlet variety native to America.

see dear good merry old Lord Longford . . . called here yesterday on his way from Longford & had not a train of sons or brothers with him as is his wont', Maria reported to one of her sisters who had just had a baby: 'He asked for you with great kindness & when I told him you were getting up he said with an expressive look – But she must not be in too great a hurry to get up – there's the danger –'.[5] In fact, a real expert at childbearing, dear Louisa Pakenham, had stayed thoughtfully with her niece when Georgiana was still a novice in the matter.

Once the children grew older, there were music masters and dancing teachers and drawing lessons at Pakenham Hall, just as there had been in the days of the Captain. The elder boys were sent to boarding school in England, to a 'remarkably nice and parental school' outside London and then on to Winchester College. In the spring holidays their father brought them all to Margate or Brighton, and bought the little ones spades and toys, noting the prices down in his pocketbook.[6] He even took Edward to see old Miss Lucretia Pakenham at Bernhurst in Sussex, whose comfortable estate was the home of his own natural child Catherine Weekes. Of his official brood, none of the children were yet reported to be sickly, or troublesome. 'We sat at Table yesterday with all my 10 children', he wrote smugly to Bess one summer holiday. 'One seldom sees such a healthy happy set.'[7]

Hercules by now had a large brood of children of his own, and Maria was delighted to find them all coming to stay at Pakenham Hall. 'He and Mrs Hercules P had been afraid to leave their children on account of the danger of cholera and Lady L invited them to come all *thirteen* including governess and servants!' This further endeared Georgiana to Maria, for whom family feeling was the most vital of all. 'This', as she remarked to Sophy, 'is something like olden times.'[8]

Perhaps domestic happiness had even diminished Longford's taste for politics. He had given up the Brunswick Clubs, and by the end of 1834 felt able to boast to Bess: 'I am well satisfied that I resisted all importunities to be an Orange Man.'[9] He resigned himself to the new Whig Government and their reforms, reporting to Bess that 'We are going on here very much better than you could expect a Protestant people who are subjected to the Detestable Triumvirate of O'Connell Littleton & Duncannon.'* He was hoping that 'quiet' would continue in Westmeath, where factionalism – aside from a dreadful episode in 1831† – had not taken strong hold of the people. He was considered a fair landlord, and did his best to create employment by a continuous programme of work on his estates. Writing to Archdeacon Pakenham in early December 1834, Henry Hamilton summed up the Longford method:

> We have just returned hither after having spent 5 weeks most comfortably and happily at Pak. Hall, Black Castle and Red House. Longford seemed quite well and in excellent spirits, as usual building, un-building and altering, adding and subtracting, exemplifying in short the 4 rules of arithmetic in practice but employing 150 people, and keeping all quiet and peaceable.[10]

Even so, with a mind to any future calamity that might overcome the family, he hid a secret cache of 800 gold sovereigns in his study in Rutland Square.‡

Like his father the old Captain, Longford saw the absenteeism of many landlords as the root cause of Ireland's troubles – and England's. 'It is indeed melancholy to see the number of wealthy British subjects shutting up all their establishments in these countries & going to spend their time & money abroad.'[11] The duty of the landlord to his tenants should dictate the pattern of his life. This was the one lesson he wished to pass on to his heir, and he wrote a private letter to Georgiana to make sure this was understood.

---

* Daniel O'Connell was now leader of the powerful Irish contingent in the Commons, Littleton – Marquess Wellesley's son-in-law – was the Chief Secretary for Ireland, and Lord Duncannon was Home Office Minister.

† A brawl at the Castlepollard fair resulted in the local police firing at the crowd. Nine people were killed outright, and several more died of their injuries. The policemen were all acquitted at trial, which caused a lasting resentment locally.

‡ The money was so well-hidden that it could not be found after Longford's death, only to be discovered by a builder making repairs to the house forty years later, and recognised as Longford's hoard by the dates on the coins and the old newspaper in which they were wrapped.

I confidently rely upon your affectionate regard for my memory, that you will pay attention to my last & most earnest wishes as to my Eldest Son . . . above all, that he may never see his name enrolled among the Absentees, to whom chiefly may be traced all that is disgraceful and all that is distressing in this Island . . .

Dearest, dearest Georgiana, instil these Principles into his Heart. – This may require some painful sacrifice, or inconvenient privations but the one must be met manfully, & the other subscribed to steadily – The reward will [be] such as an honest honorable Man will appreciate. My dear Son will be respected & regarded by all instead of being despised abroad and detested at home, as they, who neglect their Country, already are.[12]

He also made a codicil to his will, in the form of a letter to his eldest son. 'Edward *never* be an Absentee', he wrote,

Perhaps in these violent times, my end may soon be near, even from the hands of my own Countrymen. Do not let that make you an Absentee. Pains are taken to delude agitate and irritate the People, and none can answer for the consequences – Farewell my dearest Boy – God Bless Protect & Direct you – Be always useful and affectionate to your dearest Mother & believe me your truly affectionate Father.[13]

Alas for Longford's hope. The 'dearest boy' was to provide a sad series of disappointments. He had been brought in person to Winchester College by his kind-hearted father, carefully chosen by Longford over what he considered the more disreputable Eton and Harrow. 'I deem the system sound, manly and useful.'[14] But however good the discipline and care of Winchester, it could not make up for the clear evidence that Edward was no scholar.

The blow fell in July 1832 when Dr Williams, the headmaster, sent his report to Longford. 'It may be better to try a more private mode of education', Williams concluded regretfully, and Longford took the hint. Edward was brought back to Ireland for the summer. Longford's affection had not diminished. Edward continued to be a 'fine lad . . . not a dandy' in his father's eyes, and Longford continued to pay his debts without demur. By the autumn of 1834, a tutor had been found for him in a quiet village in Cornwall. The Reverend Thomas Fisher was 'intelligent, active and sensible' but not a man of the world. Although banned from going shooting, the boys had soon bribed the housekeeper to get them guns. When she changed her mind, Edward knocked her to the ground. In a passion, he threw all his clothes into a wheelbarrow and tried to run away.

The wretched Fisher begged Longford to take his son back, even though he claimed he had become extremely fond of the boy. 'How much pain [this request] has given me, I cannot express.'[15]

The patient father agreed.

The following Easter holidays, Longford and his brother Hercules had rented houses next door to each other in London. A heady programme of children's entertainments ensued – Astley's circus, the zoological gardens, the Thames 'Tunnel Panoramas' – all organised by Longford in person. In early May Longford wrote to their sister Bess that he soon planned to return to Pakenham Hall. He made a note to himself about work to be done in the garden and put it carefully into his pocketbook:

> George [the gardener] to make the Track for cascade to Hermitage & from Hermitage to moat walk. Take back the levels to Hermitage, from Walk – Weeping Ash on Moat – laurels round fence from Stable yard – Moat walk – raising hollow walk near decoy – Garden pumps – gold fish – macaws my addition to Pit – childrens' garden near oak.

He never reached Ireland. His illness was so sudden that Hercules could hardly write a coherent account of it. 'I am so astounded', he wrote to Henry Hamilton, 'by the perilous state into which our dear Longford has fallen that I hardly know what to write.'[16] It seemed that all the time Longford was bringing the boys on expeditions he 'unconsciously stood on the verge of the Grave'.[17]

Three weeks before Longford had complained to his brother of some boils on his neck, and his physician had lanced them. But it soon became clear that the boils were only an outward sign of a serious disease, diagnosed as diabetes, and that it was rapidly killing the patient. By 22 May Hercules reported that Longford could hardly stand, speak or swallow and his mind was wandering. The wound in his neck had become gangrenous, and, dosed with opium, he fell into a coma. On the 23rd the appalled Hercules wrote his final report to Bess: 'All functions of life, breathing excepted, had ceased . . . I called Poor Lady L, & soon proposed to her to join in the Prayers for the Dying . . . She cried out in utmost despair "Oh dear Colonel Pakenham is it come to this!", and then joined in with the utmost fervour.'[18] Longford died in the early hours of the morning.

Longford's body was sent over to Ireland in a lead coffin. His two elder sons, Edward and William, led the procession to the family mausoleum at Killucan. A great throng of tenants had gathered to pay their final respects – and to feast at the local inn after the burial. As for Maria Edgeworth, she was genuinely affected.

Oh my dear Fanny we have heard of Lord Longford's death – and very *very* sad we are for the loss of that excellent man. Little did I think when but a few weeks ago he was sitting in the library beside Aunt Mary – she so ill – he to all appearance in such jocund health, little did I think that she would outlive him, that he would be gone so soon!!! So very soon – that I then received his last cordial shake of the hand, his last affectionate Pakenham look . . .

Naturally, Maria's thoughts flew to Georgiana: 'How shocked she must be – ten children – and her eldest only 17 . . . She is a woman of strong mind & strong sense of duty – God help her!'[19]

Lady Longford could not travel to Ireland. In a state of near-paralysis, she refused to leave her room. As Hercules put it, 'being thrown from a Round of the highest social amusements into Deep unlooked for Mourning'[20] had been like a physical blow. It seemed nothing could console her, not even religion. 'To me all happiness in this world is for ever closed,' she wrote to Henry Pakenham, 'a premature old age has blighted all my happy anticipations . . . Whilst he was with me I thought it impossible to love him more, but since he went I am sensible that I never valued him half enough & I cannot but think that it is a judgement upon me . . . a life of repentance & tears is all that is left to me!'[21]

For the good Colonel, the work of securing the future of Long-ford's estate was more than enough to keep him busy. There were immediate decisions to be made, debts to be paid, the complications and secret codicils of his brother's will. How would Georgiana react when she discovered the several interesting annuities that were being paid out to Longford's natural children? What would become of Pakenham Hall if she could not bear to return to it? Above all, he had to find a way to steer Edward through the pitfalls that his inheritance brought with it. He had been left an arduous task, but he put his shoulder to the wheel.

Epilogue

On 6 June 1835, a neighbour of the Longfords wrote home from abroad.

> I can hardly tell you with what pain & grief I saw in this day's newspaper the death of poor Lord Longford . . . How inscrutable are the ways of God – this man with a large family in the full sphere of usefulness both Publick & Private is taken off and others . . . left . . . He has left a blank in the country, not easily to be filled up. I shall be most anxious to hear how poor Lady L bears up & whether she will give up the country.[1]

What happened to the old house and garden which Tom and Georgiana had worked so hard to improve? A report on the park by a Mr W. Vicars Griffith in 1837 shows how quickly a decline set in there. Longford's newly planted oak trees were either dead or dying, with 'only two or three' still surviving, the labels of the dead trees hanging sadly on their skeletons. The flower garden had been attacked by rabbits, the vines in the greenhouses were 'very unhealthy' and, most miserably of all, the American Garden had fallen into a decay. 'The rose beds in this garden are full of remarkably sickly plants – covered with moss', Griffith noted with disapproval.[2] Nobody knew if the young heir would return to the estate.

For Tom Longford's four siblings, long lives still lay ahead. Hercules, with his pretty Emily and nine children, remained close to the great Duke and was honoured for his military achievements with a KCB and the position of Governor of Portsmouth. Two scholarships at

Queen's University survive in his and Emily's names, set up in their memories by their son Arthur in 1876. In his lifetime, General Hercules remained the 'pattern for military heroics' that Maria Edgeworth had long ago thought him, so much so that five of his six sons went into the Army. He died suddenly at home on 7 March 1850, where the little church he had built on the shore of Lough Neagh still carries a plaque to his memory. A few months after Hercules' death, on 6 August, the eighty-one-year-old Duke of Wellington gave two of Hercules' daughters away at their double wedding. Luckily Hercules did not live to see three of his military sons die in service. One, on his way out to the Crimea, wrote a touching letter describing the strong tradition in which the boys had been raised: 'the thought of our Father, and all he saw & went through and how anxiously & often we had looked at the medals on his coat and then I think perhaps I too may earn the same'.[3] Langford Lodge was demolished in the twentieth century, after a brief period as an RAF base during the Second World War.

Hercules was followed to the grave a year later by his eldest sister Bess Stewart, to whose careful squirrelling of all family letters so much of what we know is owed. Their younger sister, cheerful Caroline Hamilton, remained plump and childless, and died a much loved aunt in 1854, leaving her money to her numerous nephews.

Henry Pakenham, the youngest of the 'Napoleonic' generation, survived them all. Henry remained in the Church, becoming 'Double Dean' of the two great Dublin cathedrals, St Patrick's and Christ Church. He would have liked to have risen higher, and once wrote to his brother-in-law, the Duke, to suggest it. 'One word from you, Arthur, and I could be a Bishop.' The Duke is said to have replied with his usual brevity: 'Not one word, Henry, not one.' Today Henry's stone face can be seen on the right of the doorway of St Patrick's Cathedral. It was he who persuaded his friend the millionaire philanthropist Sir Benjamin Lee Guinness to pay for its restoration, which began in 1860. He died at the age of seventy-six on Christmas Day, 1863.

Old Admiral Pakenham of Coolure lived just a year after his nephew

Tom Longford. Maria Edgeworth gives a nice description of his twinkling old age, when she went to visit him in 1834. He was standing on the steps of Coolure in an embroidered skullcap 'which was not *very* ugly but looked as if it had been made by one of his daughters of bits of old carpet'. He hugged Maria to his breast and immediately began to gossip. His mind was 'quite alive' the whole time – 'now don't Admiral go to your old scandal',[4] Maria admonished him. Another story describes how in old age he would arrange for mock naval battles to take place on the lake, which he would watch from the top floor through his telescope. His descendants are so numerous it is impossible to count them.

Georgiana, who had now become the Dowager Countess, lived until 1880. Always a nervous character, she became briefly addicted to morphine in the months following her husband's death – 'I sometimes sit and fancy his face of love is still looking at me', she wrote tearfully to Bess – but the duty of chaperoning three daughters soon gave her a reason to stir herself. She remained, as Longford had first boasted, 'prudent', living scrupulously within her widow's pension on the south coast of England. Occasionally, with her children in tow, she visited her neighbour, the wealthy spinster Miss Lucretia Pakenham of Bernhurst, near Hastings, in the hope that Miss Lucretia's property might be left to one of her little ones. Lucretia was said to be very much affected by the sight of all the poor bereaved children. No mention of Lucretia's ward, Catherine Weekes, ever appears in Georgiana's letters. Yet Catherine, the natural daughter of the late Lord Longford, was half-sister to Georgiana's own ten children, and must have thought of them with interest. When she eventually inherited Bernhurst herself, she left it in her will to Lord Longford's youngest child.

Maria Edgeworth gives us one more passing glimpse of Georgiana, which shows she had softened in her view of her old neighbour. One spring, they both happened to be in London at the same time. Maria had left the Dowager her card.

> . . . knock knock – double trouble – Lady Longford! – and here she came in quite warm in her manner and looking all alive – I never saw

Lady L so agreeable and ready to talk . . . I did ask her if there were any hopes of seeing her again at P Hall – 'Oh yes – I hope so – I do not know why people have all settled for me that I am not to go back to Ireland . . .'[5]

But in fact Georgiana never returned there to live.

Maria herself became more conservative in her politics as she grew older, showing a strong dislike for the 'Ultra-Reform Liberalists', who she was convinced would have let in a 'ragamuffin democracy'.[6] She devoted herself to her tenants at Edgeworthstown, and saved the estate that her spendthrift brother Lovell had nearly ruined. Although she has never achieved the fame of her near-contemporary and admirer, Jane Austen, her novels continued to be read widely in the nineteenth century. She died in 1849, having done much in her last years to help the cause of famine relief. In 2006 a bronze statue of her was erected in Edgeworthstown, where her old home is now a convent.

As for Tom Longford's son and heir, Edward did his best to be the good landlord and improver that his father would have wished. His mother was determined that he should be a success: 'I do not think there is the least chance of my dear Edward being an absentee, but he certainly never shall if I can prevent it!' she wrote to her brother-in-law. Perhaps Georgiana adored him a little blindly, writing to Bess that she hoped to see 'dear Longford revived in him'. Yet sadly Edward seemed to have inherited his father's less admirable qualities.

A few months after he became Lord Longford, he was found to have struck up an 'unsuitable' friendship with the gamekeeper at Pakenham Hall, who was selling him spirits from an illegal lakeside distillery. And Edward was already sowing his wild oats, a concerned uncle Hercules wrote to his fellow trustee: 'I have already had some talk with him respecting women, we must not expect him to be much more controlled than others, but I think he will follow my Father's advice as to prudence at *Home*.'[7] Poor Hercules always hoped for the best.

And Edward wasn't bad at heart. He was generous to his siblings, and conscientious to the wishes of his father on the delicate subject of the latter's illegitimate children, even increasing their annuities. When Catherine Chapman, his father's last illegitimate daughter who had been conceived in 1814, appealed to his agent from a debtor's prison, he did his best to help. Even with no wife or children to keep him company he loved Pakenham Hall and was never a true 'absentee', dividing his bachelor life between London and Westmeath. And his doting mother remained as attached as ever to him. 'Nothing can exceed Edward's delight in Pakenham Hall', Georgiana wrote proudly to Bess in 1844, 'and no wonder certainly for it remains always in my recollection as the beau ideal of all earthly enjoyment! He amuses me much talking over his household arrangements just like a person of 50!'[8] In fact, when the landscape designer James Fraser came to publish his *Guide Through Ireland* in 1838, it appeared that the decline of the estate had been arrested: 'The demesne . . . is kept in the highest order . . . The comfortable cottages . . . scattered along the public roads, will strike the traveller, and evince the kindness and liberality shown by this noble family to all whom they employ.'[9]

It was probably Edward's other life in London that led to his early and sordid death in Limmer's Hotel in Oxford Street. It is clear from several family hints that at some stage he 'got the venereal', and probably he died of syphilis – or the treatment for it. After his death, Edward's doctor sent his executors a bill for £729, with a suggestion that it would be wise to pay if the new Lord Longford wanted to avoid embarrassment.

But Edward's brother, William Lygon, who inherited the title, was a clever, practical soldier who rose to become a General. He sorted out the old house at Pakenham Hall and the estates in a manner which would have pleased his father and grandfather. His main legacy was drains, under the fields and all through the house – if you look at the 1860 plans there are no less than sixteen lavatories, strategically placed and ingeniously fed from lead rainwater tanks in the roof. William's son in turn became a Brigadier and was killed in the First World War, leading his men up a slope at Gallipoli towards the Turkish guns. ('Don't keep ducking, Fred,' were his last recorded words to a fellow officer, 'it upsets the men, and it doesn't do any good.') Did he remember his great-uncle Ned heading the charge at Salamanca, or dying in a forlorn hope at New Orleans? After that, any military genes seem to have gone into retreat. Edward, the 6th Earl, displayed a different brand of bravery by refusing to join the corps at Eton, which no one apparently had ever done before. And he infuriated his fellow Anglo-Irish by refusing to stand for 'God Save the King' at the Dublin Horse Show and becoming an ardent supporter of the new Irish State. Edward's brother Frank, the 7th Earl,* also showed a new kind of courage in his dogged defence of the rights of prisoners over many years.

What other genes can I trace from that distant generation of brothers and sisters born to the mother of heroes? A love of books certainly: the old house groans with them, the accumulated reading matter of over 250 years; recent generations of Pakenhams have even taken to writing them themselves. A love of trees and plants: there are groves of new oaks and beeches sheltering the house, and Georgiana and Tom's garden, rescued from laurels and brambles, is now newly planted and replenished. Maybe also a kind of restless energy and desire to be at the forefront of things. Not to sit quietly at home. And maybe the stubborn streak of eccentricity which Kitty showed as she sat, white-haired and in unfashionable white muslin, in the grand drawing rooms of London, believing passionately against all evidence that she understood her famous husband better than anyone.

* My grandfather, who died in 2001.

SELECT BIBLIOGRAPHY

All volumes are published in London or Dublin, unless otherwise stated. Editions are as used.

Airlie, Mabell, Countess of, *In Whig Society* (1921)
Airlie, Mabell, Countess of, *Lady Palmerston & Her Times* (2 Vols, 1922)
Anglesey, Marquess of, *One-Leg: The Life and Letters of Henry William Paget, 1st Marquess of Anglesey* (1961)
Annual Register
Arbuthnot, Harriet, *The Journal of Mrs Arbuthnot*, ed. by Francis Bamford and the Duke of Wellington (2 Vols, 1950)
Arbuthnot, Mrs Stewart-Mackenzie, *Memories of the Arbuthnots of Kincardine-shire & Aberdeenshire* (1920)
Aspinall, A, (ed.), *The Correspondence of Charles Arbuthnot*, Camden 3rd Series LXV (1941)

Bagot, J., *George Canning and His Friends* (2 Vols, 1909)
Barrington, Jonah, *Historic Memoirs of Ireland* (1835)
Barrington, Jonah, *Historic Memoirs and Secret Anecdotes of the Legislative Union* (1835)
Barrington, Jonah, *Rise and Fall of the Irish Nation* (1833)
Bartlett, Thomas and Jeffery, Keith (eds), *A Military History of Ireland* (Cambridge, 1996)
Bartlett, Thomas; Dickson, David; Keogh, Dáire; Whelan, Kevin (eds), *1798: A Bicentenary Perspective* (2003)
Beckett, J.C., *The Making of Modern Ireland* (1966)
Bence-Jones, Mark, *Life in the Irish Country House* (1996)
Berry, Miss, *Extracts of the Journals and Correspondence of Miss Berry, 1783–1852* ed. by Lady Theresa Lewis (3 Vols, 1865)

Bessborough, Earl of, and Aspinall, A. (eds), *Lady Bessborough and Her Family Circle* (1940)

Blake, Mrs Warrenne, *An Irish Beauty of the Regency: Journals of Hon. Mrs Calvert 1789–1822* (1911)

Boase, F., *Modern English Biography* (6 Vols, 1965)

Bond, R. Warwick (ed.), *The Marlay Letters* (1937)

Boylan, Lena, *Castletown and its Owners* (1978)

Broughton, Lord (J.C. Hobhouse), *Recollections of a Long Life* (4 Vols, 1911)

Burghclere, Lady, *A Great Man's Friendship: Letters of the Duke of Wellington to Mary, Marchioness of Salisbury, 1850–1852*, ed. by Lady Burghclere (1927)

Burke's *Peerage & Baronetage* (106th ed., 1999)

Butler, H.J. and Butler, H.E. (eds), *The Black Book of Edgeworthstown and Other Edgeworth Memories 1585–1817* (1927)

Butler, Iris, *The Eldest Brother: The Marquess Wellesley, the Duke of Wellington's Eldest Brother* (1973)

Butler, Marilyn, *Maria Edgeworth: A Literary Biography* (1972)

Butler, Marilyn, Gen. Editor of The Pickering Masters, *The Works of Maria Edgeworth* (12 Vols, 1999 and 2003)

Campbell, Gerald, *Edward and Pamela Fitzgerald* (1904)

Carver, Lord, 'Wellington and his Brothers', 1st Wellington Lecture (University of Southampton, 1989)

Casey, Christine and Rowan, Alistair, *The Buildings of Ireland: North Leinster* (1993)

Castlereagh, Robert Stewart, Viscount, *Memories and Correspondence of Viscount Castlereagh, Second Marquess of Londonderry*, ed. by his brother, Charles Vane, Marquess of Londonderry (12 Vols, 1848–53)

Clark, Isabel C., *Maria Edgeworth: Her Family & Friends* (1949)

Clarke, Desmond, *The Ingenious Mr Edgeworth* (1965)

Codrington, Sir Edward, *Memoir of the Life of Admiral Codrigton*, ed. by Lady Bourchier (2 Vols, 1873)

Cole, J.W., *Memoirs of British Generals Distinguished During the Peninsular War* (2 Vols, 1856)

Cole, M.L. and Gwynn, Stephen (eds), *Memoirs of Sir Lowry Cole* (1934)

Connell, B., *Portrait of a Whig Peer* (1957)

Cornwallis, Charles, *Correspondence of 1st Marquis Cornwallis*, ed. by Charles Ross (3 Vols, 1859)

Creevey, Thomas, *The Creevey Papers*, ed. by Sir H. Maxwell (2 Vols, 1904)

Croker, John Wilson, *The Croker Papers*, ed. by Louis J. Jennings (3 Vols, 1884)

Cullen, Seamus and Geissel, Hermann (eds), *Fugitive Warfare: 1798 in North Kildare* (Kildare, 1998)

DeNora, Tia, *Beethoven and the Construction of Genius: Musical Politics in Vienna, 1792–1803* (California, 1995)

Dickson, D., *The Gorgeous Mask, Dublin 1700–1850* (1987)

Dillon, Sir W.H., 'A Narrative of My Professional Adventures, 1790–1839', ed. by Michael A. Lewis, *Navy Records Society*, Vol. 93 (1953)

Duffy, Michael and Morriss, Roger (eds), *The Glorious First of June 1794* (Exeter, 2001)

Edgeworth, Frances Anne, *A memoir of Maria Edgeworth, with selections from her letters, by . . . Mrs Edgeworth; edited by her children* (3 Vols, 1867)

Edgeworth, Maria, *Maria Edgeworth: Letters from England*, ed. by Christina Colvin (Oxford, 1971)

Edgeworth, Richard Lovell and Maria, *Memories of Richard Lovell Edgeworth* (2 Vols, 1820)

Esdaile, Charles, *The Peninsular War* (2003)

Faulkner's Dublin Journal (various)

Fortescue (Dropmore) papers, Vol. IV, HMC (1905)

Fortescue, Sir John, *Correspondence of King George the Third from 1760 to December 1783* (6 Vols, 1927–8)

Foster, Roy, *Modern Ireland* (1989)

Fraser, Flora, *The Unruly Queen: The Life of Queen Caroline* (1996)

Fraser, James, *Guide Through Ireland* (1838)

Fraser, Rebecca, *A People's History of Britain* (2003)

Gash, Norman, *Mr Secretary Peel* (1961)

Gash, Norman, *Wellington Anecdotes* (1992)

Gash, Norman (ed.), *Wellington: Studies in the Military and Political Career of the First Duke of Wellington* (Manchester, 1990)

Geoghegan, Patrick M., '"An Act of Power & Corruption?" The Union Debate', *History Ireland 2000*

Geoghegan, P.M., *The Irish Act of Union* (1999)

Girouard, Mark, 'Modernising an Irish Country House', in *Country Life*, 23 December 1971

Gleig, G.R., *A Narrative of the Campaigns of the British Army at Washington and New Orleans* (1821)

Gleig, G.R., *Personal Reminiscences of the 1ˢᵗ Duke of Wellington* (1904)

Granville, Castalia, Countess of (ed.), *Lord Granville Leveson Gower, 1ˢᵗ Earl of Granville, Private Correspondence* (2 Vols, 1916)

Grattan, William, *Adventures with the Connaught Rangers 1809–1814*, ed. by Charles Oman (2003)

Greville, Charles, *The Greville Memoirs 1817–1837*, ed. by H. Reeve (3 Vols, 1875)

Gronow, *The Reminiscences and Recollections of Captain Gronow*, ed. by John Raymond (1964)

Hamilton, George, *A History of the House of Hamilton* (1933)

Hamilton, John, *Sixty Years' Experience as an Irish Landlord* (1894)

Hare, Augustus, *Life & Letters of Maria Edgeworth* (2 Vols, 1894)

Hathaway, E., (ed.), *A Dorset Rifleman: The Recollections of Rifleman Harris* (Swanage, 1995)

Hewitt, Esther (ed.)(PRONI), *Lord Shannon's Letters to his Son* (N. Ireland, 1982)

Hibbert, Christopher, *Wellington: A Personal History* (1997)

Hill, Constance, *Maria Edgeworth & Her Circle in the Days of Buonaparte & Bourbon* (1910)

Holland, E.V.F., *Elizabeth, Lady Holland, to her son, 1821–1845*, ed. by Giles Stephen Holland Fox-Strangways, 6ᵗʰ Earl of Ilchester (1946)

Holland, Elizabeth Vassall, *Lady Holland's Journal*, ed. by the Earl of Ilchester (2 Vols, 1908)

Holmes, Richard, *Redcoat: The British in the Age of Horse and Musket* (2001)

Hoppen, K.T., *Elections, Politics and Society in Ireland 1832–85* (Oxford, 1984)

Hunt, W. (ed.), Sir John Blaquiere, *The Irish Parliament 1775* (1908)

Hurst, Michael, *Maria Edgeworth and the Public Scene* (1969)

Hyde, H., Montgomery, *The Rise of Castlereagh* (1933)

Hyde, H., Montgomery, *The Strange Death of Lord Castlereagh* (1959)

Ilchester, Countess and Stavordale, Lord, *The Life and Letters of Lady Sarah Lennox, 1745–1826* (2 Vols, 1901)

Ilchester, Lord (ed.), *Journal of the Hon. Henry Fox, 4ᵗʰ and last Lord Holland, 1818–1830* (1923)

Irish Sword – The Journal of the Military History Society of Ireland (various)

James, W.M., *The British Navy in Adversity* (1926)

Jennings, Louis J. (ed.), *The Correspondence & Diaries of John Wilson Croker* (3 Vols, 1884)

Johnston, E.M., *Great Britain and Ireland, 1760–1800* (Edinburgh, 1963)

Johnston-Liik, E.M., *History of the Irish Parliament 1692–1800* (6 Vols, Belfast, 2002)

Jupp, Peter, *British and Irish Elections 1784–1831* (1993)

Kelly, James, *Prelude to Union* (Cork, 1992)

Kincaid, John, *Adventures in the Rifle Brigade* (1847)

Latocnaye, Chevalier de, *A Frenchman's Walk Through Ireland 1796–7*, trans. by John Stevenson (Belfast, 1917)

Layard, George Somes (ed.), *Sir Thomas Lawrence's Letter-Bag* (1906)

Lecky, W.E.H., *A History of Ireland in the Eighteenth Century* (1972)

Leinster, Emilia Mary Lennox Fitzgerald, Duchess, *Correspondence of Emily, Duchess of Leinster 1731–1814*, ed. by Brian Fizgerald (3 Vols, 1949–57)

Lennox, Lord William, *Three Years with the Duke, or Wellington in Private Life*, by an ex-aide-de-camp (1853)

Londonderry, Edith Marchioness, *Frances Anne: The Life and Times of Frances Anne, Marchioness of Londonderry, and Her Husband, Charles, Third Marquess of Londonderry* (1958)

Londonderry, Marquess of, *Story of the Peninsular War* (1848)

Longford, Elizabeth, *Wellington: Pillar of State* (1972)

Longford, Elizabeth, *Wellington: The Years of the Sword* (1969)

Loudon, J.C., *The Gardener's Magazine*, Vol. XI, 1835

Lyons, J.C., *Grand Juries of Westmeath* (Ledestown, 1853)

Machin, G.I.T., 'The No-Popery Movement in Britain, 1828–1829', *The Historical Journal*, VI, 2 (1963), pp. 193–211

Macintyre, Angus, *The Liberator: Daniel O'Connell and the Irish Party 1830–47* (1965)

Mackintosh, Sir James, *Memoirs of the Life of Sir James Mackintosh*, ed. by his son (2 Vols, 1835–6)

Malcomson, A.P.W., 'The Irish Peerage and the Act of Union 1800–1971', in *Transactions of the Royal Historical Society, 2000*, 6th Series, Vol. X

Malcomson, A.P.W., *The Pursuit of the Heiress* (Belfast, 2006)

Marcus, G.J., *A Naval History of England* (1961)

Mavor, E., *Life with the Ladies of Llangollen* (1984)

Maxwell, Constantia, *Country & Town in Ireland Under the Georges* (1940)

Maxwell, Constantia, *Dublin Under the Georges* (1936)

Maxwell, Sir H.E., *The Life of Wellington* (2 Vols, 1899)

Maxwell, W.H., *History of the Irish Rebellion in 1798* (1845)

Mayne, E.C., *The Life and Letters of Anne Isabella, Lady Noel Byron* (1929)

McDowell, R.B. (ed.), *Historical Essays (1938–2001)* (2003)

McLoughlin, M., *The Last Speech and Dying Words of Martin McLoughlin* (pamphlet, 1798)

Moody, T.W and Martin, F.X. (eds), *The Course of Irish History* (Cork, 1967)

Moore, Sir John, *Diary of Sir John Moore*, ed. by Sir J.F. Maurice (2 Vols, 1904)

Moore, Thomas, *Memories of Lord Edward Fitzgerald* with a preface and many supplementary particulars by Martin MacDermott (1897)

Morley, S., *Memories of a Sergeant of the Fifth Regiment of Foot* (Cambridge, 1999)

Napier, General Sir Charles, *Life and Opinions of Sir Charles Napier* by General Sir William Napier (1857)

Napier, General Sir Charles, *Lights and Shades of Military Life* (2 Vols, 1846)

Napier, General Sir George, *Passages in the Early Military Life of General Sir George T. Napier*, ed. by his son, W.C.E. Napier (1884)

Napier, General Sir William, *History of the War in the Peninsula* (6 Vols, 1828–40)

Napier, General Sir William, *Life and Letters of Sir William Napier*, ed. by H.A. Bruce (2 Vols, 1864)

Napier, Priscilla, *The Sword Dance: Lady Sarah Lennox and the Napiers* (1971)

Naval Chronicle 1799–1818

Nugent, Lady Maria, *A Journal of a Voyage to, and residence in, the Island of Jamaica, from 1801 to 1805, and of subsequent events in England from 1805 to 1811* (2 Vols, 1839)

O'Conlain, Micheál, *The Castlepollard Notes* (Westmeath Archaeological and Historical Society, 1996)

O'Dwyer, F., *Lost Dublin* (1981)

O'Ferrall, Fergus, *Catholic Emancipation* (1985)

Paget, Julian, *Wellington's Peninsular War* (1990)

Pakenham Letters, ed. by Thomas Pakenham, 5th Earl of Longford (1914)

Pakenham, Thomas, *The Year of Liberty* (1969)

Pakenham, Valerie, *The Big House in Ireland* (2000)

Palmerston, Lady, *Lady Palmerston & Her Times*, ed. by Mabell Countess of Airlie (2 Vols, 1922)

Peel, Robert, *The Private Letters of Sir Robert Peel*, ed. by George Peel (1920)

Pickles, Tim, *New Orleans 1815: Andrew Jackson Crushes the British* (1997)

Picton, Sir Thomas, *The Life of Sir Thomas Picton*, ed. by H.B. Robinson (2 Vols, 1835)

PRONI, Eighteenth-century Irish Official Papers in Great Britain compiled by A.P.W. Malcomson (Belfast, 1990)

Ralfe, James, *Naval Biography of Great Britain* (4 Vols, 1828)

Reilly, Robin, *The British at the Gates: The New Orleans Campaign in the War of 1812* (New York, 1974)

Reynolds, James A., *The Catholic Emancipation Crisis in Ireland* (1954)

Ritchie, C.I.A., 'The Louisiana Campaign', *The Louisiana Quarterly*, Vol. XLIV (Jan–April 1961)

Roberts, Andrew, *Napoleon and Wellington* (2001)

Robins, Joseph, *Champagne and Silver Buckles: The Viceregal Court at Dublin Castle 1700–1922* (2001)

Rodger, N.A.M., *The Wooden World* (1988)

Romilly, S.H. (ed.), *Romilly–Edgeworth Letters 1813–1818* (1936)

Ryan, G., *Our Heroes* (1855)

Shelley, Frances, Lady, *Diary of Frances, Lady Shelley*, ed. by Richard Edgecumbe (2 Vols, 1912–13)

Smith, Harry, *Autobiography of Lt-Gen. Sir Harry Smith*, ed. by G.C. Moore Smith (2 Vols, 1902)

Staël, Madame de, *The unpublished correspondence of Madame de Staël and the Duke of Wellington*, ed. by Victor de Pange, trans. by Harold Kurtz (1965)

Stanhope, Philip Henry, 5th Earl, *Notes of Conversations with the Duke of Wellington, 1831–1851* (1889)

Stanley, Maria Josepha, *The Early Married Life of Maria Josepha Lady Stanley*, ed. by J.H. Adeane (1899)

Sudley, Lord (ed.), *The Lieven–Palmerston Correspondence, 1828–56* (1943)

Tillyard, Stella, *Aristocrats: Caroline, Emily, Louisa and Sarah Lennox 1740–1832* (1994)

Tillyard, Stella, *Citizen Lord, the Life of Edward Fitzgerald* (1997)

Trench, Melesina, *The Remains of the late Mrs Richard Trench*, ed. by her son, the Dean of Westminster (1862)

Wakefield, Edward, *An Account of Ireland, Statistical and Political* (2 Vols, 1812)

Walker's Hibernian Magazine (1772–1812)

Webster, Sir Charles (ed.), 'Some Letters of the Duke of Wellington to his brother William Wellesley-Pole', *Camden Miscellany* Vol. XIII, 3rd Series, Camden Series Vol. 79 (1948)

Wellesley, Muriel, *The Man Wellington Through the Eyes of Those Who Knew Him* (1937)

Wellesley, Muriel, *Wellington in Civil Life* (1939)

Wellington, *The Dispatches of Field Marshal the Duke of Wellington, KG, during his various campaigns . . . from 1799 to 1818*, ed. by J. Gurwood (13 Vols, new edition, 1837–9)

Wellington, *Despatches, Correspondence & Memoranda of Arthur Duke of Wellington (New Series) 1818–1832*, ed. by A.R. Wellesley, 2nd Duke of Wellington (8 Vols, 1867–80)

Wellington, *Supplementary Despatches and Memoranda of Field Marshal Arthur Duke of Wellington, KG*, ed. by A.R. Wellesley, 2nd Duke of Wellington (15 Vols, 1858–72)

Wellington, *A Selection from the Private Correspondence of the First Duke of Wellington*, ed. by G. Wellesley, 7th Duke of Wellington (Roxburghe Club, 1952)

Wellington, *Wellington & His Friends: Letters of the 1st Duke of Wellington to Rt Hon Charles and Mrs Arbuthnot, etc.*, ed. by G. Wellesley, 7th Duke of Wellington (1965)

Wilson, Ian, *Donegal Shipwrecks* (Coleraine, 1998)

Woods, James, *Annals of Westmeath, Ancient and Modern* (1907)

Woolgar, C.M., 'Wellington's *Dispatches* and their Editor, Colonel Gurwood' (University of Southampton, Wellington Exhibition)

Woolgar, C.M. (ed.), *Wellington Studies II* (University of Southampton, 1999)

Young, Arthur, *A Tour in Ireland, with general observations on the present state of that kingdom . . . 1776, 1777, 1778* (2 Vols, 1780)

NOTES

The following abbreviations are used:

BL. Add. MSS – British Library Additional Manuscripts
BOD – Bodleian Library, Oxford
HMC – Historical Manuscripts Commission
JA – Journal of Mrs Arbuthnot
LSA – Lucinda Stewart Archive
NAI – National Archives of Ireland
NLI – National Library of Ireland
NLW – National Library of Wales
LONGFORD – Longford MSS at Tullynally, Castlepollard, Ireland
PRONI – Public Record Office of Northern Ireland
TCD – Trinity College Dublin
WMSS – Wellington Manuscripts (Stratfield Saye Preservation Trust)
WD – Wellington: *Dispatches* (ed. by J. Gurwood)
WDNS – Wellington: *Despatches, Correspondence & Memoranda (New Series)*
WSD – Wellington: *Supplementary Despatches* (ed. by A.R. Wellesley)
WP – Wellington Papers at Southampton University

Where no source is given, the reader can assume the quotation is from Longford MSS.

PROLOGUE

1 Lord Longford's Naval Journal.
2 Longford to Lord Mulgrave, 6 June 1777. Private collection.
3 Longford to Lord Mulgrave, 7 December 1776. Private collection.
4 Sir John Blaquiere in *The Irish Parliament 1775*, ed. W. Hunt, p. 46.

5 Journal of Henry Temple, 1st Viscount Palmerston, 1788. *Portrait of a Whig Peer* by Brian Connell, p. 365.

6 *Memoirs of Richard Lovell Edgeworth*, Vol. I, p. 71.

7 Lord Longford's Naval Journal, 17 June 1778.

8 Lady Louisa Conolly to Emily Duchess of Leinster, 14 July 1778, from Castletown. *Correspondence of Emily, Duchess of Leinster*, ed. Brian Fitzgerald, Vol. III, p. 303.

9 Lady Louisa Conolly to Lady Sarah Bunbury, her youngest sister, 12 September 1779. PRONI MIC 238/Reel I, extracts from Bunbury Letter Books, Suffolk Record Office, Bury.

10 *Naval Biography of Great Britain* by James Ralfe, Vol. II, p. 260.

11 Longford to William Cornwallis, 3 March 1782. HMC MSS in various collections Vol. VI (1909), p. 328.

12 Edward Michael had appealed to King George III four years before with the request that 'Lady Longford his mother may be created Countess of Longford whenever a Promotion takes place in the Irish Peerage, with limitation to his Brother in case of failure of issue Male by himself', 26 February 1781. *Correspondence of King George The Third*, ed. Sir John Fortescue, Vol. V, no. 3272, p. 200.

13 Mrs Greville, a cousin of the Pakenhams, to Emily Leinster, 31 August 1782. NLI MS 631, fol. 36.

14 Journal of Sophia Fitzgerald, NLI MS 35,012(1).

15 Sarah Napier to Susan O'Brien, undated 1789. BL Add. MS 51354, fol. 795.

16 The Royal Classic School. Young describes it in his *Tour of Ireland* as a 'building admirably adapted for its purposes . . . a better contrived [building] is no where to be seen. Schoolroom 56 x 28ft, dining room & dormitory "spacious and well-ventilated", room for 100 borders'. Vol. II, p. 159.

17 A memoir in the Armagh County Museum describes how Longford tied his fag's ankles to his wrists and pulled him bumpily down the stairs. He adds, however, that Longford would reward him with plum cake for this trial, and 'allowed no one to molest me but himself'. Blacker MSS Vol. I, p. 177.

18 Madame Blondel stayed with the family for several years, and was treated with great respect. The 'necessarys' for her rooms and the children's when she was installed came to an extravagant £19 12 shillings and 3 pence (account book entry, 29 September 1779).

19 Edgeworth papers, NLI Edgeworth MS 23, 505.

20 E.g. 1784, 'Miss P. ordering copy of Madame de Genlis *Les Veilles du Chateau*'. LONGFORD.

21 Published in 1782.

22 *A Frenchman's Walk Through Ireland 1796–7* by de Latocnaye, trans. John Stevenson, p. 24.

23 Note in Eleanor Butler's journal, 27 January 1788, when Wesley visited her at Llangollen. *Life with the Ladies of Llangollen* by E. Mavor, p. 27.

24 Quoted in *The Eldest Brother* by Iris Butler, p. 10.

CHAPTER ONE

1 Lady Longford to Mrs Elizabeth Stewart, PRONI Stewart of Tyrcallen Papers, D/3319/13/1.

2 James Stewart to Henry Stewart, undated. LSA.

3 Longford letters to Bess Stewart from Europe, December 1793–November 1795. PRONI D/3319/4.

4 Information from subscription list published in *Beethoven and the Construction of Genius* by Tia DeNora.

5 2nd Earl Longford to Archdeacon Henry Pakenham, 7 May 1835. LONGFORD.

6 Lady Sarah Napier to Duchess of Leinster, 8 January 1794. *Correspondence of Emily, Duchess of Leinster*, ed. Brian Fitzgerald, Vol. II, p. 341.

7 Lady Sarah Napier to Duchess of Leinster, 6 April 1794. Ibid., p. 350.

8 Duchess of Leinster to Lady Sarah Napier, 29 March 1794. NLI MS 13022 (Vol. IV of Brian Fitzgerald typescript of Leinster correspondence).

9 From 'Proceedings of His Majesty's Ship Invincible from 28th May to 1st of June inclusive'. BL Add. MSS 23207, fol. 81.

10 Quoted in 'A Narrative of My Professional Adventures', Vol. I, by Sir William Henry Dillon, *Navy Records Society* (1953), p. 137.

11 Lady Sarah Napier to Susan O'Brien, 6 January 1793. *The Life and Letters of Lady Sarah Lennox*, ed. the Countess of Ilchester and Lord Stavordale, Vol. II, p. 88.

CHAPTER TWO

1 6 January 1797. NLI MS 38, 920/2.

2 George John Spencer to 2nd Earl Camden, 11 February 1797. Centre for Kentish Studies, Pratt MSS U840 C126/4.

3 Louisa Pakenham to Sophia Fitzgerald, 20 March 1798. Lennox/Fitzgerald/Campbell papers, NLI MS 35, 004 (18).

4 14 March 1798. Lady Sarah Napier's journal, *Memoirs of Lord Edward Fitzgerald* by Thomas Moore, p. 258.

5 The daughter of a previous Lord Lieutenant of Ireland, John Hobart, 2nd Earl Buckinghamshire.

6 Loiusa Pakenham to Sophia Fitzgerald, 27 May 1798. Lennox/Fitzgerald/Campbell papers, NLI MS 35, 004 (18).

7 3rd Lady Holland wrote in her journal, 23 May 1798. Quoted in *The Life and Letters of Lady Sarah Lennox*, ed. the Countess of Ilchester and Lord Stavordale, Vol. II, p. 299.

8 28 May 1798, T. Wade to Revd Thomas Prior, Trinity, Dublin. TCD MS 9308/596.

9 This figure has been debated. Thomas Pakenham's *Year of Liberty* cites the above, whilst *A Military History of Ireland*, ed. Thomas Bartlett and Keith Jeffery, says: 'Perhaps 25,000 rebels' and 'some hundreds of soldiers had been slain' (p. 287).

10 Louisa Pakenham to Sophia Fitzgerald, 29 May 1798. NLI Lennox/Fitzgerald/Campbell papers, MS 35, 004 (18).

11 Louisa Pakenham to Sophia Fitzgerald, 29 May 1798. NLI Lennox/Fitzgerald/Campbell papers, MS 35, 004 (18).

12 Emily Bunbury, née Napier, wrote an account in 1832. NLI Conolly–Napier papers, MS 34, 922.

13 Louisa Pakenham to Sophia Fitzgerald, 20 July 1798. NLI Lennox/Fitzgerald/Campbell papers, MS 35, 004 (18).

14 Lady Louisa Conolly to William Ogilvie, 10 July 1798. *Memoirs of Lord Edward Fitzgerald*, p. 458.

15 Sarah Napier to Duke of Richmond from Castletown, 26 August 1798. Ibid., p. 460.

16 See Lady Louisa Conolly to William Ogilvie, 10 July 1798: 'What could be so wise as trusting to an honest man, an experienced military man, and, above all, an unprejudiced man, who cannot have imbibed any of our misguided passions?' Ibid., p. 458. Also see: 'How he [Lord Cornwallis] *does* hate being Lord Lieutenant! I do not wonder at him. He has made a bargain with us not to call him Excellency. What a good man he must be to undertake so horrid a situation for the sake of doing right.' Lady Louisa Conolly to Thomas Conolly, 15 August 1798 from Castletown, after Lord Cornwallis paid a visit. NLI Conolly–Napier Papers, MS 34, 922 (13).

17 Marquess Cornwallis to Major-General Ross, 2 July 1799. Cornwallis, *Correspondence*, Vol. III, p. 121.

18 Battle of 27 August 1798, known as the 'Races of Castlebar'.

19 Harriet Barker to Chambre Brabazon Barker (29 August) 1798. TCD Barker Ponsonby Papers, P2/3/5.

20 Baronstown.

21 Bess Stewart Memoir. LSA.

22 Thomas Pakenham Vandeleur writes January 1799 from Capetown to Henry Stewart: 'particularly anxious to hear of my friends the female part I mean, as to the Men I know you are all ready & willing to take your own parts – But the poor Women I hope & trust are all safe in England, as I know of no other place where they can be looked upon as out of danger'. PRONI D/33196/1–11.

23 Maxwell's *History of the Irish Rebellion in 1798*, p. 265, says 6,000 rebels.

24 See *Memoirs of Richard Lovell Edgeworth*, Vol. II, p. 221.

25 *The Last Speech and Dying Words of Martin McLoughlin*.

26 *1798: A Bicentenary Perspective*, ed. Thomas Bartlett, David Dickson, Dáire Keogh, Kevin Whelan, p. 603 says that over 400 were executed between 8 and 10 September in Longford.

27 Maria Edgeworth to Sophy Ruxton, 19 September 1798. NLI MS 10, 166, fol. 196.

28 Richard Lovell Edgeworth to Daniel Augustus Beaufort, 29 September 1798. NLI MS 10, 166, fol. 198.

CHAPTER THREE

1 NLI Londonderry MS 886 (marked 'copy'), 13 June 1798.

2 Alexander Knox to Lord Castlereagh, December 1798. *Memoirs and Correspondence of Viscount Castlereagh*, ed. Charles Vane, Vol. II, p. 45.

3 The Bill at this stage did not mention the Union by name, but the idea was mooted in the Lord Lieutenant's address. The opposition leader, George Ponsonby, moved an amendment to it, pledging the House to maintain a 'free and independent legislature'. It was the division on this amendment that the Government won by a single vote, losing by five votes when it was brought up again on the 24th.

4 *The Rise and Fall of the Irish Nation* by Jonah Barrington, Vol. II, p. 301.

5 George Nugent Temple Grenville, who had twice been Lord Lieutenant of Ireland: 1782–3 and 1787–9. Arthur Wellesley had been his aide-de-

camp. Buckingham to Lord Grenville, 23 January 1799. Fortescue (Dropmore) papers, HMC Vol. IV (1905), p. 451.

6 12 February 1799, Longford to Lord Castlereagh. *Memoirs and Correspondence of Viscount Castlereagh*, Vol. II, pp. 173–4.

7 'Fee-simple' means absolute possession. Lord Castlereagh to Lord Camden, 24 July 1799. PRONI T2627/4/114. Quoted in P.M. Geoghegan's, *The Irish Act of Union*, p. 84.

8 Cornwallis to Ross, 20 May 1799. Cornwallis, *Correspondence*, Vol. III, pp. 100–1.

9 Patrick M. Geoghegan, '"Act of Power & Corruption"? *The Union Debate'*, *History Ireland* 2000.

10 Lady Louisa Conolly to Countess of Roden, 11 September 1799. PRONI MIC. 147/9, Vol. 19.

11 *Historic Memoirs of Ireland* by Jonah Barrington (1835), Vol. II, p. 369.

12 Lord Lieutenant Cornwallis to Major-General Ross, 2 August 1800. Cornwallis, *Correspondence*, Vol. III, p. 285.

CHAPTER FOUR

1 Cornwallis to Ross, 18 December 1800. 'I cannot in conscience in duty to my country abandon the Catholic question, without which all we have done will be of no avail.' *Correspondence*, Vol. III, p. 313.

2 Colonel George Napier to Hon. John Staples, 3 November 1801. PRONI D/1449/12/239.

3 Lady Enniskillen to Arthur Cole, 4 August 1802. PRONI Cole Papers, D/1702/12/3.

4 Lady Louisa Conolly to Sophia Fitzgerald, 2 August 1802. NLI Lennox/Fitzgerald/Campbell papers, MS 35, 004 (5).

5 Admiral Thomas Pakenham to Viscount Dunlo, 3 June 1803. TCD Conolly papers, MS 3981/1457.

6 Admiral Thomas Pakenham to Viscount Dunlo, 3 June 1803. TCD Conolly papers, MS 3981/1457.

7 Louisa Conolly to Duke of Richmond, 14 May 1803. NLI Conolly–Napier papers, MS 40, 242 (20).

8 Louisa Pakenham to Sophia Fitzgerald, 9 September 1803. NLI Lennox/Fitzgerald/Campbell papers, MS 35, 004 (18).

9 Lady Louisa Conolly to Lady Sarah Napier, 26 July 1803. NLI Conolly–Napier papers, MS 40, 242 (19).

10 Admiral Pakenham to Under-Secretary Marsden, 23 July 1804. NAI, SOC 1030/52. I am indebted to Seamus Cullen for these references.

11 Lady Sarah Napier to Lady Susan O'Brien, 26 October 1804. *The Life and Letters of Lady Sarah Lennox, 1745–1826*, ed. the Countess of Ilchester and Lord Stavordale, Vol. II, p. 177.

12 Lady Sarah Napier to Lady Charleville, 30 August 1805. *The Marlay Letters*, ed. R. Warwick Bond, p. 89.

13 Emily Napier to Anne Staples, 28 July 1806, PRONI Bunbury papers, T/3795/5/2; originals SROB Bunbury letter books.

14 Serena Holroyd to Maria Josepha Stanley, 3 December 1806. Cheshire Record Office, Stanley of Alderley papers, DSA/39/Part 4.

CHAPTER FIVE

1 NLI Edgeworth MS 23, 505.

2 Dean William Cole to Arthur Cole, 2 October 1802. PRONI Cole Papers, D/1702/12/3.

3 Dean William Cole to Arthur Cole, 1 July 1803. PRONI Cole Papers, D/1702/12/13/12.

4 Dean William Cole to Arthur Cole, 20 October 1802. PRONI Cole Papers, D/1702/12/3.

5 Journal of Helen Hamilton, January 1803. LSA.

6 Bess Stewart Memoir. LSA.

7 Serena Holroyd to her brother Lord Sheffield, undated, *c*.1803. Cheshire Record Office, Stanley of Alderley papers, DSA/20.

8 Ned to Harry Stewart from Clifton, 5 February 1805. LSA.

9 Bess Stewart Memoir. LSA.

10 *Sixty Years' Experience as an Irish Landlord* by John Hamilton, p. 1.

11 Lady Louisa Conolly to Emily Leinster, Castletown, 16 July 1809. PRONI MIC. 238, SROB Bunbury letter books.

12 Bess Stewart Memoir. LSA.

13 Mrs Edgeworth to Sophy Ruxton, 13 April 1806. NLI 10, 166, fol. 511.

CHAPTER SIX

1 Mrs Frances Greville to Duchess of Leinster, 23 February 1785 or 1788. NLI MS 631.

2 Arthur Wesley to Catherine Pakenham, undated, *c*. spring 1794. *Private Correspondence of the Duke of Wellington*, ed. G. Wellesley, pp. 1–2.

3 Maria Edgeworth to Lady Romilly, August 1815. BOD MS Eng. Misc. c.905.

4 Arthur Wellesley to Olivia Sparrow, August (1801). *Private Correspondence*, pp. 3–4.

5 10 September, 30 September 1805. Lady Maria Nugent's *Journal of a Voyage* . . . , Vol. II, pp. 326, 328.

6 Charlotte Edgeworth to Emmeline King, repeating account of Sophy Ruxton, 25 April 1806. NLI MS 10, 166, fol. 512.

7 Kitty Pakenham to Olivia Sparrow, 8 October 1805. *Private Correspondence of the Duke of Wellington*, p. 7.

8 Mrs Calvert's diary: 'I hear that when someone told Sir Arthur he would find her much altered, he answered that he did not care; it was her mind he was in love with, and that could not alter.' Frances Calvert was the daughter of Edmond Sexten Pery, a prominent MP and Kitty's father's old friend. *An Irish Beauty of the Regency*, ed. Mrs Warrenne Blake, p. 67.

9 Undated. NLI Townley Hall papers, MS 10, 377(3).

10 Sophy Ruxton to Mrs Edgeworth, 28 April 1806 (misdated as 1805 in calendar). NLI MS 10, 166, fol. 460.

11 Sophy Ruxton to Mrs Edgeworth, 28 April 1806. NLI MS 10, 166, fol. 460.

12 Sophy Ruxton to Mrs Edgeworth, 28 April 1806. NLI MS 10, 166, fol. 460.

13 Arthur Cole to Florence Balfour, undated. TCD Townley Hall MS 3761/ 1–22.

14 Mrs Edgeworth to Sophy Ruxton, 13 April 1806. Edgeworth papers, NLI MS 10, 166, fol. 511.

15 Sophy Ruxton to Mrs Edgeworth, 28 April 1806. NLI MS 10, 166, fol. 460.

16 Mrs Edgeworth to Sophy Ruxton, 13 April 1806. NLI MS 10, 166, fol. 511.

17 Maria Edgeworth to Mrs Edgeworth, quoting Dr Beaufort, 1 May 1806. NLI MS 10, 166, fol. 515.

18 Maria Edgeworth to Miss Margaret Ruxton, 23 May 1806. NLI MS 10, 166, fol. 517.

19 Maria Edgeworth to Sophy Ruxton, 13 April 1806. Edgeworth papers, NLI MS 10, 166, fol. 511.

CHAPTER SEVEN

1 The point is made by A.P.W. Malcomson in 'The Irish Peerage and the Act of Union 1800–1971', in *Transactions of the Royal Historical Society, 2000*, 6th Series, Vol. X.

2 Ned to Catherine Longford, 9 September 1801. *Pakenham Letters*, ed. Thomas Pakenham.

3 Maria Edgeworth to Charles Sneyd Edgeworth, 25 December 1807. BOD MS Eng. lett. c.703, fols 55–9. In the same letter to Henry Edgeworth she wrote: 'I wish you were here at this instant . . . this is really the most agreeable family and pleasantest and most comfortable castle I ever was in.'

4 Honora Edgeworth to Sophy Ruxton, December 1806. NLI MS 10, 166 fol. 602.

5 Some genealogists make him the grandson of the Bishop; see *A History of the House of Hamilton* by George Hamilton.

6 Maria Edgeworth to Honora Edgeworth, 30 November 1809. NLI Edgeworth MSS, 10, 166, fol. 719.

7 Maria Edgeworth to Charlotte and Mary Sneyd, 9 March 1810. NLI Edgeworth MSS, 10, 166, fol. 740.

CHAPTER EIGHT

1 From Maria Edgeworth to Sophy Ruxton, c.11 February 1807. 'This moment we have the following billet from good Lady Eliz.Pakenham: Our Edgeworth friends will rejoice to hear that dear Kitty W– is well & had a stout boy the 3rd of this month.' NLI MS 10, 166, fol. 568.

2 Serena Holroyd to Maria Josepha Stanley, 29 April 1807. Cheshire Record Office, Stanley of Alderley papers, DSA/39/Part 4.

3 It had come about because the incumbent MP, William Smyth of Drumcree, had resigned on 25 February, after twenty-four years.

4 Arthur Wellesley to Lady Elizabeth Pakenham, 1 June 1807. WSD Vol. V, pp. 69–70.

5 *Sixty Years' Experience as an Irish Landlord* by John Hamilton, p. 2.

6 5 July 1807, quoted in Elizabeth Longford, *Wellington: The Years of the Sword*, p. 127.

7 Ned to Catherine Longford, 25 December 1807. *Pakenham Letters*, ed. Thomas Pakenham.

8 Kitty Wellesley to Marquess Wellesley, 19 August 1808, from Phoenix Park. BL Add. MS 37315, fol. 54.

9 Maria Edgeworth to Sophy Ruxton, September 1808. NLI Edgeworth MSS, 10, 166, fol. 643.

10 The Radical William Cobbett exclaimed: 'It is evident that *he* [Wellesley] was the prime cause – the only cause – of all the mischief, and that from the motive of thwarting everything *after he was superseded*. Thus do we pay for the arrogance of that damned infernal family'. *The Creevey Papers*, ed. Sir H. Maxwell, p. 89.

11 Ned to Catherine Longford, 22 September 1808. *Pakenham Letters*.

12 Sir Hew Dalrymple and Sir Arthur Wellesley. Maria Edgeworth to Frances Edgeworth, October/November 1808. NLI MS 10, 166, fol. 645.

13 See Byron's *Childe Harold's Pilgrimage*, XXVI: 'And ever since that martial synod met, Britannia sickens, Cintra, at thy name;/And folks in office at the mention fret,/And fain would blush, if blush they could, for shame.'

CHAPTER NINE

1 See Voltaire's *Candide:* 'All is for the best in the best of all possible worlds'.

2 Ned to Catherine Longford, 10 February 1808 (aboard the *Flora* transport). *Pakenham Letters*, ed. Thomas Pakenham.

3 Ned to Catherine Longford, 3 August 1802, St Kitts. *Pakenham Letters*.

4 Journal of Helen Hamilton, August 1803. LSA.

5 25 December 1807. *Pakenham Letters*.

6 Journal of Helen Hamilton. LSA.

7 Maria Edgeworth to Miss Ruxton, from Coolure, February 1807. NLI MS 10, 166, fol. 568.

8 Honora Edgeworth to Sophy Ruxton, December 1807. NLI MS 10, 166 fol. 602.

9 Maria Edgeworth to Henry Edgeworth, 25 December 1807. BOD MS c.703, fols 55–9.

10 Honora Edgeworth to Sophy Ruxton, December 1807. NLI MS 10, 166, fol. 602.

11 Maria Edgeworth to Sophy Ruxton, 15 April 1808. NLI MS 10, 166, fol. 631.

12 Maria Edgeworth to Mrs Ruxton, 2 February 1809. NLI MS 10, 166, fol. 667.

13 Maria Edgeworth to Mrs Ruxton, February 1809. NLI MS 10, 166, fol. 671.

14 General Arthur Wellesley to Lieutenant-General Gordon, 15 October 1808. WSD Vol. VI, p. 160.

15 *A Dorset Rifleman*, ed. E. Hathaway, p. 109.

16 Ned to Catherine Longford, 16 August 1809, a week before he left. *Pakenham Letters*.

17 Longford to Bess Stewart, 1 May 1809. LSA.

CHAPTER TEN

1 Longford to Major-General Sir Arthur Wellesley, 3 January 1808. Wellington papers at Southampton University, WP1/187/16.

2 Maria Edgeworth to Mrs Ruxton, 11 January 1809. NLI MS 10, 166, fol. 662.

3 The fate of spinsterhood did not suit her; Mrs Edgeworth quoted a visitor as exclaiming: 'Oh! What a mother was lost in her!!!' Mrs Edgeworth to Louisa Beaufort, 11 February 1807. NLI MS 10, 166, fol. 567. Lady Louisa Conolly reported that Lady Eliza had pinched her maid until she was black and blue – perhaps out of frustration.

4 Maria Edgeworth's phrase. She considered the children happy proof of her belief that to 'excite strong affection in the minds of children for their parents is most wise – as well as most pleasant in early education'. To Sophy Ruxton, *c*.11 February 1807. NLI 10, 166, fol. 568.

5 *Sixty Years' Experience as an Irish Landlord* by John Hamilton, p. 2.

6 Maria Edgeworth to Mary Sneyd, November 1811, NLI 10, 166, fol. 829.

7 Maria Edgeworth to Mary Sneyd, November 1811, NLI 10, 166, fol. 829.

8 Frederick Lamb (later Lord Beauvale) to his sister Emily Lady Cowper (later Lady Palmerston), 12 September 1808. Quoted in *Lady Palmerston & Her Times* by Mabell, Countess of Airlie, Vol. I, p. 35.

9 Maria Edgeworth to Mary Sneyd, November 1811. NLI 10, 166, fol. 829.

10 First volume published in 1809, included *Ennui, Madame de Fleury, The Dun* and *Manoeuvring*.

11 Maria Edgeworth to Honora Beaufort, 11 December 1809. NLI 10, 166, fol. 721.

NOTES TO PP. 101-108

CHAPTER ELEVEN

1 Ned to Catherine Longford, 26 October 1809, *Pakenham Letters*, ed. Thomas Pakenham.
2 Castlereagh to Arthur Wellesley, 2 April 1809. WSD Vol. VI, pp. 210–12.
3 Ned to Catherine Longford, 16 November 1809. *Pakenham Letters*.
4 To William Wellesley-Pole Wellington confessed that he had been hit, but not hurt. 'Never was there such a Murderous Battle!!' 1 August 1809. From Camden Miscellany 3rd Series, Vol. XVIII (1948), p. 18.
5 Ned to Catherine Longford, Alvesca, 10 July 1810. *Pakenham Letters*.
6 Lady Sarah Napier to Lady Susan O'Brien, 25 October 1809. This was a rare critical remark about Wellington. *The Life and Letters of Lady Sarah Lennox, 1745–1826*, ed. the Countess of Ilchester and Lord Stavordale, Vol. II, p. 229.
7 Kitty to Bess, 15 August 1809. LSA.
8 Maria Edgeworth to Charlotte and Mary Sneyd, 9 March 1810. NLI Edgeworth MSS, 10, 166, fol. 740.
9 Her name is known because of a letter she wrote to Longford in 1815.
10 The Duke commented in 1812 that 'The Peninsula is the grave of horses; and I have lost 14 upon a stud generally of 10 in three Years.' WMSS, 26 March 1812.
11 Ned to Longford, 16 March 1811. *Pakenham Letters*.
12 Hercules to Longford, 8 April 1811. *Pakenham Letters*.
13 *Adventures with the Connaught Rangers* by William Grattan, ed. Charles Oman, p. 70.
14 Wellington to William Wellesley-Pole, 15 May 1811. Supp. Desp. VII, 123. Charles Napier had much the same thought: 'Take Lord Wellington away and we are *generalless*.' *The Sword Dance* by Priscilla Napier, p. 324.
15 Maria Edgeworth to Sophy Ruxton, June 1811. NLI MS 10, 166, fol. 810.
16 Mrs Edgeworth to Fanny Edgeworth, 18 October 1812. NLI MS 10, 166, fol. 873.
17 Undated. LONGFORD.
18 See Byron's *Childe Harold*, XLIII: 'Oh Albuera, glorious field of grief!' The battle took place on 16 May 1811.
19 When Beresford wrote his dispatch to the Horse Guards, Wellington declared, 'This won't do, write me down a victory.' Earl Stanhope, *Notes of Conversations with the Duke of Wellington*, p. 90. The Duke had a hand in rewriting the dispatch, which was sent out on 22 May.

20 Undated. LSA.

21 Ned to Longford, 25 July 1811. *Pakenham Letters*.

CHAPTER TWELVE

1 Reported by midshipman of the sloop *HMS Talbot*, in a letter to his uncle. Quoted in *The Times*, 19 December 1811.

2 Letter to Henry Stewart, 9 December 1811. LSA.

3 Report of William Fletcher. Ph.D. thesis, John O'Raw.

4 Kitty to Marquess Wellesley, undated. BL Add. MSS 37315, fol. 143.

5 Lady Louisa Conolly to Sophia Fitzgerald, 21 December 1811. NLI Lennox/Fitzgerald/Campbell papers, MS 35, 004 (5).

6 Maria Edgeworth met her in London over a year later. Maria shows no sign of resentment that Ned Pakenham had been rejected; in fact it may have been convenient, since she jokingly proposed Annabella as a wife for her brother William: 'William, look sharp!'. Annabella had £12,000 per annum. Maria Edgeworth to Fanny Edgeworth, 18 May 1813. Quoted in *Maria Edgeworth: Letters from England*, ed. Christina Colvin, p. 66.

7 Quoted in *The Life and Letters of Lady Byron* by Ethel Colburn Mayne, p. 26.

8 Kitty to Hercules, 1 April 1812. *Pakenham Letters*, ed. Thomas Pakenham.

9 Wellington to Hercules, 5 January 1812. *Pakenham Letters*.

10 General Robert Craufurd had commanded in Ireland during the civil war of 1798 and had led Hercules on the retreat to Vigo in 1809.

11 A Highlander stands over their joint memorial tablet in St Paul's.

12 Hercules to Longford, 16 March 1811, *Pakenham Letters*.

13 Quoted in Elizabeth Longford, *Wellington: The Years of the Sword*, p. 273.

14 Picton remained a faithful friend to Hercules. He took leave of the latter just before the Battle of Waterloo with a strange premonition of his own death. ' "God bless you!" Said the General as he shook him warmly by the hand; "if we never meet again, you will at all events *hear* of me!" ' He was killed at Waterloo. *Life of Sir Thomas Picton*, ed. H.B. Robinson, Vol. II, p. 339.

15 *Sixty Years' Experience as an Irish Landlord* by John Hamilton, p. 15.

16 Kitty to Hercules, London, 29 April 1812. *Pakenham Letters*.

17 *Life of Sir Thomas Picton*, Vol. II, p. 142.

18 *Dictionary of National Biography*, ed. Leslie Stephen (1895), p. 84.

19 'I knew . . . something very serious was about to happen when an article so precious as the leg of a roast fowl was thus thrown away.' General Alava in *The Croker Papers*, ed. Louis J. Jennings, Vol. II, p. 20.

20 There are several sources for this anecdote. William Napier's version was: 'if you will give me one grasp of that conquering hand', which seems rather long-winded, given the circumstances.

21 *History of the War in the Peninsula* by General Sir William Napier, Vol. V, pp. 169–70.

22 S. Morley, *Memoirs of a Sergeant of the Fifth Regiment of Foot*, pp. 114–15. Cited by Charles Esdaile in *The Peninsular War*, p. 395.

23 John Kincaid, *Adventures in the Rifle Brigade*, p. 165.

24 Henry Pakenham to John Hamilton, 26 October 1863. TCD Brownhall papers.

25 Ned to Catherine Longford, 30 August 1812. *Pakenham Letters*.

CHAPTER THIRTEEN

1 24 August 1812. *Extracts of the Journals and Correspondence of Miss Berry, 1783–1852*, ed. Lady Theresa Lewis, Vol. II, p. 506.

2 Kitty Journal, 9 September 1812. WMSS.

3 Bathurst to Wellington, 20 August 1812, WSD, Vol. VII, p. 407.

4 Kitty to Bess Stewart, Harley St, 10 April 1813. PRONI D/3319/8/1.

5 Kitty to Bess Stewart, Harley St, 10 April 1813. Ibid.

6 Maria Edgeworth to Sophy Ruxton, 16 May 1813. NLI MS 10, 166, fol. 919.

7 11 May 1813. *Memoirs of the Life of Sir James Mackintosh*, p. 267.

8 Mrs Edgeworth to William and Emma Beaufort, 16 July 1813. NLI MS 10, 166, fol. 941.

9 Serena Holroyd to Maria Josepha Stanley, 13 December 1813. Cheshire Record Office, Stanley of Alderley papers, DSA/39/Part 5.

10 Dr Carpendale to Harry Stewart, 13 August 1813. PRONI D/3319/7/1–11.

11 Ned to Harry Stewart, 9 January 1814. PRONI D/3319/7/1–11.

12 Hercules to Harry Stewart, 26 December, no year. PRONI D/3319/7/1–11.

13 Lady C. Enniskillen to Arthur Cole, *c.* January 1814. PRONI Cole Papers, D/1702/12/7/1–8.

14 Maria Edgeworth to Sophy Ruxton, September/October 1814. NLI MS 10, 166, fol. 1035.

15 John Hamilton, *Sixty Years' Experience as an Irish Landlord*, p. 11.

16 *The Strange Death of Lord Castlereagh* by H. Montgomery Hyde, p. 167. Castlereagh, who had by then become Lord Londonderry, killed himself 12 August 1822. At the time it was noticed with what anatomical precision the suicide was carried out. See Chapter Twenty.

CHAPTER FOURTEEN

1 Quoted in *Sixty Years' Experience as an Irish Landlord* by John Hamilton, p. 12.

2 *Pakenham Letters*, ed. Thomas Pakenham.

3 Sir Harry Smith.

4 *Autobiography of Lt-Gen. Sir Harry Smith*, Vol. I, p. 232.

5 Ibid., p. 236.

6 Smith met the Duke at Cambrai in France in 1816, and told him the whole story of the campaign at New Orleans; he was particularly horrified that the men had fired 'in column'. Like many a soldier before him, Smith was intimidated by the Duke's brisk approach. 'How I longed to tell him how I loved and admired his brother-in-law . . . But although I talked of "the General", I never made use of the magic word . . . "Pakenham".' *Autobiography of Lt-Gen. Sir Harry Smith*, Vol. I, pp. 304–5.

7 Major MacDougall remained fiercely loyal to Ned: when another veteran, Reverend George Gleig, published an attack on General Pakenham's plans some years later, he replied sternly, 'Sir Edward Pakenham fell, not as has been usually supposed, after an utter and disastrous defeat, but at the very moment when the arms of victory were extended towards him.' *Literary Gazette*, 12 April 1828.

8 Dispatches of Captain Wylley, General Pakenham's military secretary. LONGFORD.

9 Duke of Wellington to Earl of Longford. LONGFORD.

10 Duke of Wellington to Lady Shelley. *Diary of Frances, Lady Shelley*, ed. Richard Edgecumbe.

11 *Passages in the Early Military Life of General Sir George T. Napier*, ed. by his son, W.C.E. Napier, pp. 239–40.

12 Longford to Bess, 3 June 1815. LSA.

13 *Dublin Evening Post*, 16 March 1815.

14 29 and 30 April 1823, Dr A. Hunter to Duke of Wellington. Southampton papers WP1/760/15 & 17.

CHAPTER FIFTEEN

1 Lord Bathurst was Secretary of State for War. Maria Edgeworth to Mrs Ruxton, 23 August 1812. NLI MS 10, 166, fol. 869.

2 Maria Edgeworth to Mrs Ruxton, 13 October 1814. NLI MS 10, 166, fol. 1036.

3 Lady Bessborough to Lord Granville Leveson Gower, Paris, 1 November 1814. Lady Bessborough was sister to Georgiana, Duchess of Devonshire, and mother of Lady Caroline Lamb, and had conducted a long but discreet love affair with Lord Granville. *Lord Granville Leveson Gower . . . Correspondence*, ed. Castalia, Countess of Granville, Vol. II, p. 507.

4 9 February 1816, referring to the previous year. BOD MS Eng. Misc. c.905, Romilly letters, fols 112–209.

5 Kitty to Caroline Hamilton. LSA.

6 24 March 1819. Maria Edgeworth to Mrs Ruxton, quoted in *Maria Edgeworth: Letters from England*, ed. Christina Colvin, p. 185.

7 25 October 1814. *Memoirs of the Life of Sir James Mackintosh*, Vol. II, p. 315.

8 *An Irish Beauty of the Regency* by Mrs Warrenne Blake, p. 244. 20 March: 'on Friday, Sir James, Edmond Knox, and John arrived from Paris. They had come off in a violent hurry, as did the Duchess of Wellington, and *shoals* of English on account of Bonaparte's advance.'

9 Kitty to Harry Stewart, Dublin, 6 April 1815. LSA.

10 Ibid.

11 Maria Edgeworth to Sneyd Edgeworth, 10 May 1815. NLI MS 10, 166, fol. 1098.

12 Maria Edgeworth to Mrs O'Beirne, 31 May 1815. NLI MS 10, 166, fol. 1102.

13 Longford to Bess, 12 June 1815. LSA.

14 Hercules to Harry Stewart, 8 May 1815. PRONI Stewart papers D/3319/7/1–11.

15 Serena Holroyd to Lord Sheffield, 24 January (1809). Cheshire Record Office, Stanley of Alderley papers, DSA/20.

16 To Bess Stewart, 12 June 1815. LSA.

CHAPTER SIXTEEN

1 '[Caroline Hamilton] was present one day at the Duke of Wellington's when Blücher and Ld Melbourne (then *Lamb*) and Lady Caroline were at the dinner – a bust in plaister of Paris of the Duke had been placed on

the table to be judged of – It had been just sent by some young French artist – Lady Caroline exclaimed against it as not doing the Duke justice snatched it up and dashed it to pieces on the floor – her husband said to himself, but loud enough for Caroline Hamilton who sat next to him to hear the words 'Very foolish indeed!' Maria Edgeworth to Fanny Wilson, 23 November 1834. BOD MS Eng. lett. c.708, fol. 33.

2 Lady Romilly to Maria Edgeworth, 9 August 1815. *Romilly – Edgeworth Letters*, p. 110.

3 Maria Edgeworth to Lady Romilly, 18 August 1815, BOD MS Eng. Misc. c.905 (B).

4 Caroline Hamilton account in LSA.

5 To Bess Stewart, 21 March 1816. LSA.

6 Maria Edgeworth to Harriette Sneyd, 4 August 1816. NLI MS 10,116, fol. 1189.

7 Maria Edgeworth to Lady Romilly, 9 February 1816. BOD MS Eng. Misc. c.905 (B).

8 William Wellesley-Pole to Charles Bagot, 5 July 1816. 'Whenever [the Duke] appears he is follow'd and Huzza'd as much as he was in 1814, and great notice has been taken of him by Carlton House, etc.' J. Bagot, *George Canning and His Friends*, Vol. II, p. 29.

9 Kitty to Eleanor Butler, 18 July [1816]. NLW MSS 22977D, fols 83–4.

CHAPTER SEVENTEEN

1 Maria Edgeworth to Mrs Ruxton. NLI MS 10, 166, fol. 1194.

2 23 August 1813, Lowry Cole from Peninsula (enclosed in letter from Ned). *Pakenham Letters*, ed. Thomas Pakenham.

3 Fragment: Maria Edgeworth to ? (Mrs Sneyd Edgeworth?) *c.* September 1815. NLI MS 10, 166, fol. 1145.

4 Ned to Longford, 1 February 1813. *Pakenham Letters*.

5 Ned to Longford, 2 May 1813. *Pakenham Letters*.

6 Ned to Longford, 18 October 1813. *Pakenham Letters*.

7 'I truly regret the circumstances which have made the following arrangements expedient but I deem it a duty to make reasonable provision for the several parties who have been placed by me in a situation to require it.' Private letter to Henry Hamilton and Dean Henry Pakenham, 12 July 1830. LONGFORD.

8 Catherine Enniskillen to Arthur Cole, *c.* January 1814. PRONI Cole Papers, D/1702/12/7/1–8.

9 John Reginald Lygon – who became 3rd Earl Beauchamp – had married Charlotte Scott in 1814.

10 Richard Lovell Edgeworth quoted by Maria in letter to Mrs Ruxton, 25 August 1816. NLI MS 10, 166, fol. 1194.

11 Maria Edgeworth to Lady Romilly, 23 December 1816. BOD MS Eng. Misc. c.905 (B).

12 Longford to Mr G. Swan, 10 August 1816. LSA.

13 Draft letter to Lord Beauchamp enclosed with previous letter to Swan. Lord Beauchamp made no objection to Longford's proposed jointure or annual allowance of £2,000 to Georgiana in the event of his death – with £20,000 to be settled on younger children.

14 Longford to Swan, 21 August 1816. LSA.

15 Maria Edgeworth to Mrs Ruxton, 25 August 1816. NLI MS 10, 166, fol. 1194.

16 Ibid.

17 Longford to Richard Lovell Edgeworth, 8 February 1817. NLI MS 11, 132 (2).

CHAPTER EIGHTEEN

1 Undated, but marked 'received 20 Jan, 1818'. LONGFORD.

2 To William Wellesley-Pole, 20 February 1816. Published in 'Some Letters of the Duke of Wellington', Camden Miscellany Vol. XVIII, p. 37.

3 Undated. Wellesley Papers, BL Add. MSS 37416, fol. 331.

4 Her brother was the Duke of Richmond, the ex-Lord Lieutenant of Ireland. She was not a reliable witness: Pamela Campbell, daughter of Lord Edward Fitzgerald, called her 'prejudiced, worldly, entrenched by prejudice upon prejudice, till her very soul is straightened within the narrow limits of the Ministers, their wives and her own Family'. Pamela Campbell to Emily Eden, NLI Lennox/Fitzgerald/Campbell papers, MS 35, 016(1–4).

5 Maria Edgeworth to Sophy Ruxton, 19 September 1818, quoted in *Maria Edgeworth: Letters from England*, ed. Christina Colvin, pp. 102–3.

6 Maria Edgeworth to Mrs Ruxton, 24 March 1819. Ibid., p. 185.

7 Engraved portrait of Lord Longford used in frontispiece of Vol. II.

8 Maria Edgeworth to Sophy Ruxton, 2 April 1819. *Maria Edgeworth: Letters*, p. 91.

9 Kitty to Mrs Mackintosh, 16 August from Stratfield Saye. BL Add. MSS 63090.

10 Kitty to Bess Stewart, 1 January 1821. PRONI D/3319/8/6.

11 Kitty to Bess Stewart. LSA.

12 *The Life of Wellington* by Sir H.E. Maxwell, Vol. II, p. 260.

13 19 April 1820, quoted in *Wellington: Pillar of State*, by Elizabeth Longford, p. 75.

14 5 May 1821, ibid.

15 9 July 1821, ibid., pp. 76–7.

16 Kitty to Lord Bristol, 25 May 1822. By kind permission of Suffolk Record Office, SROB 941/56/72 pt.

17 Kitty to Bess Stewart, 1 January 1821. PRONI D/3319/8/6.

CHAPTER NINETEEN

1 Longford to Bess Stewart, 6 September 1820. Westmeath County Library, P/P/4.

2 To Kitty, 14 March 1820. WMSS.

2 See *The Buildings of Ireland: North Leinster* by Christine Casey and Alistair Rowan, p. 257.

4 Edward 1817, William 1819, Thomas 1820. Another seven children followed.

5 Hercules to Kitty, undated, must be spring/summer 1820. WMSS.

6 Longford to Edward Conolly, from Dublin, 26 September 1820. LONGFORD.

7 Bess Pakenham to Richard Pakenham, from Castletown, 3 May 1821. LONGFORD.

8 Louisa Pakenham to Lady Harriet Clancarty, 21 April (1822). National Archives of Ireland, Trench family correspondence, 999/347/2.

9 13 June 1821. LONGFORD.

10 *The Times* of London.

11 20 August 1821, Mrs Chichester Fortescue to Martha Fortescue. Original held at the Somerset Record Office (DD/SH/C/1189/347). Quoted with permission.

12 See 'The Court of Dublin Castle' in *Historical Essays*, ed. R.B. McDowell.

13 William Saurin had been appointed in 1807 by the Duke of Richmond.

14 Maria Edgeworth to Mrs Ruxton, 21 January 1824. BOD MS Eng. lett. c.717, fol. 153.

CHAPTER TWENTY

1 From Apsley House, 2 May 1822 to Mrs William Foster. *A Selection from the Private Correspondence of the First Duke of Wellington*, ed. G. Wellesley, pp. 14–15.

2 29 August 1822. *JA* Vol. I, p. 185.

3 27 June 1822. Ibid., p. 168.

4 'Wellington's *Dispatches* and their Editor, Colonel Gurwood', ed. C.M. Woolgar.

5 To Frederick Lamb from Countess Cowper, 10 September 1822. *Lady Palmerston & Her Times* by Mabell, Countess of Airlie, Vol. I, p. 103.

6 Wellington to Mrs Arbuthnot, quoted in *Wellington: Pillar of State*, by Elizabeth Longford, p. 95.

7 Kitty to Marquess Wellesley, Stratfield Saye, 8 December 1822. BL Add. MSS 37315, fol. 273.

8 9 October 1822, quoted in *Sir Thomas Lawrence's Letter-Bag*, ed. George Somes Layard, p. 171.

9 14 November 1822. Quoted in *Frances Anne* by Edith Marchioness of Londonderry, p. 98.

10 Lord Liverpool to Charles Arbuthnot, 21 October 1822. A. Aspinall (ed.), *The Correspondence of Charles Arbuthnot*, Camden 3rd Series, Vol. LXV, p. 35. The next letter is 1 November.

11 Lady Cowper to her brother Fredrick Lamb, 16 January 1823. *Lady Palmerston & Her Times*, Vol. I, p. 106.

12 Lady Frances Shelley's phrase. *Diary of Frances, Lady Shelley*, ed. Richard Edgecumbe, Vol. II, p. 311.

13 Kitty to Lord Oriel, undated, *c.* April 1825. PRONI D/207/67/65.

14 Perhaps it was very wise that he did. Kate's husband William Foster was reported to be pompous and tactless by Maria Edgeworth, a mere 'fribble of a parson'. Caroline Hamilton had dreaded lest 'Willy F should instruct the Duke of Wellington in the art of war . . .'. Maria Edgeworth to Mrs Edgeworth, 1 May 1825. BOD MS Eng. Lett. c.699, fols 11–14.

15 The Duke of York had died on 5 January 1827. Lady Holland wrote to her son on 9 February 1827: 'The D. of Wellington is very near dying, and several others.' *Elizabeth Lady Holland, to her son, 1821–1845*, ed. Giles Stephen Holland Fox-Strangways, p. 59. Someone did: Lord Liverpool had a stroke when he heard Canning was ill and died on 28 December 1828.

16 Sir Robert Peel to Lady Peel, 22 January 1827. *The Private Letters of Sir Robert Peel*, ed. George Peel, p. 96.

17 Ibid., p. 110.

18 *Diary of Frances, Lady Shelley*, Vol. II. p. 311.

19 27 October 1825. *JA* Vol. I, p. 423.

20 26 January 1826. Ibid., Vol. II, p. 6.

21 *Diary of Frances, Lady Shelley*, Vol. II, p. 312.

22 The King had appointed George Canning as Prime Minister on 9 April, and Wellington had resigned in protest. Kitty to Mrs Arbuthnot, Stratfield Saye, 1 May 1827. Correspondence of Charles Arbuthnot, Camden 3rd Series, Vol. LXV, p. 87.

CHAPTER TWENTY-ONE

1 Captain John Armstrong to Hercules Pakenham, 30 June 1823. LONGFORD.

2 Speech by Colonel H. Pakenham in reply to second reading of Sir Francis Burdett's Catholic Relief Bill, 19 April 1825.

3 Lady Cowper to Frederick Lamb, 24 May 1825. *Lady Palmerston & Her Times*, ed. Mabell, Countess of Airlie, Vol. I, p. 118.

4 Kitty to Bess, 28 February 1828. LSA.

5 *The Greville Memoirs*, Vol. I, p. 254.

6 24 September 1828. Princess Lieven to Countess Cowper, *The Lieven–Palmerston Correspondence, 1828–56*, ed. Lord Sudley, p. 3.

7 9 October 1828. *JA* Vol. II, p. 212.

8 1 August 1828, to George IV.

9 Wellington to Mrs Arbuthnot, 23 September 1828. *Wellington & His Friends*, ed. G. Wellesley, p. 84.

10 9 October 1828. *JA* Vol. II, p. 213.

11 Wellington to Bathurst, 24 November 1828. WDNS, Vol. V, p. 280.

12 Lady Margaret Chapman to Longford, 28 October 1828. LONGFORD.

13 Speeches from pamphlet printed 1828 in Dublin. NLI.

14 Newcastle letter to Lord Kenyon, 18 September 1828.

15 Longford to Duke of Wellington, 8 November, Southampton papers WP1/966/3.

16 Duke of Wellington to Lord Francis Leveson Gower, 21 October 1828. Southampton papers WPI/964/3.

17 Maurice Fitzgerald to Wellington, WDNS, Vol. IV, pp. 584–8.

18 King George IV to Wellington, 17 November 1828. WDNS, Vol. V, p. 268.

19 *The Greville Memoirs*, Vol. I, p. 176.

20 Cited in *The Catholic Emancipation Crisis in Ireland* by James A. Reynolds, p. 168. Other sources give larger numbers, e.g. K.T. Hoppen in *Elections, Politics and Society in Ireland 1832–85* gives 216,000 to 37,000.

21 *Diary of Frances, Lady Shelley*, ed. Richard Edgecumbe, Vol. II, p. 188.

22 Maria Edgeworth to Fanny Wilson, 13 April 1829. BOD MS Eng. lett. c.708, fols 33–4.

23 Maria Edgeworth to Sophy Ruxton, 21 April 1829. BOD MS Eng. lett. c.719, fols 85–8.

24 3 May 1829, Hercules to Kitty. WMSS.

25 Henry Pakenham to Kitty, undated, 1829. WMSS.

26 7 April 1829. WMSS.

27 28 April 1829. WMSS.

28 Estates worth £1,500,000 a year according to *Modern English Biography* by F. Boase.

29 Hercules to Henry Stewart, 9 July 1829. LSA.

30 Duke of Wellington to Sir Thomas Pakenham, 12 June 1829. Southampton papers, WPI/1029/25.

31 Longford to Downshire, 3 December 1829. PRONI D/671/C/12/423.

32 Maria Edgeworth to Surgeon General of Ireland Sir Philip Crampton, 9 July 1830. TCD Crampton MS 4177/159.

33 Wellington to Hercules, 7 October 1832. Southampton WPI/1236/4.

34 7 October 1829. WMSS.

CHAPTER TWENTY-TWO

1 24 February 1830, to Bess. LSA.

2 16 February 1830. *JA* Vol. II, p. 336. Mrs Arbuthnot blamed Kitty for not doing her wifely duty when the Duke was so busy, and looking after his private affairs. At the time, Wyatt's bill for the improvements to Apsley House had come in, to the Duke's annoyance. Mrs Arbuthnot put another nail in Kitty's coffin with the remark: 'his wife has not sense enough [to help him] & rather encourages his servants & people to cheat him. Not that she is extravagant in herself for she is generally dressed like a beggar, but from mere folly.'

3 Charles Arbuthnot to Lord Cowley, 11 April 1830. Camden 3rd Series LXV, 1941, p. 125.

4 24 May 1830. *JA* Vol. II, p. 359.

5 Kitty to Bess Stewart, Apsley House, 23 July 1830. PRONI D/3319/8/8.

6 Kitty to Longford, Apsley House, 12 November 1830. PRONI T/3007/20.

7 Kitty to Bess Stewart, Apsley House, 15 November 1830. PRONI T/3007.

8 Kitty to Bess, Stratfield Saye, 29 November 1830. PRONI T/3007/21.

9 Ibid.

10 Maria Edgeworth to Mrs Edgeworth, 22 January 1831. *Letters from England*, ed. Christina Colvin, pp. 475–7.

11 Kitty to Bess, 21 February 1831, PRONI D/3319/8/10.

12 Longford to Bess, 18 April 1831. PRONI D/3319/9/46.

13 Maria Edgeworth to Mrs C.S. Edgeworth, 30 January 1831. *Letters from England*, p. 479.

14 Longford to Bess, 24 April 1831. PRONI D/3319/9/47.

15 Hercules to Bess, 3 May 1831. PRONI D/3319/9/51.

16 24 April 1831. *Wellington & His Friends*, ed. G. Wellesley, p. 94.

17 *Memories of the Arbuthnots of Kincardineshire & Aberdeenshire* by Mrs Stewart-Mackenzie Arbuthnot, p. 224.

18 30 April 1831, to Mrs Edgeworth. *Letters from England*, pp. 26–7.

19 Duke of Wellington to Mrs Arbuthnot, *Wellington & His Friends*, p. 95. Mrs Arbuthnot didn't live much longer than Kitty. She died very suddenly of cholera on 2 August 1834. When Kitty's sister Caroline heard the news she thought only of Kitty's benevolent disposition. 'Our precious sister was enabled to forgive her all the sufferings she inflicted on her.' Caroline to Bess, 8 August 1834, PRONI D/3319/10/1–27.

CHAPTER TWENTY-THREE

1 'W.C': correspondent in *The Gardener's Magazine*, Vol. XI, 1835, ed. J.C. Loudon.

2 Maria Edgeworth to Sophy Ruxton, 15 November 1832. *Life & Letters of Maria Edgeworth* by Augustus Hare, Vol. II, p. 197.

3 Maria Edgeworth to Sophy Ruxton, 19 September 1832. BOD MS Eng. lett. c.719, fols 126–7.

4 Maria Edgeworth to Sophy Ruxton, 19 September 1832. Ibid.

5 Maria Edgeworth to her half-sister Lucy Robinson, 6 February 1833. BOD MS Eng. lett. c.714, fol. 47.

6 'Spades for children' listed in red account book. LONGFORD.

7 Longford to Bess, 13 July 1834. PRONI D/3319/10/1–27.

8 Maria Edgeworth to Sophy Ruxton, 19 September 1832. BOD MS Eng. lett. c.719, fols 126–7.

9 Longford to Bess, 16 November 1834. PRONI D/3319/10/10.
10 Henry Hamilton to Henry Pakenham, 3 December 1834. LONGFORD.
11 Longford to Bess, 18 April 1834. PRONI D/3319/10/1–27.
12 Longford to Georgiana, Pakenham Hall, 2 July 1830. LONGFORD.
13 LONGFORD.
14 Longford to Hercules and Henry Pakenham, 25 April 1831. LONGFORD.
15 Reverend Thomas Fisher to Longford, 18 August 1834. LONGFORD.
16 Hercules to Henry Hamilton, 22 May. LONGFORD.
17 Hercules to Henry Hamilton, 27 May. LONGFORD.
18 Hercules to Henry Pakenham, 3 June 1835. LONGFORD.
19 Maria Edgeworth to Fanny Wilson, 30 May 1835. BOD MS Eng. lett. c.708, fols 30–35.
20 Hercules to Henry Pakenham, 6 July 1835. LONGFORD.
21 Catherine Longford to Henry Pakenham, 13 June, from Portland Place. LONGFORD.

EPILOGUE

1 To William Barlow Smythe of Barbavilla from a Smythe relative in Florence, 6 June 1835. Smythe of Barbavilla papers at NLI MS 41,602(4).
2 Report by W. Vicars Griffith, 15 December 1837, in Leinster Street. LONGFORD.
3 Edward William Pakenham became a Captain in the Grenadier Guards and at the Battle of Alma 'first jumped over the embrasure of the Russian Battery'. At Inkerman, he 'defended at the head' and was killed on 5 November 1854. *Our Heroes* by G. Ryan, pp. 67–8.
4 Maria Edgeworth to Fanny Wilson, 7 February 1834. BOD MS Eng. lett. c.708, fols 13, 15.
5 Maria Edgeworth to Mrs Edgeworth, 14 March 1841. BOD MS Eng. lett. c.702, fols 31–8.
6 Maria Edgeworth to Charles Sneyd Edgeworth, 12 February 1835. BOD MS Eng. lett. c.703, fols 227–32.
7 Hercules to Henry Hamilton, 19 June 1835. LONGFORD.
8 LONGFORD.
9 James Fraser's *Guide Through Ireland* (1838). This was the same James Fraser that Longford had employed in 1832, so most likely to be partial in his description.

INDEX

Lodging a Case to Hornsby.

Winchester College School.

By Mr Silchester

T. W. Dowell

... Silchester
... Pakenham
... Pakenham

2/8 1 11

1832 Longford

To the Right Honourable
Thomas Earl of Longford
Pakenham Hall Westmeath
Longford Castle Ireland

... destroy this letter I beg you to send the
enclosed to Lord Hobart — Pray
buy for me four quarters of tickets
for the next English Lottery